The Golden Bridge

New Directions in the Human-Animal Bond

Alan M. Beck, series editor

Dedicated to all North Star's children
and the dogs who help them to find their way.

Justin and North Star's Flash.
Photo by Pei-Pei Ketron.

Contents

Foreword

It takes courage and great passion to be a pioneer; both perseverance and faith are needed to map uncharted territory.

In *The Golden Bridge,* Patty Dobbs Gross leads us on an extraordinary journey of heart and mind, allowing us an inside look at how specially bred and trained dogs help to facilitate communication for children with autism and other developmental disabilities, as well as to support children who must face the pain of a loss or serious illness.

Created as a guide to help parents deal with the social, emotional and educational issues of raising children with challenges, *The Golden Bridge* focuses on possibilities and explores the many ways an assistance dog can make a profound difference in young lives. Myths and labels within the world of autism are explored, dissected and redefined. Thinking "outside the box"—pushing past barriers of intolerance and misunderstanding—is the cornerstone of this groundbreaking work.

As an adult living with a physical and developmental disability, I have encountered many attitudinal roadblocks in my own life's journey. I identify with many of the struggles outlined in this book, especially the social isolation that has at times made me feel like bruised fruit on a produce stand, too often bypassed for a healthier looking specimen. Although I initially sought to use an assistance dog to mitigate my physical disabilities, I found that my dog became the most astute facilitator in bridging the fears and misunderstandings that separated me from the rest of society. In this capacity, my assistance dog has provided me with the most valuable gift of all: even out in public, I no longer feel socially isolated. People who might normally avoid eye contact now seek my attention to find out more about my dog; he is an icebreaker, a bridge, and a shared focal point to begin conversations. When my dog is with me, it is somehow safer for people to approach me than when I am alone.

Children have long been fascinated by my unusual physical appearance as a double leg amputee. Open and curious, children ask pointed questions to help understand what my life is like: "How do you drive?" "Does it hurt?" "How do you go to the bathroom?" I love answering these questions, and do not find them in any way invasive—they are honest questions, born of genuine interest in all things new and unique. Adults, however, have learned that it's socially unacceptable to bring attention to a disabling condition, so for fear of saying something inappropriate, most find it easier to pretend I don't exist.

Having an assistance dog beside me as I go about my daily life opens up so many doors of communication. Dogs are child magnets, and luckily even more fascinating than my missing body parts, so conversations begin with questions about my dog. This allows the children's parents to relax, and not worry about their child asking me what they assume will be an inappropriate or embarrassing question. I am grateful for the opportunity to segue into a conversation about my physical disability, and show that I'm open to answering questions and sharing information about what life is like without having legs, and all the ways my dog helps me to stay independent and healthy. My assistance dog allows me to be proactive in communicating with both children and adults, and he offers me social opportunities I'd never experienced before his arrival. I've come to understand that being paired with an assistance dog is less about how the dog helps me physically and far more about the many invisible ways my canine partner has brought me into the mainstream of life. On days when physical pain leads to emotional overload, my dog is my silent security blanket; pressing his body next to mine and allowing me to focus on his presence in a very tactile way. The rise and fall of his chest with each breath, the soft silkiness of his fur, the gentle warmth of his tongue allows me to redirect the pain and quell emotional anxiety, preventing me from spiraling downward into depression.

It takes a special dog to be able to offer this level of physical, mental, emotional and social facilitation. In *The Golden Bridge,* Patty Dobbs Gross details the breeding, training, and placement of dogs that will become facilitators for children with a host of life's challenges. Her approach of a "three-way partnership" of the dog, the child, and the family sets each member of the partnership up for success in a positive way. Understanding that dogs are social animals, Patty Dobbs Gross embraces the "It Takes a Village" concept of how each family member's individual contribution is essential for a successful placement. She offers a solid foundation for how this can be achieved, step-by-step. Although the book's focus is on how assistance dogs can mitigate children's challenges, the advice shared within its pages will be immensely helpful for anyone involved in breeding, raising and training dogs to mitigate any type of disability at any age.

The Golden Bridge is a gift to all of us who are discovering how powerfully the human-canine bond can change our lives for the better.

Debi Davis

Preface

"A dog never lies about love."—Jeffrey Masson

All proceeds from this book will go to fund North Star Foundation, a nonprofit organization whose mission is to breed, train and place assistance dogs with children who face a variety of challenges. The majority of our clients have autism or other developmental disorders, but we have also placed North Star dogs with children who are grieving over losses, living with life threatening illnesses, adjusting to adoptive homes, or dealing with serious medical conditions. North Star dogs are carefully bred to possess temperaments conducive to working with children and our training programs are based completely on positive reinforcement.

There are many people to thank for helping me to create North Star Foundation and write this book. My parents have encouraged me to value diversity since I was small and allowed me to feel comfortable with my own differences. My husband and four children have made many sacrifices to allow me to do North Star's work, even when it cut deeply into our own time together. My friend and North Star's Assistant Director, Genevieve Nilluka, has helped to shape North Star's growth and greatly enriched our work with her sensitive and generous spirit. North Star's supporters include heads of corporations as well as children who raised coins through bake sales; our puppy raisers range from rocket scientists to stay at home parents who want to enrich their children's lives by helping those in need. All are equally appreciated.

North Star works with therapists, teachers, and family members of the children we serve; we also educate our children's classmates about the nature of the unique challenges they face. Building bridges of understanding and empathy between our children and the members of their community is important to us, as we believe there is no better way to teach tolerance than through the eyes of a puppy being trained to help. We pledge our commitment to help care for all the world's children, regardless of race, religion, gender, disability or nationality.

Despite the different heights of our supposed ceilings, we all sleep under the same sky.

Part 1

The Journey Home

1

The Golden Bridge

We need light in the darkness and sound in the
silence. We need bridges in place of walls and we
need to be encouraged to cross those bridges one step
at a time from our own world to a shared world.
—Donna Williams, Australian author with autism

This book is written for anyone who desires to help a child socially, emotionally and educationally through the use of a properly bred and trained assistance dog. It is designed to help you to locate an appropriate dog for your child through a recognized organization or independently, to craft a training plan and to create this dog's ultimate job description once inside your home.

It is written from experience, as over a decade ago we received an assistance dog named Madison from Canine Companions for Independence (CCI) to work with our son, Danny, who had been diagnosed with autism at the tender age of two. Today Danny is 18 years old and preparing to attend the University of Connecticut, where he will live in a dorm and major in communication sciences. He is respected as a talented writer and filmmaker in our town and he enjoys a small circle of close friends and a large measure of intelligence and integrity. I don't think the aging golden who still sleeps by his side can take all the credit for his successful development, but I do believe Madison contributed greatly to Danny's solid social skills and sky-high level of confidence.

These goals did not take center stage during the maelstrom of Danny's early intervention, and they were not even the specific goals we had in mind when we brought Madison home. The ways Madison helped our son came as a result of a dynamic process that involved every member of our family. We learned as much from what worked with his placement as what didn't, and all that we discovered has formed our philosophy for creating our placements at North Star Foundation.

Madison came to work with Danny in the spring of 1993; CCI's official title for him was "social dog" and he was paired in a three-way partnership with Danny and my husband, Ron. I wanted to be the one to attend the mandatory two-week training period with Danny, but I had just delivered my fourth child the week our name came up on the waiting list, and so Ron accompanied him to CCI to pick up Madison without us. It was with great regret that I watched them go, as Danny's siblings and I wanted very much to take this new journey with him. This experience taught me that with placements involving children, all family members should ideally be included in the process of acquiring an assistance dog as much as possible. A healthy family needs to share both the heartbreak as well as the joys that come with meeting a child's challenge.

We were told that to promote bonding we would need to establish that Madison was Danny's dog as opposed to his three siblings', and so we ran into our first roadblock to our placement, painfully and headlong. Her name is Jennie and she is Danny's older sister; she was only five at the time, but packed a real wallop in the pure will department, especially concerning animals. I believe CCI's policy regarding siblings is necessary due to the difficulties of bonding with an older dog, especially when we consider the importance of the dependable canine service that an adult or a child with a physical challenge requires. In these cases, dogs need to keep as their primary focus the people they are serving. However, when we tried to enforce this "hands-off" policy with Jennie, it not only didn't fly, it crashed in painful flame. For one day I tried to keep her from bonding with Madison before her plaintive sobs changed my mind.

I now believe that siblings of a child with a social, emotional or educational challenge need to be a part of any effective therapy that is to take place inside their collective home. Siblings help to bring the assistance dog into the fold of the most important social clique your child will ever attempt to enter: your family. The siblings of a child with a social challenge such as autism have more important roles to play in their families than average children, and their support and ability to teach and to lead their brother or sister, as well as the assistance dog who works with him or her, is key to a successful family group. This is why all the placements we make at North Star are family-based, with every member given a special job to perform with their North Star dog. The job assignments are created with bonding issues uppermost in mind (i.e., to facilitate bonding, jobs such as feeding will be given to the child with a challenge, but we also try to draw the rest of the siblings into the placement with jobs such as walking or grooming). The dogs we use for placements at North Star are from very people-oriented genetic lines within very social breeds, and they are encouraged to form individual bonds with every member of their immediate family, which sets us all up for success.

In traditional assistance dog programs, fully trained dogs are placed with human partners when the dogs are over two years of age. New owners must learn handling skills during a two- or three-week training session, and selection of the specific dog for the person he or she will serve is made toward the end of this session. Dovetailing the dog's prior socialization experiences with its future job description is not given high priority, and follow-up services are usually minimal. While receiving a fully trained dog is certainly more convenient, there can be drawbacks to placements created between children and older dogs not specifically socialized to work with them, and danger in placements that are not monitored closely by professionals as the years pass. Placements made to help a child socially, emotionally or educationally differ significantly from one meant to help a physically challenged adult, and so the philosophy of placement should be tailored to better meet the unique needs of the child. Training plans should be developed in tandem with the dog's natural development and abilities, and respect should be given to meeting the dog's needs as well as the child's throughout the life of the placement.

At North Star we place our dogs within the home at a younger age than typical for assistance dogs, as less intensive training is needed or desired. It is indeed possible for a dog to be too trained; I've seen dogs like this, with the uncomfortable mix of a sensitive nature and correction-based training, waiting tensely for the next command and frightened of failure. We want to take this energy and work with it to encourage creativity in a dog's approaches to seeking attention from a child. We also take full advantage of the superior bonding that comes with following an earlier timetable for pairing and placement. This opportunity allows us to create early and specific socialization goals appropriate for the dog's ultimate job description, and to begin work on them immediately. This also allows early visits to take place between the puppy and the child, with rich opportunities to educate and prepare them both for their future working relationship.

Creating placements when the dog is still young can help to facilitate the strongest bonds possible, along with ensuring that the dog's early training and socialization will match the child's needs for the dog in question. By the age of two years, a dog's temperament and abilities are well established. What if the dog has not had exposure during the early months to the child in question, or the specific challenges that child presents? With no experience in how to interpret behaviors that many children with autism display, the dog may react unpredictably. Children with autism or other developmental disabilities often display unusual behavior, occasionally throwing loud tantrums or failing to grant the appropriate body space that we unconsciously and consistently grant each other. Dogs depend greatly on nonverbal communication, and are apt to be uncomfortable with violation of "personal space."

A case in point: a few weeks after we received Madison, I decided to take him to a rehabilitation center for a pet therapy visit. Shortly after entering the center a woman with Alzheimer's disease approached, waving her arms and speaking loudly in gibberish. Madison growled menacingly and we beat a hasty retreat. I was mortified and confused. Here was a dog that had a very gentle temperament and was extremely well-trained; it took me a while to realize that Madison's lack of exposure to the profile of a typical Alzheimer's patient is what caused him to interpret her behavior as threatening. It occurred to me then that a dog should ideally be raised from puppyhood with exposure to his/her eventual partner, or at least with exposure to the typical behavior patterns of this future partner.

Madison came to us equipped with the skills of a working mobility assistance dog, and although his temperament proved exactly what we needed to help our son, many of Madison's skills were useless to us. (Turning the lights on and off is a cute trick, but it's tough on wallpaper.) Although Madison formed a bond with my son Danny and the rest of us, right from the start his canine heart clearly belonged to my husband, Ron. My theory is that this happened because Madison's puppy-raiser who cared for him during his first eighteen months of life was a middle-aged gentleman with no family. The powerful and early bond that formed between the two provided the template for Madison's future relationships, and now when Ron leaves on his occasional business trips our entire family must support Madison emotionally. Ideally, this is the type of deep bond a service dog should form with his child partner, not the father of the child. I believe the earlier the working pair bond, the greater the chance for achieving a deep relationship. It is out of these convictions that North Star Foundation was formed and I set out to breed, socialize, and train service dogs for children in nontraditional ways.

The vast majority of our placements have local puppy-raising families that host visits from the child the pup will serve and they support the gradual transition to the child's home. This connection between families also helps to pull the child with a challenge into the fold of his community, as most challenges children face have the potential to isolate them. The cooperation that exists between a child's parents, therapists, siblings, friends and puppy raisers, together with the puppy as fluffy catalyst, provides a powerful support system for a child with a challenge.

However, it is a very different experience to acquire an assistance dog at a young age than the more traditional approach of placing assistance dogs over the age of two, when nearly all training is complete. It takes more time and energy to train and set boundaries for the young pup, and it takes patience to teach children the skills to lead a young dog traveling like the original poky puppy up steep learning curves. Neither method is ideal; both have drawbacks that should be recognized and worked through.

Careful breeding and educated puppy selection go a long way toward reducing training time and increasing the safety of our placements, as does establishing optimal behavioral patterns right from the start. But this partnering up to complete a young dog's training isn't for every family, and we advise families that are not able to expend this time and energy to seek other organizations that provide fully trained dogs to work with their children. These fully trained dogs are expensive, and so you may find either the money you are asked to provide or fundraise prohibitively high, or else you may discover the waiting list to be dismally long, but there are circumstances that make these older, fully trained dogs worth the wait as well as the money.

There are desired qualities in a North Star dog that cannot be trained; they instead are recognized, carefully nurtured, and supported. The ability of some dogs to read human social cues is capitalized upon in North Star's breeding program. North Star dogs pay attention to the subtle cues every member of the family gives out, and I believe much of the potential for these qualities comes encoded in the genes. We have been selectively breeding dogs for North Star work that display confident intelligence, creative problem-solving ability and the potential to form strong bonds with the members of their family. The relationship these well-bred and well-socialized dogs will eventually form with their handlers and children is equally important in creating a successful placement, as being able to communicate effectively with a dog is a necessary component to any working canine partnership.

It requires a shift in thinking about traditional dog training to fully understand this concept, as traditional dog training has tended to focus on simple canine compliance rather than communication about our shared goals. I myself have been struggling to shift my paradigms about dog training; several years ago we spent a great deal of time and energy developing a technique to train dogs to block a fleeing child's escape. A North Star mom named Kathy desired to teach her son's dog, North Star's Nomar, to block her autistic son Jake's flight. Trainer Pam Murphy worked together with Kathy to achieve this goal, and ultimately they were successful; they even got Nomar to block Jake to the left or right upon her verbal cue! Training Nomar to block Jake was a major achievement, but the blocking skill must be regularly practiced and reinforced to prevent its extinction and, despite all the effort it took to design and maintain this training, to date it has never been found necessary to keep Jake within boundaries. There has been a valuable and ironic silver lining to all of Nomar's training, as the emphasis on the blocking training within the family served to demonstrate the seriousness of the issue in Jake's mind. Jake now stays within boundaries appropriately, seeking his parents' permission before leaving the yard.

Jake and Nomar can enjoy each other's company outdoors now that Jake has learned an appropriate respect for boundaries, with Nomar's assistance. In the meantime, however, four other North Star children with autism have wandered off from home and each time their North Star dogs have followed them and kept them safe in a variety of ways the dogs themselves created. One North Star dog, Flash, began to spontaneously circle his child, Justin, when he wandered away, offering him his leash with his mouth. Another North Star dog, Bailey, coaxed his boy Gavin to return to his summer beach house by nipping gently at his heels all the way home. Despite solid foundation training to stay in their respective yards, all these dogs followed their children when they wandered off their property. The intelligent disobedience of the dogs choosing to leave the property to follow their children against their specific training to stay in the yard was important, but the real value came with the creativity these dogs then displayed in their efforts to bring their children home. None of the North Star dogs were specifically trained to circle their children who were leaving the safety of their homes or to nip at their heels or hand them their leashes, but they had all been raised with lots of follow-the-leader and hide-and-seek games played with their children to set the stage for their later care-taking behavior. These North Star dogs' intelligent disobedience-in-action demonstrates the combined influence of their natural instincts along with their perceived role within their pack (i.e., their child's family). I believe these dogs demonstrated this ability due to a combination of factors that involve both nature as well as nurture:

- Good genetic potential,
- Gentle and positive training, and
- Communicative relationships with their handlers that encourage the dogs to think for themselves.

By focusing on the importance of relationship-building rather than cut-and-dried training we can better support our canine companions in their effort to think for themselves rather than just obey our commands. Obviously, the dogs need to regard us as leaders, and our North Star dogs are submissive even to the youngest children they serve, but the respect they have for their families is mutual and not tainted with any fear of physical corrections.

This is very important to our work at North Star, for our children with autism are relatively safe when they are in our sight because we are there. But most of the danger to children with autism happens when we are not there, and all four times when North Star children with autism have wandered off, their dogs have followed them and thought for themselves to figure out how to bring them home. And it is very important to state clearly that although our deepest hope is that North Star dogs will come to understand what their roles are as protectors in vulnerable children's lives, this dog should still be regarded as a safety net beneath other safety nets, and never as a babysitter paid with liver snaps.

The most rewarding aspect of my work is watching the child begin to take responsibility for his or her dog. Encouraging a child to take an active and nurturing role in raising and training a puppy is an ideal way to teach him/her empathy and responsibility. Most children with challenges have had significant care given to them in their young lives, and many seem quite delighted to experience the role reversal that a North Star placement offers them. I have seen nonverbal children run to fill up their dog's water bowl when their dog began to pant, and the pride they take in watching their dog slake their thirst is obvious. Expanding this empathy to a thirsty playmate is tricky (for playmates don't normally pant), but a wise parent will point out the more subtle signs of thirst in humans, including the phrase "I'm thirsty!" It is language that gets in the way of understanding our nonverbal children, and of them understanding us, but as luck would have it our dogs are not inclined to be verbose. Many nonverbal children are actually quite skilled at reading body language, and most are more perceptive than we might imagine. They are also more sensitive and empathetic than you may believe, and not once have I seen any child with autism be intentionally rough with his dog. The one time I heard of a child being rough with his North Star dog (which immediately ended the placement) was when a child had a major sleep disturbance and difficulty with his changing medications.

Unfortunately, sometimes empathy does not exist or develop properly in a child, and in this case an assistance dog placement would not be appropriate. Children who have poor impulse control may still be appropriate candidates for an older, more stable dog with the necessary guidance and supervision, but a young and vulnerable dog would obviously not be appropriate for them. I think it is very important to understand that children who tend to lash out physically are not good candidates for any dog, or any animal, at least until these tendencies are brought under strict control. This is for the safety of the dog as well as the child, for any animal will ultimately defend itself despite its breeding and training.

Although assistance dog placements have been helping children with social and emotional goals for over a decade, the concept of training a dog in a three-way partnership with a child with a developmental disability is still somewhat unusual. I personally witness the benefits of these placements on a daily basis, but I also greatly respect the potential dangers that exist when a child with a developmental disability is paired with any animal. With North Star's work I place great faith in the dogs we breed and raise, based on the sound principles of behavioral genetics and the positive training techniques we employ. We also spend a great deal of time educating the parents of the child in question to understand how to facilitate the bond and properly supervise the interactions between the dog and their child.

It is extremely important to provide close supervision between children and their dogs at all times. This is true for all children, but it is especially important for children with autism. The same difficulties with communication that children with autism experience with people can exist with dogs. Dogs take their cue from us regarding how their relationships with people are structured; training is just a concentrated form of communication about what behaviors we want to encourage or discourage. If a child with autism does not make it clear to his or her puppy that playful nips hurt, then the puppy will naturally nip more. Waiting for appropriate signals about limits is how this pup would approach his siblings during playtime. These nips are not necessarily aggressive, as play between puppies can involve lots of nipping and playful growling. It is important for the caretakers of any child to understand that their role is to ensure that the relationship between child and puppy is consistently gentle and mutually enjoyable. This is not just during a temporary training phase, but for the life of the dog. It is also not only a training issue for the pup, but also an educational one for the child. Engaging a child to take an active and nurturing role in raising his or her very own puppy is an ideal way to teach the child how to set limits and communicate appropriately the way he or she wants to be treated.

Parental involvement is crucial in a three-way placement of a child and a young dog or puppy, and although time-consuming, this job is not unpleasant. On the contrary, adding a well-bred and well-trained puppy or dog makes time spent working on a child's social, emotional, and educational goals more focused and fun. Attention paid when the child and the pup are together must be consistent and educated, but the parents I have come to know pay this type of attention to their children already. These parents also come to crave the emotional support their North Star dog gives them so freely. It is part of the joy of my job to watch these parents begin to understand that they get to love this dog as much as their children, and to reap the benefits of having an assistance dog in the family. The right dog can be a valuable companion in the life of any child, regardless of the challenges he or she must face. The wise parent asks for assistance in selecting the most appropriate puppy, learning positive training methods, socializing the pups correctly, and facilitating the bond that develops between the child and the dog.

Parents will also need to transfer the puppy or young dog's training into their home. Dogs are associative creatures, and teaching them to sit at a training facility or their puppy raiser's living room is not the same thing as teaching the pup to sit in his owner's kitchen. Training classes for the pup should also focus on training the owners of the dog so that the pup's training can be easily transferred to the home. Training is a dynamic, not static, process, and dogs are much more than computers to be programmed.

Allowing the child with autism to watch the clicker training of a puppy can be a path to grasping verbal language through observation. Some older children with autism get quite skilled at clicker training, especially if they are familiar with the premise of applied behavioral analysis (ABA). To be on the teaching side of this equation is refreshing to them, and dogs trained to respond to children's commands and to regard them as leaders help to raise their self-esteem.

We put considerable energy into teaching the child to interact with his or her dog in ways that enhance bonding and enrich communication. These goals are incorporated into the dog's training based on observed interactions that take place naturally. For instance, recently a young boy with autism named Ian met his North Star puppy, Duncan, in my kitchen; despite his very young age, Ian was quite communicative and automatically gave Duncan a "back off" hand sign when he came too close. Duncan sat down at this waving of arms and slight vocalization and thus a command had been born. It is important to recognize and reinforce such interactions, and to think creatively about commands, thus increasing the dog's ability to communicate with his or her child. Many North Star dogs are trained to respond to hand signs, thereby increasing the communication between child and dog if a child does not yet speak clearly. These signs don't have to follow any universally understood sign language, and I think it's best to create them based on a child's naturally occurring movements. One boy with autism quickly taught his dog that circling his finger in the air meant, "sit." For us, it was just a matter of watching the boy invent this sign, and pairing this event with a verbal command to sit, which we then quickly faded. Dogs pay great attention to our body language, and they are quick to learn and respond to hand signals if given appropriate feedback.

An assistance dog can act as a bridge between the activities of a therapy session and a child's home program, providing familiar cues and structure to pragmatic language. This helps to generalize language learned in a speech therapy session, and to translate it into conversation spoken in the larger world beyond the walls of the therapy room. Children with autism often have great difficulty in generalizing learned speech to new situations and people. This is due to their overly selective attention and tendency to respond to only a limited number of cues. Using an assistance dog as a tool for teaching pragmatic language at home and in the community can be as simple as rehearsing stock responses to the fairly predictable questions people are likely to ask when they see a well-trained dog wearing a saddle with a patch that reads "Please Ask to Pet Me." As children with autism tend to be dependent on verbal cues provided by others, this positive and predictable social interaction is a valuable tool to help with developing pragmatic speech within natural settings in the home as well as the outside community. People who may have shied away from the responsibility of starting a conversation with your child, and keeping it in motion, often relax and rise to the challenge when a dog is available to help structure the questions and comments.

North Star remains committed to assisting families throughout the life of our placements and to help design positive techniques to deal with the adolescent dog's desire to push the limits he has previously accepted with good-natured puppy charm. We keep our North Star dogs in training programs for the entire first year of a dog's life, and sometimes well into the second. Teenage dogs, like teenage children, require a different set of skills to manage, and successfully mastering these new skills is key to a smooth transition to adulthood for both dogs as well as children (and I know how hard making this training/parenting shift can be, as I now have four teenage children and two teenage dogs living under my roof!).

When creating North Star placements we seek to empower our clients to participate in forming their own training relationship with a well-behaved young dog, and any professional currently working with this child will hopefully be receptive to ways this bond can be used to help the child socially, emotionally or educationally within the context of therapy. I believe it is important to note that the biggest mistake made with animal-assisted therapy is the tendency to impose too much structure upon it, or to give it too heavy a frame. I think of my North Star dogs as simple tools for creatively capturing attention, transitioning focus, and calming anxiety. Our goals at any given time are social, emotional and educational, but dividing these concepts up into separate words can be deceiving. During the best sessions these three goals are interwoven and can't be easily pulled apart.

I have witnessed, more than created, ways that assistance dogs have a therapeutic effect on children. I believe these effects are heightened in a child with autism because of the powerful nature of communication between the dog and the child. A child with autism, like the rest of us, needs a reliable friend at the end of the day. Examining the reactions of the child to the young dog are key components in determining how this dog can help the child emotionally. One North Star dog discovered on his own that his well-timed lick to his boy's cheek disrupted an impending tantrum. Naturally he was reinforced for this, both by the boy's resulting giggles as well as the stream of treats the Mom was coached to deliver at this moment. Noticing interactions like this and then putting a dog's naturally occurring behaviors on cue help to create North Star's specific training programs.

Spending time with a dog is a nice way to structure critical down time (which can greatly reduce the frequency of meltdowns). We encourage our families to redefine "time out" as non-punitive time spent with a North Star dog reliably holding a down/stay to provide comfort and support. This can help a child to have the rough edges of his or her day smoothed over gently.

A properly bred and trained dog can modify autism's expression by stimulating an area of the brain that responds to animate objects, which has been found to be weak in the MRIs of autistic children. It also keeps a child focused on any learning plan in progress, either as a motivator or prop for the day's lesson plan. Allowing the child to watch you train a puppy can be quite an easy path to grasping verbal language through observation, and the ability to attract the child's attention seems the most important advantage here.

North Star dogs have also been used as tools to meet other therapeutic goals, such as those established in occupational or physical therapy. Sometimes this role is motivational, as some of this therapeutic work can be tough on a child. One little girl named Jessie would get a kiss from her North Star dog every time she completed a repetition of ten exercises as part of her rigorous physical therapy program, and this addition to her program has increased her ability to focus on the tasks at hand.

This book concentrates on placements between assistance dogs and children with autism, as over half the children we serve are on the autism spectrum, but North Star dogs are also helping children with a variety of other challenges as well. We have also placed North Star dogs to support children who have suffered a tragedy, faced a loss, or are dealing with life-threatening illnesses. It is more difficult for me to write about how these children are helped, for so much of how we can help children who face tragedy is simply bearing quiet witness to their loss and carving out a space for them to safely explore their feelings. North Star dogs can comfort dependably on cue, which can help in a variety of ways with children who suffer a loss or stressful event. This dog can become a tool for animal-assisted therapy, either in the context of traditional therapy sessions in a professional office or in the more casual (but no less important) atmosphere of the child's home. The grief placements I've helped to create at North Star certainly humble me, for I've learned that some days it is enough to simply hope you can distract a child briefly from his or her sorrow or pain, and to give family members who share this child's challenge a soft furry creature to focus on during a very difficult day.

A seizure alert and response that certain dogs can provide offer valuable safeguards for a child with epilepsy. Although no one can reliably predict which dogs will provide a naturally occurring seizure alert, a response can be trained from learning to recognize and reinforce this alert when it does occur. There are also methods that can increase the likelihood of an alert surfacing. Many researchers believe most dogs have the capability of alerting to seizures, but only about one in ten pet dogs of people with epilepsy seem able to learn to alert dependably for this; I believe this number would be higher if people knew how to recognize a naturally occurring alert and could then expand it to include a trained response.

Several years ago we placed a North Star dog with a young boy with a rare genetic disorder called congenital adrenal hyperplasia (a condition that causes fluctuating hormones and resulting mood swings). His North Star dog, Lily, chose to alert to this state by backing into his boy to sit on his lap. Fortunately, the boy found this amusing, but if he did not, then another alerting technique would more than likely have been created. It is the dynamics of the relationships that will determine how the communication will unfold between dog, parent and child; in this case I placed Lily with this family at the young age of nine weeks. I believed it was better for Lily to have grown up with this boy from an early age, and as the mother was home full time and both of her children were old enough to support our training goals, we selected a very early placement date for Lily. She began alert work early as well, following her boy Ryan from room to room if he was upset or feeling ill; both Ryan and his parents and sister would support this shadowing, and Lily quickly understood her role in his life. She now alerts dependably to changes in his hormone levels, and Ryan has a companion during his most difficult times. I believe that when comfortably possible, an early and supported placement with an appropriately tempered dog is optimal for setting the stage for alerting behavior to occur.

The right dog can be a valuable companion in the life of any child, despite the challenges he or she must face. It is not difficult to select the most appropriate puppy, learn positive training methods, and facilitate the bond that develops to create your own companion dog for your child. It is also easy to locate an appropriate organization to assist you if you feel you need more guidance in selection or training of your dog. Whatever method you choose, I advise you to keep safety as your touchstone and to begin your adventure with optimism, knowing you can always turn back if the path proves too thorny. Just don't let doubt be what changes your course, because weathering the storms of uncertainty is an important part of this journey.

2

Diary of an Autistic Mother

Not all who wander are lost.—J.R.R. Tolkien

I actually have no disability, at least none readily apparent or visible to the naked eye. But look closer, listen to me for a while and you might discern the characteristics and quirks of someone mildly autistic. Perhaps it will be as subtle as an inappropriate pause that interrupts our conversation, disturbing a rhythm you didn't even know existed until it was broken. Maybe it will be my penchant for following tangents, or my ability to turn our topic on a dime. Autism, at its best, offers a reprieve from society's tedious pretenses, an opportunity to peek over the fence of conformity, and a chance to feel at one with the open meadow beyond.

But being an open meadow while driving down the highway can get you killed, and sprinkling too many non sequiturs on top of a dinner party can earn you a reputation for being the one who inhaled Bill's leftover smoke. So I struggle to keep track of the details of my day, rarely taking the time to rummage through my personality for autistic tendencies. And the truth is, I actually have very good social skills; my eye contact is normally excellent, my conversation almost always appropriate and my purpose usually clear. I believe I'm enriched by my idiosyncrasies, but never feel defined by them, and I have achieved a good measure of success in my life despite these traits (or perhaps even because of them).

But I have also spent years arranging rocks in increasingly complex patterns, initially to keep my son company but later just because I felt like it. I've grown reckless with society's expectations and confused about things I used to think were certain. I feel driven to turn nonconformance into an art form, and my wardrobe is a hodge-podge of hand-me-downs somebody else pulled off the rack. I am prone to pointing out the emperor's lack of clothing, despite the consequences. (And while anarchy is sometimes considered attractive in the young, this seldom holds true for middle-aged Connecticut housewives.)

What value do we place on someone who won't, or can't, conform? Is looking presentable as important to a happy life as Sears implies? If someone contributes to a conversation by presenting a different slant on the subject, is that an odd, or a charming, thing to do?

While I'm busy asking you all these questions, I'll ask you this: are society's social expectations an intrinsic part of understanding autism? Does being a conformist color the meaning conveyed by the word? Lorna Wing once described a group of children with Asperger's syndrome, a high-functioning form of autism, as "active but odd." *Wired* magazine ran an article that referred to Asperger's as the "geek syndrome." (The premise was that underlying the explosion of diagnosed cases of autism in the Silicon Valley is the social phenomenon of geeks procreating like active but odd little bunnies.)

I think there may be some validity to this idea, but it is important to view it with through a pane wiped clean of society's fingerprints. It seems we are still busy untangling autistic tendencies from personality traits, disorders from differences, normal genetic variations from defective ones. The nature of diagnosing and treating autism is still so mired in misinformation that prejudicial opinion tainted with social values continues to fill in far too comfortably for fact.

Autism predisposed Danny to perceive the world differently; it is no surprise that he would end up altering my own perceptions as well. After all, we've spent eighteen years influencing each other. When Danny was small I believed I had to energetically interrupt his natural course of development and pull all of his thoughts my way. But how far did he end up pulling me his way, for better or for worse? I am now a much more tolerant and original thinker than I used to be, and I suspect these gifts came from the experience of raising my son. But which came first, me as the chicken or Danny's egg?

This is a relevant question. Scientists are beginning to answer it with the help of our burgeoning knowledge of genetics. There was a recent cover story in *Time* magazine that suggested that the components of autism, far more than autism itself, tend to run in families. According to Dr. Fred Volkmar, a child psychiatrist at Yale, this is especially true in cases of children with Asperger's. About a third of the fathers or brothers of children with Asperger's show signs of the disorder (and, so far as I understand, mothers are not off the genetic hook). This seems to underscore *Wired* magazine's premise, as the ability to focus unwavering attention and remain undistracted by social cues can be quite a valuable trait to possess in present-day Silicon Valley. It might be possible that people on the autism spectrum are finally becoming appreciated by our culture, at least enough to allow them to succeed as part of our mainstream as adults. And as creatures that adapt within a society live to reproduce there, this might be part of the increase in numbers of children being diagnosed with autism.

It might also be that the net we cast has become increasingly sophisticated, and has been able to catch more children than it might have in the past, but if this theory is true, then where are the unidentified Asperger children from my school days as adults? I personally remember kids being teased for their supposed similarities to computers and I've heard it said that today many adults on the high-functioning end of the spectrum can be found teaching on college campuses, unlabeled and successful, for academia is relatively safe ground for many people with autism.

Temple Grandin is a woman with high-functioning autism who has achieved a great deal of success in animal science, her chosen field of study. It should be noted that she was raised in the fifties with the help of a very intelligent and intuitive mother and a nanny who appeared to have experience raising children on the spectrum. (Although in this decade it was rare to actually have a label of autism, this nanny recognized the similarities between her previous charge and Temple and followed both her instincts as well as her experience when helping to raise her.) Temple's mother also speaks of how the village-like atmosphere of suburbia in the 1950s helped to form an effective type of early intervention that retained its community roots.

Rummaging through my own past for answers to autism's genetic roots is tricky business, for pressing relatives between slides to examine them under a microscope is a dangerous pastime. I managed to slip through my childhood without being labeled, but my brothers and junior high school enemies enjoyed pointing out my absentminded nature and the random trains of thought I was prone to hop aboard. My husband, Ron, first attracted me because of his charming disregard of social rules and his refreshing lack of guile. (I wasn't the only one who followed him around at parties to hear what he was going to say next, but I was the one who stuck around the longest.) I found him refreshing in New England's rather rigid and stifling social climate, and I still do. Together we have four amazing children, two dynamic careers and a very green lawn. Despite our outwardly successful life together thus far, do our quirks put us on the autism spectrum? Can we use our accomplishments like a shield to protect us? And assuming we can, should we even try?

If my parents, or Ron's, had taken us to even one professional who believed we had enough of the traditional hallmarks of autism to warrant giving us a label, then we would be considered autistic even today. So far, there is no blood test to be given or genetic marker to be found that can clear us once indicted. Professionals, loath as the rest of us to admit mistakes, rarely take back labels, but as luck would have it our parents had a wide definition of what they considered normal; we also had many friends who seemed to like us despite our unusual personalities (or perhaps even because of them). We flew under the radar, and today I bump into people all the time who had apparently joined us on this stealth flight. The tests they are designing today for screening children with autism are growing increasingly sophisticated, and I believe that many more children are vulnerable to being swept up onto the autistic spectrum than you might suspect. I see autistic traits in people frequently in my life and they are sprinkled into the soup of our collective unconscious, from quirky neighbors on sitcoms to Emily Dickenson, Jane Austen, and Andy Warhol (and, of course, Einstein: my favorite impressive person to point to when defending the quality of autistic thought). I have come to appreciate the refreshing color and creative thought these characters use to design our shared landscape. I worry that the tests they are designing to catch early autistic tendencies can cause many more parents undue anxiety about what it means to have them. I think casting a wider, more sophisticated net will help to locate children we can potentially help, and that this will ultimately lead to deeper acceptance for autistic adults, but this can only happen when a new paradigm is built by all of us that respects the autistic tendencies they will find.

The same thought applies to children who are intellectually challenged (who often have quite impressive social skills). I was told I should no longer use the word "retarded" by a mother with great pain in her eyes, because the word was bastardized by society, and used as a weapon on most playgrounds. I certainly know what she means. When I ask for the definition of "retarded" in the classrooms I visit I get such a predictable response: slightly shamed expressions from the young and giggling ones, with quick and knowing looks sliced across the silence in the older grades. A new word is needed to reflect what it means to be intellectually challenged in our society, but only after we've weeded out the preconceived notions that have taken such deep and shameful root at our feet.

The nature of our collective reality is to consciously define and agree upon it, hopefully refining it as the years pass. A curious lag in this flow toward enlightenment is our understanding of developmental differences. Just over a decade ago the myth of the refrigerator mother causing autism was still widely believed (this phrase was coined to describe the cold, unfeeling mother whose chilly parenting style somehow caused her child's autism). Bettleheim had crafted his own fairy story about this topic, along with the more traditional ones for children. The refrigerator mother was a character in a fairy tale meant for adults; by casting the mother of a child with autism as a tragically flawed catalyst for disaster, he kept everyone else seemingly safe from this devastating whim of fate.

Despite myself, I understand why. I have doubted my own mothering; how can I expect others not to? To have a child not meet your eyes, to be looked through as easily as a pane of glass, is unnerving. The situation begs for a reaction or solution. So neighbors, certain relatives, some probably-distant-anyway friends judge you in a way that coils around their value system like a snake. Because I nursed him until he was nearly two, all Danny's difficulties were initially chalked up to my unusually child-centered parenting. (I conceived my first child in southern California. Enough said!)

This is interesting: within the space of a decade a woman could be blamed for causing autism by being either a refrigerator or a maternal monster furnace stuck on full blast. To add to the confusion, the information I found on how to raise my son was saturated with misinformation that was often biased, and sometimes just plain wrong. For instance, one book advised ignoring echolalic speech; another stated Danny's early reading was chalked up to a splinter skill ("barking at words") that was to be ignored.

This advice was echoed over the phone in a weary tone by our developmentalist; he was responding to my discovery that 2½-year-old Danny could read any word I wrote with chalk on our driveway. This had seemed a pivotal moment to me, much like Helen Keller connecting the feeling of a cold stream of water to the way Anne Sullivan's fingers moved across her palm. I had stumbled upon a way to communicate with my son using a different medium, and I knew he comprehended at least some of what he read; the way he responded to the blue chalk "Mommy" was a dead giveaway (a most unscientific approach, I know, but time proves me correct and the developmentalist still safe from the truth inside his book-lined office). I still cringe when I remember how vulnerable I was to his advice, and how tempting it was to accept his authority, put the chalk away, and wrap the cloak of resignation even tighter around my shoulders.

Fortunately, I have a tendency to trust my instincts. Also, I am a practical girl at heart: reading was really the only way that my son and I could reliably focus on the same page, both literally as well as figuratively. It just made sense to stay in this zone with him as much as possible. (And I know I am not alone in this decision; Clara Parks joined her autistic daughter inside a literal closet for months, waiting so patiently to open the figurative door together.) I never let Danny read the phone book or encyclopedia; however, I began to go the library and took children's books home by the dozen. I lugged home these nourishing books the way other women lugged home the groceries and I read to Danny for six hours a day, treating his increasingly literate echolalia with the respect I felt it deserved.

I found it was quite important to pay great attention to Danny's day, as this was my best preparation for decoding that evening's echolalia. As Danny grew older his echolalia was gradually sanded away with each day's buffing and polishing of his speech. I felt then, and still feel, that the concept of speech and other types of therapy need to be integrated into the home program, as there is no way an hour or two a week inside one room can have a lasting impact on a child's speech.

Working outside the home, something I had been planning on since Helen Reddy sang her cheesy anthem, was now completely out of the question for me. Trusting someone with Danny, even and especially in the segregated program our town offered us, was out of the question. His best new language would often come in tangents; a phrase might be lifted from the page of a book, a snatch of dialog from his movie of the week, or an incident from his day. If I wasn't there to catch this connection it could go by the wayside, along with bits and pieces of his potential. Without this specific knowledge of how Danny was experiencing and communicating about the world, the gulf of misunderstanding between my son and me would inevitably widen. It became my life's central goal to keep this from happening, and it still is, although the truth is this relates to all my four children equally. It is exhausting, but exhilarating, to keep this level of communication and understanding with all of them.

I chose to educate Danny, along with my other children, with a child-led approach primarily because it was the most effective way to gain his elusive attention. I would call his name a dozen times without response, and I could force him to sit in a chair and meet my eyes, but cuddling up to read him a story he chose was often the only way we could actually be together. Incidental learning sounds complicated, but it can make your life much simpler to incorporate this concept into your day. Instead of teaching according to a particular timetable, I believe it is powerful to follow what a child is paying attention to and use that as a launching pad for speech and language learning. An assistance dog fits into this scenario like a hand in glove, as it naturally serves as a shared focal point of attention in any room he or she occupies.

For many years I lived inside a world created by the vivid imaginations of many talented writers, with my children and Madison for company. Surrounding a story such as "Pinocchio" with the book, video, audiotapes, stuffed characters and plastic figures gave me tools to educate Danny. These stories all had messages that were delivered in a way he could receive them, such as the fact that it is the ability to love that makes you a real boy. New products on the market include DVDs of these timeless stories, complete with prominent captions and auditory feedback. (Watching television with the closed caption feature helped Danny to learn to read visually by pairing his weak auditory processing skill with his superior visual avenues to learning.) Computer time on a desk in your living room can be regarded as every bit as important as time spent in a classroom if you have the appropriate software.

As Danny got older, we allowed him to use our video cameras, permitting him freedom to create movies and documentaries. Any kind of artistic or musical expression is helpful not just intellectually, but socially and emotionally as well. These are all avenues that children with autism can travel with power and unique speed, thereby fulfilling their need to create and express themselves. Being blocked from verbally expressing themselves is hard on children with autism (or for any child), but by providing other paths toward self-expression children with autism can, and do, thrive.

In truth, these early years raising Danny were a wonderful reprieve from the stifling structure my life had acquired even before my first child, Jennie, was born. The eighties were a time of bellying up to the Monopoly board and buying your properties; I let Ron handle all our number crunching and budget making during his many hotel nights away from us. While he and the rest of the Western world seemed preoccupied with making money, I was spending it on Disney movies and dinners out that featured more than chicken nuggets. It was my way of making time with my children by avoiding cooking and cleaning, as well as increasing Danny's experiences within the community. (I still go to Friendly's every Monday evening with Danny, come hell, high water or bounced check fees.)

I think back on these years with both a wince and a bit of awe at the often-pregnant crusader with a constellation of kids in tight orbit around her; the woman controlling the benevolent chaos seems too far removed now to be considered me. I don't know whether to pity her or admire her, and I think this was a common reaction to those around me: there was a certain charm in the sheer and adorable force of toddlers and infants. People tended to move aside, but first they usually smiled. I myself was usually happy to be the ringleader of our motley crew; we had no strict bedtime or rigid schedules for our brood in a neighborhood full of people quick to ask if our latest newborn was sleeping through the night. ("Yes!" Ron once tossed back, "in fact, yesterday he went into a coma . . . we were so proud!" He said this with mock pride and weary sarcasm, as it is not easy to live without the approval of your neighbors.)

No matter how hard we tried during those early years to keep our dignity, it often felt like we were a couple of circus clowns, throwing cream pies into each other's faces and tripping over our own huge feet. It felt like everything in our house was worn, creased or dented; sometimes things simply broke quietly and sometimes they shattered in an explosive way, like the giant and pompous crystal bowl we received for our wedding. This bowl had survived three moves from apartment to condo to house, only to splinter into hundreds of shards and chunks across the cheap tile of our kitchen floor. Danny just stood at the center of this perfect glass storm he had created, overwhelmed by the violent beauty but unaware of the social implications of his act of deliberately letting go.

Five-year-old children are not supposed to deliberately break what is obviously fragile. This is clear. They should also refrain from speaking pure gibberish or being related to someone who does. Our eventual banishment was gradual and mutual as we took comfort inside our own home. The calm that exists inside the eye of a storm enveloped us, and together we found joy behind our battened hatches.

I raised and nurtured my four children in this cocooned kind of peace. Thinking back to this time my memories fall cleanly into two camps: upstairs where I spent time with my precious brood, and downstairs where our picture window framed other people's children playing so happily together without them. We would watch those children tumble over each other like the real puppies that would later become so central to our lives; they moved with a rhythm of body language and pragmatic chatter that now seemed meaningless to me and impossible to teach to my son. Mothers stood in tight circles by the carefully planted and pruned bushes, watching their children and gossiping about mine. I would join these groups occasionally, but I had great difficulty keeping the conversational balloon tapped in the air when it floated reluctantly my way. Since autism entered my life, my previous impressive social skills had grown decidedly rusty.

I have a memory of one spring afternoon sitting on my front steps with Danny in our old house, watching child after child dressed in party clothes parade past our postage-stamp lawn. The mothers all carried brightly wrapped gifts as they hurried on by us to the lucky birthday boy's house next door. They avoided eye contact as intently as my son did and for once I was grateful for Danny's oblivious nature, as well as for my own temporary reprieve from pointing out relevant social information to him. My neighbor called me up later to invite Danny to celebrate her son's birthday in a private manner, a self-contained party limited to one strange guest. I politely declined her strained invitation and never bothered her again with over-the-fence chatter or requests for cups of sugar. My children and I stayed inside that beautiful afternoon and watched *Sleeping Beauty* yet again. Malificent's bitterness over being forgotten when everyone else in the kingdom gathered to celebrate Aurora's birth seemed perfectly understandable to me. It came more easily than sympathizing with the king and queen's task of protecting their perfect child.

I had never experienced prejudice in my life, but I was now enrolled in a crash course. It was a painful, if enlightening, experience. People tend to fall back on their personal and fearful inclinations when deciding how to approach a child with a difference. It is difficult to grant the time and non-judgmental attention that is required to gain an understanding of any child, much less a child hidden behind the cloak of a label. I recall a supposed friend, coaxed by the impunity of having a seemingly perfect child, leaving her coffee hot and untouched when Danny and her son disappeared for a moment to play in a different room. She quickly followed them, swept up her son and left, but not before giving him a quick, tight hug in some surge of appreciation for his normalcy. In the days following Danny's diagnosis I had assumed everyone was squarely on my side of the universe when it came to my son; it was always, and still is, an unpleasant shock to discover a different truth. It took me many years to understand that society still knows so little about autism that it is impossible to place true blame on any individual set of ignorant shoulders.

Incidents began to occur on the block and on the bus, and when it rains it usually pours. We discovered the antiquated special education program we were offered was shockingly primitive. They expected Dan to sit for a solid hour in a circle that was populated by every young kid in town who needed any kind of special education; medication was encouraged to help achieve this dubious goal. They would sing songs, I was told, and apparently no child was ever hurt by his own screaming. This was the same advice a pediatrician gave when presented with the problem of Danny's colic, and then again by a young intern at an early intervention program. (I left

Danny with her, despite his frantic screams, only to return to find him still shuddering from sobs in his sleep. "At least he knows now that screaming won't get him what he wants," the young therapist told me earnestly. When I doubted her shaky logic, she read to me from a book on autism. She flipped through pages with her manicured nails, quoting me chapter and verse while Danny slipped from my arms with his sleeping weight.)

Labels can both illuminate and obscure the truth. Danny did technically have colic as a baby, but I regret believing our pediatrician when he said we should shrug out shoulders, wait for that magic three-month mark, and stop trying to delve any further. I now believe I conspired with him to stop this delving into reasons behind my son's desperate communication, as I sensed there were more sinister labels that lay in wait, ready to ambush. Society forces you to cry uncle and bear the weight of a label before you can receive the help this label can offer by way of services and information. Danny's colic was actually screaming due to the disorganization of his sensory integration system; I now believe sounds came painfully magnified to his tender ears. My perplexed reports of Danny's excessive crying were dismissed at our routine doctor's appointments as being beside the point. The immunization shots the nurse gave my son while shooting me dirty looks when I tentatively questioned them are nauseating to recall. Memories of these shots being given come to me grainy and slow, like some cheap horror flick . . . they visit me unbidden at stoplights and creep into the plot of my nightmares. These shots made Danny scream and perhaps regress, and on some level I think I knew this.

I knew it! Or did I? I couldn't be sure then that the shot did anything more than offer protection—and I still can't prove it had any other effect. I couldn't stop the needle from piercing Danny's delicate skin, but I will always wish I had the courage to break the restraint of the nurse's cold look. I wish I still had time to knock that needle from her hand, sending it skittering to the floor so we could all escape. Instead I held my breath while she held him down, and then I would watch Danny scream until he gradually lost his voice. Hours later his mouth would open and the cry could be seen but not heard. Even my own heartbeat when I held his twisting body next to mine in a vain attempt to comfort must have been perceived as a form of torture. It is hard to forgive my failure to understand my son's early and desperate communication, or my own unquestioning ignorance, and after all these years it hurts to even remember it. It is also hard to forgive a society that sent someone to the moon before they could prove that the shot they injected into my baby was safe.

The screaming Danny was doing years later when he was supposed to be singing songs finally landed him in a more enlightened intervention center in a neighboring town. (Danny's screaming not only communicated his pain; it fortunately also disturbed the "normal" kids in the kindergarten class next door.) The conflicted nature of school personnel was revealed to me one afternoon at a hair salon when the customer beside me, a kindergarten teacher, spoke candidly about having the kids with special needs trickle back into mainstream classrooms. Being forced to implement a mandate is not the same thing as creating the space, designing the necessary materials and welcoming children with a difference back into the fold of mainstream education. Any parent of a mainstreamed child needs to know this is true to be certain the child's needs are truly being met by integration.

I recall observing a kindergarten class that included an adorable girl with Down's syndrome. The children were all sitting cross-legged at their teacher's feet, playing a guessing game. All the children clutched little boxes of something they had brought from home on their laps, and the object of the game was to have the other children asks questions until someone guessed correctly what was inside. The little girl with Down's syndrome could only stand before her classmates' forest of raised hands one excited moment before she blurted out with words full of delight and pride: "It's a ball!"

The teacher frowned and firmly told her she had missed the point of the game, and that now she had to sit down. Perhaps tomorrow she could try again, remembering the rules, she was told. I watched her sit back down and laboriously cross her legs, crestfallen. It occurred to me then, as it does now, that the concept of appropriate education for our children is not necessarily more expensive; it does require a shift in thinking, however, which ends up harder in some ways than merely shelling out cash.

Shifting my own thinking to stay connected with Danny was in some respects the most difficult part of raising him. Old and useless paradigms had to shatter as completely as our wedding bowl, and new ones needed to be created and forged with fire. There were several years I fell asleep to tortuous replays of tinny Disney songs, my legs kicking the covers with my repressed restlessness, only to wake up to the weight of yet another day pressing me down. Patience is like a muscle, and for the most part I was in good enough shape to allow Danny the space to learn by repetition, but there were days I ached with the effort of moving at his pace. I remember a walk we took up and down the block one terrible Tuesday morning. For two solid hours we slowly made our way up the block, with Danny stopping every few steps to line up his precious rocks. I wince when I recall the surreptitious glances framed by frilly curtains. My neighbors were watching a mother and son, both deeply immersed in the world of autism, seemingly convinced a spiral pattern of carefully chosen pebbles could be the comfortable center of their universe.

In struggling to remember the past my mind skips to this Tuesday morning like a needle to a worn groove, though I believe this memory is actually a composite of hundreds of similar mornings. I tried to remember as I moved through those days that I was doing something important, even when I was afraid this could not possibly be so. And the cavalry (i.e., my husband Ron) was probably in another state on this mythical morning. As Ron moved up the corporate ladder he frequently moved sideways on lengthy business trips, supposedly not happy to escape the turmoil at home.

There are jagged edges here, and I am bleeding on this page. Ron and I fought frequently about his demanding work schedule during those difficult years, and the scar this formed still winds its way across the face of our relationship. It is only now that I can appreciate what he was trying to tell me: we needed money to wage this war on autism. The Disney movies Danny cherished and took to bed with him like chunky black security blankets were costly. The therapists we hired because the ones the school had provided were substandard or nonexistent were expensive. I spent time with my children rather than helping Ron bring home the bacon, and we often paid other people to fry it up as well. I was a sucker for anything even remotely educational, even if I knew the check would bounce like the shiny blue therapy balls that dotted our backyard. If you're drowning you ignore the price tag on the fancy life jacket that is within arm's reach.

It is no surprise we wound up bankrupt, both financially and emotionally. We brought all four children with us to court the day our case was called, and huddled together on the floor like the masses that yearn to breath free. I felt no shame then, and I still don't as I type these words. I would spend every penny again, and MasterCard be damned. (And apparently, they have already forgiven us. We have been bombarded with new applications with attractive "low" interest rates; last week they even courted Danny.)

I eventually let Danny play with the other kids on the block, staying home or spying on him from a distance with a knot in my stomach. Sometimes his experiences were successful and he would come home glowing to patiently relay his experiences in halting, poetic language before he would go to write about them, illustrating the pages with great care. Other times he would come home upset and unable to tell me exactly why. There was a boy named Mike who lived across the street and who took Danny under his wing (much the same way we had taken Mike under our wing years before when he roamed the neighborhood as a cold, lonely and bored preschooler. What goes around, comes around). Although many kids on the block either ignored Danny or gave him a hard time when no adults were watching, Mike remained unfailingly polite. Danny mentions him in a story he wrote at age six titled "Anytime."

> Danny Was A Great Sport. He Could Run So Fast
> That He Will Never Stop Running. He Never Got
> Tired of Running. He Had A Red Bike, A Green
> License Plate on His Bike, A Black Handle.
> He Had The Word CHALLENGER On His Bike
> Too. He Liked To Show Off. "Thanks!" Said The
> Boys. "Anytime," Said Danny. And The Next Day,
> I Showed Off Again. The Boys Didn't Watch. So He
> Didn't Show Off. I Got In Michael's Way "Get Out
> Of My Way,Dan!" He Whispered. "I'm Not Playing
> With You Or Your Lives!" Danny Shouted. Poor
> Danny Went Home. He Walked His Bike On The
> Sidewalk Just In Case Of Cars. "So?" Asked My
> Mom. How Was It Going?" Great, Except I Had An
> Accident Michael Whispered To Get Out Of His
> Way. "And?" Said Mom. "And Then I Walked Up The
> Sidewalk And Went Home," Answered Danny. He
> Laid On the Couch, Looking At The Ceiling.

Here is another piece of untitled writing, generated about the same time:

> On Daniel's Day with Danny's Friend's Time, He
> Set Off To Bike To His Friends. There Was A License
> Plate On The Back Of His Bike. It Said "Awesome
> Dude!" His Friends Saw It. Their Guess Was It Was
> Awesome. They Climbed Up To The Middle Of The
> Road. They Played Hide & Seek. They Hid In The
> Very End Of The Forest. Danny Could Not Find
> Them, But He Had Another Friend That Liked
> BasketBall. He played BasketBall. They Threw Their
> Balls In The Air. When Daniel Came Back To His
> Friends They Said There Was A Jaguar Suckin'
> Blood Down. Daniel Had A Plan. His Plan Was He
> Would Go Home And His Friends Would Call Him
> Back. And It Was A Jaguar All Right . . .

A careful reading of this story will reveal he was not just teased, but ditched, and my heart sank when he solemnly handed me this slightly rumpled report about his afternoon adventure. The careful arranging of my features to reflect pride instead of the lump in my throat was not even necessary. Danny read books, not facial expressions. It was painful beyond all bounds to have no weapon to fight in this insidious new war, to be reduced to staring out picture windows and sitting on curbs as attentive and powerless as a beached lifeguard. My parents believed being ditched and teased was a rite of passage, and they counseled me to treat Danny like the resilient kid they perceived him to be. And I knew Mike was probably stage whispering his words to Dan with kind intent: "Get out of the way, Danny, you're in the middle of the road. It doesn't matter what you're trying to show me." The fact that one doesn't tend to ditch and tease a person taught in an isolated classroom down a distant hall is confusing comfort. It's true that one can't hurt someone intimately without understanding him, but does this mean you should keep your guard up or continue to break down the barriers of segregation?

All I could do was to pick up the pieces should Danny come home shattered by the destructive mix of an insensitive culture and someone else's bad parenting. I still acted as his ambassador and occasional translator of foreign phrases when I could, but as he grew older and farther away from my sphere of influence, this layer of protection peeled off.

Some of the protection I had to actively chip away, such as the time he came up to me, at the first (and last) luncheon we were ever invited to, with a toy gun and a bewildered expression. "What's this?" he asked loudly, and everyone turned to face one of the few six-year-olds on the planet that didn't know what a gun was. At this point in time Danny had memorized the names of all the states, including their capitals and chosen birds; he was also a fluent reader, crackerjack speller and gifted writer. (Fueled by panic, I had managed to pack a lot of education into my son's first six years, but I had not gotten around to teaching him what a gun was, or what you were supposed to do with it.)

I remember this moment because it was surreal. All eyes were on us as I carefully chose my words: "It's a gun, Danny. People use it to kill other people. You point it at someone and say, 'Bang, bang,' and then they pretend to die." I felt more than a touch embarrassed to have such a public lesson with the son I was hoping would blend in this lovely spring morning, but this was the simple and concrete language I needed to use when I relayed information to him. Danny nodded solemnly, wrapped his finger around the slim black trigger and pretended to kill his first friend, who chose to not pretend to die cooperatively on cue. I inwardly winced at both the awkward sight and the silence that had fallen over the room like a blanket of springtime snow. I knew then my son was still different despite all the progress we had made, and I realized for the first time the responsibility of having to teach him things most kids pick up so easily despite our efforts to hide them.

I was struck by the irony of this being the first thing I had to teach him that I did not really want him to learn. Up until then the name of the game was to cram knowledge into him so that he could spit it out on cue the next time he was tested. This day I saw that it was more than simple information I would need to relay to my son; I would somehow have to break down the complexities of our society to be able to teach my son in a way that made sense to him. I would have to communicate the most barbaric aspects of human nature, both to educate him as well as to try to keep him safe. (I still struggle to teach him complicated concepts like nonexistent weapons of mass destruction and the concept of killing people to keep other people safe, but I struggle equally to explain this to myself.)

Other people's kids, a group to which I had never given much thought, began to wield a frightening amount of power over my life and the life of my son. But as much as I wanted to hate the children who bullied with abandon, my anger ended up softening upon the sight of them; it was quickly apparent to me that the bullies had the same vulnerabilities as any other child, and usually more. Bullying was often so obviously trouble's red flag, a clear indicator of problems with empathy, a dead giveaway that they had not been treated kindly and could not incorporate kindness into their troubled hearts.

Fortunately, the incidents of discrimination Dan faced in public school were sparse, and as he got older the incidents grew rare, though this could be attributed more to who Danny grew up to be than to growth in the tolerance level of his peers. Dan is just so likable and pure in his intent; bullies have only his stammer to latch onto and jab him with verbally. One memorable day a bully jabbed him physically with a finger. When I heard this story I caught my breath, only to release it with a laugh when Danny solemnly apologized for what happened next, which involved sending the offending finger and the bully attached flying into a desk. It is easy to underestimate Danny, but you seldom do it twice.

Danny slowly became more accepted, as his peers begin to appreciate his open heart and stoic maturity. He ends up being astonishingly like my mild-mannered and exceedingly kind father. When I voiced this sentiment recently, the listener assumed I meant that my father had autistic traits, but actually the traits they share are not typically considered autistic. It makes me see how little Danny's autism has ended up shaping him as he grows into an adult, and how even this small influence is reduced every passing year.

It required a journey to raise a child with a challenge, this is true, but the path we chose and the pace we took were up to us. At times it felt like a burden to crash through trees instead of taking well-worn paths, but every footfall brought us closer together as a family. And most steps also brought us closer to rejoining the civilized world, already in progress..

3

Zen and the Art of Understanding Autism

You are a child of the universe, no less than the
trees & the stars; you have a right to be here.
And whether or not it is clear to you, no doubt
the universe is unfolding as it should.—Found in
Old Saint Paul's Church, Baltimore; dated 1692.

Over the past quarter century there has been an unprecedented increase in the numbers of children diagnosed with autism. Children with autism are crowding both special education and mainstream classrooms, siphoning off money from regular education that we are still unclear about how to spend. Meanwhile, parents of children with autism are spending tremendous amounts of their own money for unproven or downright dangerous "treatments," while the scientific community scrambles to make up for time it lost trying to thaw out chilly refrigerator mothers. (This is why I am determined to keep North Star Foundation nonprofit. When we finally discover the best treatments for children who face autism, it seems quite clear to me it shouldn't cost families a large sum of money, especially for those who don't have it to give.)

Autism is a behaviorally defined syndrome, and scientists are currently searching for its genetic marker. Most behavioral geneticists believe autism is a polygenetic disorder, with each case triggered by at least three or four interacting genes. This backs up the theory that components of autism can be passed on, probably much more frequently than its full-blown expression. Several markers will hopefully be found some day soon, all capable of combining in a variety of ways to predispose a child to autism as early as the second trimester in pregnancy. Scientists are searching diligently for these genetic holy grails, as their discovery could lead to earlier identification of autism, more appropriate behavioral and psychological treatment plans, and custom-designed medications. But don't hold your breath waiting for this scientific understanding to filter down to help you to form your child's treatment plan anytime soon; the most recent article I read spoke about "junk DNA" found on genes that seems to have nothing specifically to do with any chromosomes they cling to, but has been associated with autism nonetheless.

Until scientists are able to locate and identify genetic markers associated with autism, parents will continue to discover their child's autism the old-fashioned way. They will probably have a child develop normally until approximately eighteen months before uncomfortable diagnostic appointments are made. Eighteen months is a long time to think you can predict your child's future; this is quite late in the game for parents to just begin to understand what challenges lie before them. The most painful aspect of Danny's diagnosis came during the months preceding it, my mind trying desperately to deny what my heart already knew. Most pediatricians are not prepared to recognize the first signs of autism, even if they appear before the legendary eighteen-month mark.

Ours was no exception. As Danny's screaming continued long past colic's three-month window, our pediatrician's explanations began to creep toward overindulgent parenting. If I had been a single parent the explanations might have been different. The problem might have been lack of male role models or a dearth of quality attention. (Parents of children newly diagnosed with autism are about the most vulnerable creatures on earth. Great care should be taken to keep observations and value judgments of any child with difficult behavior free from the taint of our own prejudice.)

The recent increase in diagnosing children with autism might be traced to the fact that autism has features that can help a person to survive in our increasingly visual society. Most children with autism are quite talented on the computer due to their visual skills and superior ability to focus on the screen for long periods of time, and this increases their ability to secure employment as adults. Meanwhile, our society is inching closer toward accepting people with differences, at least enough to support them in their attempts to be mainstreamed, to marry and to raise a family. Having a successful life does not necessarily require social approval as it did in the past, when good social skills were more intrinsic to survival.

But good social skills still have great value, because the ability to read and respond to the social cues around you is important to your happiness, as well as to your freedom and safety. Until fairly recently people with even mild degrees of autism might not have lived as functioning members of our society, much less gotten married and had children. Toddlers with Danny's profile were routinely confined to group homes and institutions where they grew up pale, medicated, and completely unprepared for life outside the two dimensions of the television screen. Evolution normally moves quite slowly, but with the rapid growth of technology in our new millennium there has been a leap in the ability of a person with autistic traits to not just survive, but to thrive.

It is interesting to note that some components of autism, such as the ability to focus unwavering attention or see past limiting social expectations, can have great survival value. Nature does not necessarily view the genes we will eventually find correlated to autism as defective; it is we who attach the value judgments and survival value to any genetic profile. A touch of attention deficit disorder might have come in handy to the sailors who braved those choppy seas on their way to conquer our new world. But their descendents' first grade teachers might not value this restless and impulsive nature when they find it in little boys forced to sit for hours in little plastic chairs.

The latest research also suggests it is not only autism, attention deficit disorder or eye color that can be inherited, but also such intangible qualities as social skills, level of introversion and some more difficult to define concept we normally associate with character. A study recently published in the journal *Science* reports that a gene has been found that can help predict which abused children will become violent or antisocial adults. Eighty-five percent of abused children with a variant of this particular gene were eventually diagnosed with conduct disorder as adults. (Behavioral scientists are still at a loss to know why the other 15 percent of children with this gene grow up to beat the odds, but most believe it is proof that it is the interplay of nature and nurture that weave the total person.)

What do we do with this information as a society? Do we continue to blame the kids who land in prison instead of college, or the kids who sits alone at recess drawing circles in the air, rather than helping them to figure out how to play the genetic hands they were dealt? Do we let insurance companies, police departments and school systems know our children's genetic makeups so that they can better target their surveillance or save a couple of bucks?

Or should we try to understand what being genetically predisposed means, and how it can give us great power to help children find their way to a happy and healthy adulthood, despite the difficult path they must walk to get there?

Ironically, as our society evolves it also grows more stressful, discriminating and demanding; in the past children with a degree of autism may have spent their entire lives in some small town without ever being diagnosed or "treated" for autism. (I would imagine they were given the treatment by their peers, however. I believe people with mild degrees of autism or retardation compose the last minority it is somehow acceptable to blame and punish for their imposed role of outcast.)

Autism exists on a continuum, and all spectrums eventually stretch into apparent normalcy. Following this train of thought, the skyrocketing increase of children diagnosed with autism may simply reflect our increasing sophistication in detecting and diagnosing the subtle differences among us, but the truth is probably more complicated than any of these theories alone. While some of the skyrocketing numbers can be chalked up to improved recognition and reporting of children with autism, or explained by complicated genetic theories, it is growing clear there may also be an environmental component as well. As Nancy Minshew, director of the Collaborative Program of Excellence in Autism at the University of Pittsburgh points out, "you can't have a genetic epidemic. So the increase would have to be a genetic-environmental interaction."

Pollutants can be internal or external; chemicals can be fed to, injected into, or inhaled by our children, even and especially when they are in utero, with devastating consequences. Few would disagree that vaccines and pesticides have also helped to keep our children healthy and safe, but caution should rule this day, even if this caution is belated. The link between childhood vaccines and autism has been thoroughly researched, but with such conflicting results that it is alarming. Is it possible for us as a society to put money aside when we consider the question of whether the shots we routinely give our babies are safe? I wish I could believe the answer was yes, but I am not certain this is so.

Ironically, the mercury is not associated with the vaccine itself, but is actually in the medium of the vaccine, acting as a preservative (thimerosal). Mercury poisoning and autism have nearly identical symptoms: self-injurious behavior, social withdrawal, lack of eye contact, lack of facial expression, hypersensitivity to noise and touch, and repetitive behaviors.

There have also been questions raised about the hepatitis B vaccine and the rhogam shot currently given to Rh-negative pregnant mothers; both these shots in the past have contained mercury.

There are theories that a certain percentage of children are unable to process even small amounts of mercury in their systems, which may cause confusing results in small-scale studies of childhood vaccines and autism. Courchesne and his colleagues have presented data linking autism to an unusual pattern of brain growth shortly after birth. They found that infants who later develop autism tend to have a slightly reduced head circumference at birth compared to normal infants, but undergo a rapid growth in head circumference during the first two years of life. This growth spurt is so strong that by the time they leave toddlerhood, autistic children's brains tend to be larger than normal.

Not every child who has larger-than-average head circumference growth during the first two years of life goes on to develop autism, however, and my two youngest children are living proof of this fact. Perhaps the high rate of brain growth from birth to two years of age is an antecedent of autism, but an additional trigger is needed to induce autism's expression. Courchesne and his colleagues conclude that the causes of autism may lie in factors that lead first to reduced head circumference at birth and the subsequent rapid spurt in brain growth, rather than factors that are not experienced until behavioral signs of autism are evident, such as exposure to mercury in vaccines; however, these shots, or another, yet to be discovered factor, may set autism in motion.

In July 1999 the U.S. Public Health Service and the American Academy of Pediatrics issued a joint statement recommending the removal of thimerosal from vaccines, but even my own much respected pediatrician was unclear which shots he was due to give my children at their last appointment contained thimerosal and in what amounts (or what amounts are considered safe). If you do a Google search on the subject of thimerosal in vaccines you will find a confusing jumble of conflicting results from a large variety of studies. Recently Robert F. Kennedy Jr. wrote an article in *Rolling Stone* magazine that speculates about the politics and possibility of a cover-up of the danger of thimerosal in vaccines, so this leads me to believe that the jury is still out (and hopefully not being tampered with).

Of course, it is not only mercury inside our syringes that can hurt our children; mercury from power plants taint our oceans and poison the fish we eat. This mercury has shown up in higher concentrations in pregnant women who live on the coasts of our country, where I spent most of my child-bearing years. Although I remember eating tuna sandwiches for lunch nearly every day (for everyone knew fish was brain food), I also recall standing in front of the Atlantic Ocean twenty years ago, my heavily pregnant belly facing Chernobyl the day it melted down.

Other people have concerns about specific toxic chemicals, including the ones that lace our gardens or rest quietly in our kitchen cabinets. I don't recall voting on what pesticides would be sprayed in the common areas of the condominium complex we lived in when I conceived Danny, but I do recall rushing my cat to the vet after she nibbled on some leaves from a beautiful plant by our front door. I am also aware of several babies conceived around the time that we conceived Danny who had multiple disabilities, including brain abnormalities, along with strange rashes that appeared on babies allowed to crawl on our lush green lawn. I had been lulled into thinking that strangers who kidnap were the biggest danger my children faced. Radon, pesticides and toxic preservatives are fairly new and subtle threats; perhaps I was too busy locking the doors and memorizing faces on milk cartons to keep my children safe from real harm. We need well-designed, independent (read: not associated with profit!) scientific investigation of the biological mechanisms of vaccines, chemicals and pesticides that surround us; the dearth of proper research has led to a lack of accountability and progress in detecting potential danger to our children.

All this searching to discover the root cause of Danny's autism, combined with the difficulty of proving it to anyone, has always paralyzed me. And though it's been years since I was plagued by depression, even writing this chapter has made me sad. It all feels like quicksand; facts shifting beneath my feet give me the feeling we are sinking, not moving ahead in our understanding of the cause and etiology of autism. Looking backwards to discover the reasons for your child's autism can cause you to tumble into a painful psychological trap. Dr. Wakefield, clinical professor of medicine at Stanford University, calls this "diagnosing causation." There are probably many causes of autism, ranging from genetic to environmental; placing blame, on yourself or others, is a tricky business. Without proof, a theory can quickly slide into mere speculation.

The same frustrating sense of doubt exists when considering treatments for autism. Parents of children with autism are among the most motivated people on the planet to search for a cure for what ails their child, second only to parents of children with a potentially terminal illness, and this fact makes them exceedingly vulnerable to charlatans and advice peddlers. There is no shortage of available (and expensive) treatments for autism, including behavioral modification programs, vitamin supplements, dietary changes, experimental psychiatric medications, auditory training, behavioral opthamology, sensory integration and chellation. Every parent of a child with autism has to find his or her own way through this maze of potential cures and treatments; I have dabbled through this list with mixed results, struggling to first and foremost do no harm.

When Danny was three a book was published about a young boy who supposedly had cerebral allergies to milk. At the time milk was a necessary staple in Dan's diet; I believe he only went one horrific day without it in his entire life. To follow a theory blindly despite evidence it isn't working is a real danger for any parent. I only held out a day before realizing Dan needed his milk more deeply than I needed to explore this latest theory. Over a decade later I read another theory that natural vitamin A therapy may reconnect the retinoid receptors critical for vision, sensory perception, language processing and attention. For many years milk was Danny's only form of vitamin A, due to the typically limited diet of a child with autism, and I am left with an important reminder to move carefully despite the intensity of my good intentions.

When Danny was six we briefly gave him mega-doses of vitamin B and magnesium, and years later we put him on a short trial of the medication Risperdal, but both these forays were tentative and short-lived. Without identifying any "defective" genes we cannot be sure a medication is correcting any specific chemical imbalance or merely acting as a placebo. (Although I do not sell the placebo effect short, the price you pay in side effects may not be worth it.) Mega-doses of vitamins and prescription medications are to be approached very cautiously and under the guidance of someone you trust wholeheartedly. Side effects can be cumulative and unpredictable, and safer, more intelligently designed medications are hopefully right around the corner. With exceptions, I would rather focus on behavioral modification and creating appropriate environments for children with autism, as opposed to drugging them into accepting an environment that may not be ideal. Just as pain is there to warn us of physical danger in our environment, a child's bad behavior can be an important clue to psychological danger. (Keep this in mind with typically developing children as well!)

Auditory training, conducted by Dr. Binet in Montreal, seemed to help Danny with his hypersensitive hearing, but I approached this treatment like a mother instead of a scientist. Without applying the scientific method it is impossible to be certain it helped, but I am convinced it did him no harm. The training consisted of having him listen to a specially filtered tape twice a day for a ten-day period. The fact that Dr. Binet lived in Montreal is either important or incidental. How can you know? In between our sessions we spent valuable time alone as a family, in a beautiful Canadian chalet that offered us hope, optimism and a hot tub. This alone was worth the time and trouble.

Although we tried other therapies and treatments in fighting Danny's autism, results were less than encouraging and the stress of implementing them may have caused more harm than good. If a cure has been discovered for autism it happened without my knowledge, but my feeling is that any cure will rest squarely upon the firm ground of genetic research, custom-designed medications, appropriate and sensitive education, sensory integration techniques and successful education of all children regarding tolerance to differences they may find in their classmates. With the war on autism, victories are measured in inches. This is because there is so little to conquer, so much to accept, and just one real enemy: intolerance.

Communicating with a child with autism must be done in a gentle manner where each person leads as well as follows. For us this could seem as graceful as a dance, but at times Danny's strong will was a horse that was infinitely easier to ride when we were going in the same direction. Convincing myself I wanted to go there anyway was a skill I honed. Being flexible about my destination and timetable was necessary, and the ability to check the reins to avoid a power struggle eventually became second nature to me. (Just take an eight-week-old puppy out for her first walk and you will immediately know what I am talking about here. Some places you just have to agree to go to together, or not at all.)

As my son Danny grew older and more verbal I was able to ask him questions about the source of his anxiety when he was small. He used to have many intense fears as a child that caused a great deal of his tantrums and upsets; for instance, he had a deep fear of a mechanical game called Rock 'em Sock 'em Robots, and for a long time he couldn't go into a toy store because of this phobia. Over a decade later I asked him about this, and he explained quite eloquently his confusion about what was alive and what was not; if I could turn back the clock I would try harder to communicate simple messages such as Rock 'em Sock 'em Robots are not alive, despite the fact that they pummel each other, along with a detailed explanation of how batteries work. (Although I am quite certain I explained this to Danny verbally, my theory of his continuing fear of mechanical games was that my explanation was sketchy and incomplete. I share this confession with you now as a cautionary tale: rock-solid certainty about anything concerning a child with autism, including our ability to communicate with him, is a luxury we cannot afford.)

I gave Danny great freedom and materials for him to create his own stories and design his own books; in retrospect this was perhaps the best thing I did for him when he was small. I am always delighted when I see a child with autism display a strong interest in letters and books, and quite anxious to get him to learn to read in order to create a vital avenue to learning about the world. With material at his disposal such as paper, tape, markers, glue and glitter he would make daily journals of his adventures that I am quite certain helped him to process the social information he needed to keep up with his peers. From a very young age Danny had a "voice" in his writing, and it was easy to see that his ability to express himself with the written word helped him both to learn about as well as to cope with his sometimes bewildering social universe.

Here is a story I saved from when he was just seven and fresh from an exciting play date with some other children in the neighborhood:

The Social Sphere

Danny was at the bus stop collecting shiny rocks. Later, alley and ben, 5 and 3 years old came to the bus stop and joined him. After they brought him 2 rocks that sparkled all over. That just gave danny an idea. he would go to bryan's house and would pickhimup to go to danny's clubhouse. Bryan said"cool!" danny showed him around the clubhouse. Then they saw ryan at bryan's house. They went to pick him up and show him around the clubhouse. "this clubhouse is really cool!' he said. Then bryan showed danny and ryan around his clubhouse. "cool" they both said. They went back to bryan's drive way and played with blocks that had holes in them. After that, they went in the woods and played Indians. They found a log that looked like a hawk. They made it bryan's vehicle (but not a real vehicle) they tried to push it down. Then,1 other kids came along. His name was jesse. They all screamed "JESSE'WE NEED YOUR HELP!" jesse tried to help. He pushed and pushed. But it didn't go over. it stayed. so they pushed with all the power they had. and they did it! they all layed on the log and screamed"WE ARE THE STRONG MEN!!" they did it again with all their power, but it didn't go over. but they figured out what was wrong. There was a tree in the way. So bryan bent it and jesse and danny pushed with all their power again,but danny's shirt was attached to a part of the log,and the log pushed danny over the log. Jesse, ryan,andbryan all said"ARE YOU ALL RIGHT?" they all asked. "ya,i am all right." Said danny. Danny said"I think we should not play Indians anymore."

I used to wait by the picture window or perched on a lonely curb until Danny finally came home from these journeys, only relaxing when he was deep in the process of creating a story or book about them. It would be years before I truly understood how educational it was for him to create these books. Education, in the appropriate form, should happen both inside and beyond the walls of the classroom. Many teachable moments young children experience are part of sensitive transitions connected with waking up, winding down, or going to sleep. Seizing these opportunities will greatly increase the young child with autism's base of knowledge and skill at communicating. Knowing how to support a child with autism through difficult transitions and dark days will hopefully reduce or eliminate the amount of psychological trauma that can chip away at the best of childhoods.

For now the painful diagnosis of autism relies largely on personal observations. Labels are determined by the results of developmental I.Q. tests along with parental and educator interviews. They are also influenced by the changing tide of perception. When Danny was diagnosed, the powers-that-be were getting ready to redefine the definition of all the conditions on the autism spectrum. Any offered label seemed penciled in because tomorrow your child could be called something different. I ended up welcoming this shifting sand of opinion. This pulled back the curtain, as Toto did to reveal that the wizard was a simple man, and clarified what was behind this bumbling nature of labeling. This deeper understanding of the wizard's fallibility allowed me to focus on what was truly important: how my son learned best, and how to support him through the challenges he would be facing.

Autism should be seen as a spectrum disorder. It is deceptive to draw firm lines between people who have it and those who don't; I frequently run across people who have autistic traits without even realizing it. Bert on *Sesame Street* has some autistic tendencies (the paper clip thing is a dead giveaway). People with autism exist on a bell curve, though not at the populous middle; they did not drop from the sky. This is why I tend to use the term "child with autism" rather than "autistic child." (I think of it as analogous to "child with glasses," as opposed to "glasses child.") As Danny grows up I can see that his autism only reflects his learning style, never substituting for his substance.

The psychological challenge of accepting their child's label is often the first major hurdle parents must leap in their quest to help their child. They will need to do this before being granted the services their community can offer (or privately, to seek the knowledge this label can grant them). Labels and predictions of future development are necessary evils in the life of any child with a challenge, but I advise parents to keep them in perspective. No label can change who a child is, but it can strongly influence how parents and professionals will see him or her. I think most professionals are genuinely kind in not wanting to raise a parent's hopes for a bright future when delivering their report. Their reasons vary from unselfish to pragmatic, but they should keep in mind that losing all hope is the biggest threat that parents of a newly diagnosed child will face.

Warning parents not to aspire for their child with autism is cruel, but it's also just plain bad advice. No one can honestly know any child's potential, and numbers can be crunched and shaped to fit any theory. I am not advocating dismissing test results or refusing to listen to predictions; I am only pointing out that any child is a shiny new package capable of many happy surprises as he or she opens up. There are many ways to enjoy life and contribute to each other's existence, and as luck would have it, conventional normalcy is not a prerequisite for this. If parents are left without hope for the future, they are left without the energy, enthusiasm and imagination it will take to survive the long journey that awaits them.

I don't believe anyone has designed an I.Q. test for a very young, nonverbal child with autism that can reliably predict future intelligence. This is because a child's potential is still in the process of being realized, and nothing is set in stone with very young children. (Also, bear in mind that children with autism often do poorly on developmental tests that are language-based.) Over a decade ago I spent many hours observing a psychologist through a one-way mirror at the Yale Child Study Center as she struggled to try to pinpoint Danny's I.Q. and make predictions about his future. She was a very kind, intelligent and sensitive woman who proved invaluable to us in helping to understand our son, but her conclusion that Danny had borderline intelligence and would never be able to be mainstreamed was as devastating as it was misleading. Time has proven her wrong, but I do not place any blame here. Her task was as impossible as a fortune-teller's, no matter how powerful or prestigious her crystal ball. Who could know what potential lay deep underneath the layers of Danny's autism at the time, or what tools we were going to fashion to find it? It is the slope of the developmental line that matters most, which is created by plotting the scores of diagnostic tests given to a child in a consistent manner over many years.

Often, just knowing that a child exists somewhere on the autism spectrum can be very helpful in understanding a range of behaviors, especially for confused parents who may have questions that are difficult even to form. They may have wondered why their unusual child can read nearly any word he sees while seeming to have trouble even noticing the baby sister who is chortling and waving her fists just a foot away. They have probably ignored the way their child pinches them long after he should have learned to stop, or the way he repeats an action without tiring, eyes glazed, throwing wild tantrums when thwarted. They have tried to catch their child's eye, coax a word, quell the panic when speech finally does emerge, inward and garbled, with occasional recognizable words embedded like jewels in concrete. It feels disloyal to question their child's normalcy, even and especially within their own minds. Often it is an event that finally triggers a conscious recognition, perhaps a family gathering where the difference between their child and his startlingly precocious cousins is painfully obvious.

Autism impacts the child's development primarily by the way it influences attention and sensory integration. Autistic symptoms can be seen more clearly and in a more typical fashion with the very young. Lining up objects meticulously, showing emotional reactions to inanimate objects, displaying precocious interest in letters and numbers, and limited eye contact are all early red flags. Breaking the autism down into its specific learning differences in Danny was quite helpful to us; weaving these strands of knowledge into the fabric of his day created the beautiful pattern of our lives together. We came to respect him because of, not despite, his learning and perception differences. Danny always had a full inner life and wide range of emotions along with a strong desire to connect with the larger world. But while his words could be halting and his communication style undeniably different, his thoughts were always refreshingly free of the simplest pretense. People with autism are nearly incapable of lying, for it takes good social skills to manipulate the truth. (Danny's first attempts at lying were sweet moments for me, charming and awkward proof of his progress).

Playing tug-of-war with autism is a delicate affair. At any moment you could theoretically yank the rope to your side, but this would not necessarily leave you the winner. The child with autism is at a heightened risk of developing genuine emotional problems from the strain of living in a world that he has such trouble understanding. Our assistance dog, Madison, was always on hand to help smooth out the rough edges of a day, and

I like to think I was frequently available as well (although, unlike Madison, I am only human).

Children with autism are expensive children, both emotionally and financially. It is important to prioritize your goals for everyone in the family. The child with special needs should not be the white-hot center around which everyone in the family revolves; the goal is to integrate the children with autism completely into our society, beginning with the people who love them the most. There is only so much time, energy and money available to any family, and these resources should be spread evenly as butter on bread. (Caution: Unless you are careful, and even if you are, there will be a few years when you will be the dry toast in this analogy. Convincing your partner to take turns being toast with you may increase the odds that the unique experience of co-parenting your special child will bring you closer together, not farther apart. Trust me, your relationship will definitely go one way or the other. But ask any soldier about the intimacy that develops when you have lain in the trenches together if you have any doubts about the possibility of having this bring you closer.)

Keep your mind open when searching for what interests you can support with your child, and try to create genuine enthusiasm about the topic that he or she wants to explore. Sharing these interests will allow you to stay squarely in the communication zone. On the surface this sounds easy, but if you have ever seen *Bambi* seventeen million times you will know what I'm talking about when I say that it's not. However, if I hadn't shared his early passion I might have missed the meaning behind Danny's first complete sentence, "I think we'd better go home now." This was said in the middle of a hike, and he meant to say, "Hey, Mom, guess what? It looks like it is going to rain, and I believe we'd better turn back." Luckily I had *Bambi* memorized and knew Danny had borrowed that phrase to communicate his knowledge of a darkening sky. He was barely three and still speaking in single, functional words, so this sentence was as startling as the moment when Danny had arranged his colorful magnetic letters so carefully on the fridge to read "FBI Warning."

Should you let children with autism have free rein with creating patterns and repeating actions? What of deliberately scattering patterns, as one North Star dog (Cassie) was prone to do with her child's autistic pattern-making? Is this a good thing, or bad? I wondered when this was reported to me. Robbie's mother was convinced this was a good thing, but some people believe repetitive actions are a functional part of developing the damaged brain, an exercise that must be performed to strengthen function of healthy areas. Other people believe this autistic tendency is to be interrupted as consistently as possible and they will make deliberate efforts to do so. Still others believe the tendencies of the child with autism are to be copied in order to enter his or her world. Raun Kaufman was diagnosed with autism and retardation at 18 months, but his parents worked with him in a home-based, child-centered program they devised for him. They attempted to accept Raun's autistic behavior instead of trying to root it out, and they tried to enter and accept the world of his perceptions. This idea of working with a child's autism instead of fighting it tooth and nail was quite radical 25 years ago, and it is still unusual today.

I took a moderate approach, interrupting when the time seemed right and welcoming any help that came my way to do so. Dogs are wonderful distractions, as long as they don't cross the line into annoying interruptions. They will take their cues from us, as we communicate to them what our expectations are when interacting with a child with autism.

I always took great care to treat Danny's intense interests with respect when I could, and these interests were often behind the wild tantrums he occasionally threw; in retrospect, I can see that he knew how critical it was to follow his heart's hunger in life. When language was enriched and communication improved to the point that he could pursue his interests unblocked, his behavior improved dramatically. An increase in Danny's ability to handle frustration came with his ability to comprehend "first we do ____ [fill in the blank] ____, then we go home. . . ." Grasping this concept was a ledge that allowed us to catch our breath as we climbed the challenge of dealing appropriately with his early difficult behavior. Danny has infinitely more capacity to face life's trials now, but there are still areas where his patience with delay is thin. These areas nearly always revolve around areas that he has had a deep interest in since early childhood, such as video and computers.

Although some degree of cognitive impairment usually exists in the child with autism, this is not always the case. The figure usually quoted is that 75 to 80 percent of autistic children are mentally retarded, but this figure will more than likely drop when proper early intervention is more consistently employed. I think the different degrees of cognitive impairment as well as varying sensory integration problems are behind some of the difficulty in typecasting the child with autism, as both of these issues will impact the child's development. However, any child with any degree of autism or cognitive impairment will benefit from participation in an appropriate early intervention program designed to help him achieve his potential. I maintain that the child's E.Q. (emotional quotient) should also be paid great attention, in school and as part of his IEP (individualized education program), especially concerning behavioral issues and peer relationships. (In fact, great care should be taken to increase all children's E.Q., for children who are familiar with and respectful of their own emotions are inclined to be more tolerant toward others. I am convinced that intolerance is the biggest and most disturbing disability of them all.)

Integration in classrooms and playgrounds can be the best choice for a child with autism, or the worst. It all depends upon the approach, along with the specific child and his particular challenge. We found that any school or social group we sent our son to had a philosophical underpinning concerning special education; we came to examine this and refer to it later if issues arose. I am relieved and more than a bit proud to note that I have not had any skirmishes with schools or teachers since we moved to Mansfield nearly a decade ago. This is largely due to the fact that we all ascribe to a similar philosophy on integration issues, we all keep Danny's well-being uppermost in our collective mind, and we take the time to communicate through any differences of opinion until we can discover valuable middle ground.

Parental instincts should be strengthened in regard to deciding how to best educate children with autism; parents' opinions about what works best for their child should be blended with professional opinions to craft a treatment plan for the child with autism at school and at home. In the absence of scientific knowledge, anecdotal evidence needs to be collected and carefully examined. This is not an area where anyone gets to pretend he knows all the answers.

At home parents can have a great deal of influence over their child's education. Pointing out relevant social information and modeling appropriate behavior (especially when communicating strong emotions) is crucial in helping to improve the child's ability to respond appropriately in social situations. Parents should know, and take comfort in the knowledge, that children with autism often feel as deep an attachment to their caretakers as do their siblings, but they tend to show their love in unusual ways and at odd moments, especially when young. Responding in an appropriate way to this unexpected demonstration of affection is important; valuing the differences children have in their priorities and modes of self-expression is crucial to raising any happy and emotionally healthy child.

Relationship-based rather than goal-oriented treatment should be stressed with children on the spectrum, with lessons for little ones made to be as fun as possible. Social and emotional goals should be seen as important as those for education, and ambition should be tamed lest it decide to rule (and spoil) the day. Nurturing children with autism to become empathetic and compassionate seems the true goal in our struggle to help them to develop their full potential. Not rote, memorization-induced empathy, such as training them to parrot the correct answers to artificial scenarios, but true compassion, where the thoughts behind the feelings are lined up with our personal definition of caring for those we love. Teaching children with autism to care for their dogs is quite valuable for them, along with accepting the responsibility of receiving unconditional love. As luck would have it, this ends up a very simple task for the vast majority of children with autism that we serve at North Star.

As with my other children, I tried to take my cue from Danny's behavior when untangling a knot of fear. There were thoughts behind those fears and fledging phobias, and I would try to trace them back; while some of them ended up linked by misperceptions that I could correct (i.e., Rock 'em Sock 'em Robots could not leap up and punch people), others remained encased in fear, which Dan had to scramble over like a stone. He became good at this, and his resiliency and knowledge of himself was instrumental to allowing us to help him grow up strong and emotionally healthy. It became my task for many years to uncover and correct misperceptions, and gradually this effort faded to series of simple and natural conversations about his day. We still touch base occasionally, Danny and I, to see if anything is bothering him that I can help to smooth by way of correcting information gathered or rearranging the frame that he put around it. As much as possible, I avoid situations that make him uncomfortable, as I believe stress and social pressure are as toxic as chemicals.

The most difficult thing about this philosophy when children with autism are small is the tension of letting go of the polite crust of social behavior enough to truly value your child's differences, even those that make little intrinsic sense to you and others. The next step past this insight is to allow your child to share these differences with the larger world despite the potential for pain. It changes you to do this, and my opinion is that this change is for the better.

Following his interests has led Danny to possess an in-depth knowledge of movies and computers as a teenager, and I believe it has made his childhood happier. That alone would have made it all worth the effort. I might not have come to this conclusion if the result of following his own lead had sent him down sterile corridors leading to empty rooms. But Dan has always been his best teacher and therapist. All of his intense interests as a young boy are now lush offshoots of his earlier splinter skills. I believe that based on this observation, great attention should be paid to splinter skills in the young child with autism when constructing a blueprint for his or her education.

We relied on our common sense in raising Dan, being careful to keep an open mind about the relative value of things in our universe. We were not always consistent; often instinct or exhaustion forced us to be flexible despite the goal of structure. We sometimes bent the rules to avoid tantrums and other times we stood firm in the face of his awesome will. But it should be noted that my most painful memories of raising Dan are not of crumbling in the face of a meltdown, but of stubbornly standing too firm. The cruelty of angry, poorly timed or ill-chosen consequences can seduce you into writing a power play rather than a script for kind and intelligent parenting.

What follows is a poem Danny wrote the summer after his graduation from middle school; it is in large part what gave me the confidence to let him attend our town's large high school, as his level of insight of both himself as well as others was both apparent and reassuring to me.

4

Life as a Computer

Danny Gross

I am like a computer,

The outside plainness and inner complexity of me can scare some people away.

But the people who give me a chance find out how pleasant and helpful I really am.

I can seem complicated at first, but become simpler with use.

I am access to a whole other world with unlimited potential.

I help them with more than they ever could imagine.

I am an escape for them when they want to forget their troubles.

I can get them to places they've never seen before.

Some people are skilled with me, and some are not.

Some people do not know how to use me,

and if they do it wrong, I will not help them.

If they add additional things to me, I will be of more use to them.

Sometimes I freeze or I crash and I provide a disservice to them.

Sometimes that happens because they pushed a wrong key or deleted a wrong file.

Otherwise, it is an error that they did not cause or could not prevent.

(I will make sure I always work right afterwards and never let it happen again).

I can be shut off, but if they come back to me and turn me on again, I will be there.

I do everything I do in a completely different world, in a way they've never seen.

I will always help them and provide for them until I cannot anymore.

As they give me a try once, they find themselves doing it again,

and again.

If they go even one day without me they will find themselves diminished.

But if they know to use me, and how, they will be greatly rewarded.

5

Assistance Dogs and Children with Autism

Your friend is your needs answered.
He is your field which you sow with love
and reap with thanksgiving.
And he is your board and your fireside.
For you come to him with your hunger,
And you seek him for peace.
—Kahlil Gibran

Recent research has demonstrated that children with autism display social behaviors toward their pets more readily than they do toward their human companions; some of these reported behaviors are quite atypical according the accepted definition of autism. Children with autism were found to pay frequent attention to their pets, often in amounts not normally granted to people. These lucky animals were also the recipients of a surprising amount of empathy and high levels of nurturing by their young owners. At a paper presented in Switzerland at the Seventh International Conference on Human-Animal Interactions, Animals, Health and Quality of Life, children with autism were found to display behaviors toward their pets that they rarely, if ever, displayed toward human companions, and some of these behaviors are contrary to DMS-IHR diagnostic criteria for autism. The children's mothers were asked to assess their children's behavior across a number of relationship dimensions with themselves, with one other important person in the subject's life, and with the pet. These dimensions include greeting, proximity seeking, confiding, companionship, sensitivity to the needs of others and play. Despite the supposed autistic aversion to being touched or hugged by people, children with autism frequently sought pets out for tactile comfort, on their own terms and timetable. Greater sensitivity toward the needs and feelings of the animal was also noted, together with a lack of anger and aggression directed toward them. With guidance, children can draw upon the knowledge gleaned from a relationship with a pet to deepen their understanding of the infinitely more complicated nature of human interactions.

Children with autism are inclined to pay attention to the inanimate world at the expense of the animate one; as a result they have great difficulty learning to infer the emotions and perspective of others. Failure to do this is referred to as "mindblindness," which I consider a core feature of autism. A slew of new research on young babies' social and emotional development shows them ready to read facial expressions. By reading emotional responses, doctors have begun to discover ways to tell if a baby as young as three months old is showing early signs of autism. "Instead of just asking if they're crawling or sitting, we're asking more questions about how they share their world with their caregivers," says Dr. Chet Johnson, chairman of the American Academy of Pediatrics' early childhood committee. "Do they point to things? When they see a new person how do they react? How children do on social and emotional and language skills are better predictors of success in adulthood than motor skills are."

It may well be that psychologist William James's description of a typical infant's view of the world as a "one great blooming, buzzing confusion" may relate more to a child with autism than a typical child. A strong, well-developed ability to connect with the world, and to parents in particular, is especially important when babies begin making their first efforts at speech. Babies that receive immediate and appropriate feedback in response to their attempts to communicate babbled more and advanced more quickly than those who didn't. Increasing this appropriate feedback for children on the autism spectrum, even when the communication attempt is clumsy or tangential, is a powerful way to develop their communication skills. Having a dog within the home can also provide a moving focal point of attention to increase opportunities for incidental language learning.

I believe that an assistance dog can help children with autism to communicate in several ways, and perhaps the most important is to encourage them to focus on the animate world longer than they might have if left to their own devices (trying to ignore a social puppy is nearly impossible for anyone, autistic or not). By being gently encouraged to shift their attention back and forth from animate to inanimate, this valuable skill is strengthened. The key here is to be gentle and respectful of the child's emotional state and frame of mind, and to find a puppy or dog that will understand the behavior needed for the child to trust him or her. The child's attention should be coaxed and courted, never forced. North Star puppies and dogs consistently try to capture the attention of children with autism, being deliberately careful not to overwhelm the child. (This is why the right temperament is crucial; there would be little or no benefit and some potential harm in having a dog that ignores social cues.) In reviewing my training tapes, I am impressed with how even the young puppies I breed have an intuitive sense of how far to push the envelope to gain the child's attention. Some puppies and young dogs even come to have skills superior to the children they were helping; they seem to eventually relish and recognize their role as teacher. They spend a good amount of time simply observing the child and tentatively trying out various approaches or introductions to new games with the children they serve.

Encouraging a child to leave a cherished inanimate world, even for a few minutes, can be hard unless you have an alternative safe and enjoyable place to offer their attention to go, but your sympathy for a child with autism should be sprinkled with plenty of good cheer and bravado. The fluid movements and golden charm of a well-bred and well-trained puppy or dog provide plenty of interesting interruptions and lessons about dealing with the random nature of life in a positive manner. I believe this lesson is far more easily learned with the natural movements of a puppy rather than our clever but artificial interventions or in a series of humorless, top-down lessons.

An assistance dog placement also encourages children with autism to understand the puppy's perspective to help them develop empathy. Children with autism usually have great difficulty picking up the subtle social cues we send to each other in an attempt to broadcast our frame of mind, so it is not surprising that their developing sense of empathy may lag behind their typically developing peers. By a year of age, most average babies are becoming increasingly sophisticated social learners, following others' gazes to discern what's important in the environment, and reading facial expressions to glean the mood of the people around them. Part of developing empathy and social skills may come from the ability to discern emotions from the facial expressions of the people around them, an ability that is strikingly poor in children with autism. "Most textbooks still say that babies younger than six months don't recognize emotions," says

Diane Montague, assistant professor of psychology at La Salle University in Philadelphia, but her research on four-month-old infants has led her to believe that typically developing babies younger than six months find meaning in facial expressions.

Much attention has been paid to keeping children with autism on par intellectually with their peers, but not as much attention has been paid to keeping them on par with their peers socially and emotionally. Perhaps learning to read facial expressions is as important a skill for them to master as reading print. Although facial expressions can be difficult for children with autism to comprehend, most can easily recognize a dog's wagging tail as reflecting her happy and social state of mind. I've even seen a child with autism who was unable to provide a rejoinder to my verbal invitation to play return a pup's play bow after only a few minutes of observation. Understanding their pups' emotions based on their easier style of communication permits children with autism to develop their empathy by increasing their ability to nurture and respond to their pets' needs (this can happen as simply as a child recognizing that his dog's panting indicates thirst and bringing him a bowl of water.)

The nonverbal avenue of interacting with a dog is an important advantage here, as sometimes spoken language can get in the way of successfully communicating with an autistic child. For a child with autism who has had an exhausting day struggling to communicate in a manner that is foreign to him, spending time with his dog is a powerful way to replenish his energy and shore up his self-esteem. The concept of "time out" can be redesigned to be offered to the child and his dog in a positive manner before behavior reflecting inner turmoil causes unfortunate isolation or punishment for the child.

Children with developmental disabilities need to learn by observing typical children at play, as important areas of their brains can be active and engaged in learning even if they are not participating directly. Where the child is choosing to direct his attention is key for this observation to happen. Encourage interaction between your puppy/dog and your other children and invite your child with autism to participate or simply observe. A lively pup or dog is often a bouncy social referencing point that everyone in the room can share.

Dr. Steven E. Gutstein is a psychologist and autism specialist who has created a groundbreaking program called Relational Developmental Intervention. His program teaches social skills to children with autism in a way that respects their social and emotional growth. (His book, *Solving the Relationship Puzzle,* is truly fascinating.) As parents of children with autism attempt to guide and frame the interactions they have with their child as part of an RDI program, a dog can provide an important blend of exciting novelty and familiar structure, someone with whom they can "share the excitement." Several families are currently incorporating their North Star dogs into their child's RDI program: Mitchell is a six-year-old boy with autism who reads to his North Star dog every night, being careful to let her see the pictures before each turn of the page. (Rita doesn't have much interest in the pictures Mitchell shows him, of course; she is just holding a down/stay and is trained to look where he points.) Another family uses their North Star dog as a shared social referencing point, with the adventures they share as stories in the making.

A valuable way to set the stage for the arrival of a new puppy in the home is to write a "social story" to prepare the child with autism for the coming interactions with the puppy or dog. Social stories provide important information to children with autism that will be difficult for them to glean from the actual social encounter; they tend to be better able to process information delivered through the written word as opposed to the subtle verbal cues or body language most typical children rely upon. Writing stories that contain these missed cues and messages can greatly help a child with autism to fill in the gaps of his knowledge, thereby reducing anxiety and increasing the probability of successful social encounters. These stories need not be elaborate or fancy; most parents of children with autism are familiar enough with their child's level of cognition to compose a paragraph or so about what he needs to know about any upcoming event.

I believe this is a good method for teaching visual learners how to care for and treat their puppy, and allows the self-reflection a child needs to allow emotional growth to take place. You might also take a crack at writing your own book, scaled down or brought up to your child's level of understanding, with photos or pictures you've drawn to complement the carefully chosen text. This is a wonderful way to connect with a child with autism.

Here is an example of a story a mother named Meta wrote for her son Gavin, who has autism, on the eve of his North Star dog Bailey coming to live with him:

Bailey Comes Home

Bailey is coming home today! For the past two weeks Bailey has been at Patty's puppy school learning to not jump up. Patty, Ron, Chris and Kelsey will bring her back to our house at 2:00 this afternoon. We will be happy to see all of them. We will be especially happy to see Bailey.

> We will try to remember to tell her to sit when she comes
> over to us. Bailey will try to remember to sit instead of
> jumping up. As soon as Bailey sits we will say hi to each
> other, and we will be very happy to be together again. I
> will jump on the trampoline with Chris and Kelsey.

This story greatly helped Gavin to reduce his considerable anxiety over the transition of Bailey from our house to his, and during the transition months several more were written and illustrated to keep Gavin on the same page as the rest of us. Writing about the developing relationship with North Star dogs can be rich and imaginative; if you create these "social stories" in a photograph album you can easily slip in photos or created pictures to illustrate the ongoing story.

One of the biggest gifts that parenting Danny bestowed was the art of knowing how to forgive people (quickly and with your whole heart); an important quality we seek when selecting puppies for North Star's work is this very trait of being able to forgive quickly. This is also a trait we try to encourage and support with North Star's children within the framework of the placement. Many children with autism are capable of developing the ability to perceive and understand other perspectives if these lessons are approached with confident patience. A child's recognizing and appropriately responding to his or her dog's weaknesses and failures is a valuable aspect of any North Star placement. Due to the comparative simplicity of their intellect and behavior, dogs' perspectives are quite a bit easier for the child with autism to understand. A dog wags his obvious tail when he's happy, and as Jeffrey Masson reminds us, they "never lie about love." In my experience, dogs and children with autism are natural communicators because of their breathtaking honesty.

We don't want the child to stop there, naturally, but being able to successfully respond to his dog's frame of mind and nonverbal messages creates a valuable stepping stone to the larger undertaking of comprehending people's complicated and sometimes capricious points of view and methods of communication. Gaining an understanding of individual mindsets along with the general consensus of the group is necessary for a child to learn in order to develop social competence.

Developmental scientist Bob Emde refers to a concept called "We-go," which refers to a group ego that provides more safety, power, and significance than can be experienced alone. This important goal can be achieved by blending a child's emerging identity as a social being with his or her dog. One young boy, Caleb, who received a North Star dog named Shiloh, asked his mother to embroider North Star's logo, which appeared on Shiloh's saddle, onto his jacket. Caleb's wanting to belong was quickly recognized and built upon, and now his trainer Rachel and mother Michele both have similar shirts, and I've ordered one for myself for the next time I visit him. According to Dr. Gutstein, "this desire to belong to a group grows in a child, so too does his understanding that he must coordinate himself in specific ways to maintain his status and membership." For Caleb this means adopting the rules of etiquette in treating Shiloh gently, and to remember what he has been taught about giving Shiloh commands and rewards. The simple concept of positive rewards and appropriate feedback dovetail with similar goals that have been set for Caleb at home as well as at school.

Another important role the child with autism can learn with his or her puppy is the care-taking or teaching role. Most children with autism are quite used to being taken care of, and of being on the receiving end of ABA; switching roles with their dog is a very educational and affirming experience for them. It also encourages the development of empathy, which is usually poor in children with autism due to the difficulty they have in keeping other perspectives in mind.

But it's my opinion that the most powerful way a well-bred and well-trained dog can help a child with developmental differences is to offer dependable and unconditional love. This love is a powerful antidote to the poison of intolerance most children with a challenge are apt to receive from their less enlightened peers. Children with developmental differences cannot learn social skills in a vacuum, yet their opportunity to experience social contact is sadly limited.

Children with autism are struggling to find ways to relate to their peers, a goal that relies on kind children to successfully achieve. Shiloh will be accompanying Caleb to school this year to help him achieve his social goals, but it is not just Caleb who will be crossing the bridge that Shiloh provides: a well-trained dog in school is a kid magnet, and the attention that will be pulled Caleb's way will be an invaluable and necessary resource for him. The social skills he has developed from raising Shiloh will be easily transferred from puppy to peers; linking lessons learned from the backyard to the playground will be literally child's play. Having an aide or parent structure play between Shiloh and Caleb at recess will be a tremendous help, as Caleb still has trouble understanding the spontaneous rules of free play. Caleb's peers will hopefully use Shiloh as a bridge to connect to a great kid whom they may have overlooked due to his differences. Caleb will in turn use the lessons Shiloh taught him about respect and empathy to develop relationships with his peers that will be so important to his successful social future.

It is important to understand how dogs communicate, both to train them effectively as well as to use them in the most appropriate way. Turid Rugaas, who studies dogs in Norway, has identified a concept called "calming signals" that she calls an international canine language. Her book, *On Talking Terms with Dogs: Calming Signals,* identifies over 30 calming signals, including slowing down, arching upon approach, licking lips, turning the head, looking away, standing sideways, or sniffing the ground.

These calming signals attempt to mitigate stress and cement relationships within members of a pack (which includes you and your child with autism). Teaching your child how to read these calming signals in your dog is an excellent springboard to further lessons on reading people's nonverbal communication. Meanwhile, your puppy or dog will be watching you and your child for signs of stress, with an inclination to reduce this when spotted; you can help your pup figure out what calms your particular child and praise him to the skies when he makes attempts to do so. Capitalizing on this naturally occurring tendency is the cornerstone of many North Star placements. For example, teaching your dog to sit in front of your child, perhaps even laying his head on his lap, when he appears upset is an example of an appropriate, stress-free way to relate to your child. One young boy with autism recently had a breakthrough by interrupting his own tantrum when he correctly perceived that his dog was attempting to comfort him. This young boy consciously allowed this comfort to happen, and he then took an active role in soothing himself and reinforcing his dog for his efforts.

Most dogs communicate with each other using short one-note barks; they tend to talk to each other about social events, where they fit in the pack, how they're feeling and what they want. When dogs make noise it is usually for a reason, mostly having to do with communicating alarm or fear. Dr. Feddersen-Petersen at Christian-Albrechts-University in Kiel, Germany published the results of a study comparing vocalizations in 11 European wolves and 84 dogs from 9 breeds. Her results demonstrate how different barks express different emotions, including loneliness, fear, distress, stress and pleasure; these barks alert other dogs, people or animals to changing external circumstances. Noisy barks relate to "defensive and offensive threats, social insecurity, or physical distress." A dog that is barking repeatedly and monotonously is simply communicating about something nonthreatening, but if the bark moves to a lower register, becoming slower and more deliberate, that dog is beginning to perceive a threat. A dog at play makes a distinctive, breathy exhalation that can trigger playfulness in other dogs, says researcher Patricia Simonet of Sierra Nevada College in Lake Tahoe. She and her students analyzed recordings of dogs at play and pinpointed several broader-frequency exhalations that seemed to induce play in both the laboratory and the field. When the researchers broadcasted this sound (Simonet calls it a laugh), puppies often picked up toys or trotted toward a presumed playmate.

Dog communication with people has evolved into a complicated range of harmonic notes. A group of European researchers that includes Dr. Feddersen-Petersen are studying vocal communication between dogs and people, and they are finding that dogs are capable of sophisticated communication. Harmonic barks are used as a signal for social play, as well as for making social contact. Harmonic barking is used primarily between dogs and people, and it is in the process of evolution. "This work on barking is extremely careful and extremely important because it calls attention to the complex social life of dogs that we have barely begun to comprehend," says Dr. Marc Bekoff, an ethnologist at the University of Colorado who studies canids and cognition in animals.

Your puppy's vocalization is only one way it has to communicate with your child, but I do not count it among the most important. Certain lines of dogs are more inclined to communicate vocally with people, and my theory is these vocal lines are more inclined to communicate nonverbally as well. North Star dogs tend to be big talkers, but we cultivate this quality with caution. We try to limit our dogs' vocalizations to our greeting times, and although they might sprinkle the rest of the day with communicative noises, we respond to these sparingly to avoid creating a whiny dog. However, a desire to vocalize harmonically as a way of talking to you or your child should be capitalized upon; merely speaking back to establish the rhythm of speech is valuable. Children with autism who watch or participate in this amusing exchange are bound to learn a great deal about the necessary turn-taking required with pragmatic language.

In regard to qualities such as tolerance, empathy, and forgiveness, dogs are the best teachers and role models for all of us; there is no need to underscore these lessons your dog will teach your child unless you desire to elaborate or expand on this topic. Despite a nasty penchant for eating the garbage when your back is turned, your dog may well end up the most valuable and least expensive therapists you will ever employ.

Children with autism can learn a variety of social lessons through interactions with their puppies and dogs, from pragmatic language to the valuable social skill of taking turns. I have found this work surprisingly easy and believe the hardest part is to resist the tendency to interfere with the process by doing and saying too much. When a play session between a child and his assistance dog is going well, my role is mostly to observe and perhaps point out relevant information to either the child or the dog to increase communication and interaction. For instance, if a puppy takes a toy that the child seems to want back, I might offer the child the proper verbal command to tell the dog to give back the toy. Or I may verbally point out the obvious to increase the child's verbal skills ("You are laughing and having fun playing with Star!"). Sometimes I act as referee, reminding either the dog or the child not to invade the comfort zone of personal space. Learning to read a dog's body language and teaching the child to respond to this language in appropriate ways is at the heart of animal-assisted therapy for children with developmental disabilities.

Animal-assisted therapy works best when a puppy or dog can be shared with others in a child's world. In a study of peer social initiations, researchers found social behavior particularly difficult to teach children with autism and to carry over into a child's everyday life. This is because mastering appropriate social behavior is more than just learning a set of skills; it is a dynamic, ongoing process to learn how to communicate socially. The poorly developed social skills of young children with autism are influenced by a variety of biological and environmental influences (such as not enough opportunity to learn social skills due to segregation). Finding kind and sensitive children to form a peer group for a child with autism to join, playing in both structured and unstructured ways, can make a huge difference in the eventual social behavior of a child with autism.

You will hopefully have better luck than I finding this ideal peer group; I had no such luck in my little town so many years ago and I ended up creating Danny's first and most important peer group myself. The three siblings I created for Danny were the best gifts I could have ever given him, as they have taught him lessons that would have proved impossible to teach him myself. I have come to know dozens of siblings of the children North Star serves, and I am consistently amazed by the depth of character that they possess. These children have developed a deep sense of empathy and tolerance, sometimes before they have even mastered the task of tying their shoes. In an age when many people (and most world leaders) are struggling simply to tolerate each other, siblings of children with challenges are the peacemakers that we can only hope will inherit this earth.

They are touchstones to normalcy in a family that grows weary of being different; they tend to be wise beyond their years, compassionate to a fault, and light years ahead of the rest of us in understanding the universe. Most siblings of children with challenges take the heat and energy that radiates from their love for their special brother or sister and use it to develop character with the strength of forged steel. Their adolescent years are spent both garnering social approval as well as learning to live without it; this dichotomy compels them to dig beneath the surface of the usual teenage experience. The early lessons they learn about the nature of love will give an added depth to all their future relationships (especially the important one they will have with themselves).

When parents of children with autism first visit me hoping to receive a North Star dog to help their child, my first question is about how their child reacts to animals in general, and to dogs in particular. Stories of specific dogs they have known that drew their child out are particularly heartening, and I pay great attention to what temperament this specific dog had, and how their child related to him or her. I then observe the child with my own dogs (who are trained to approach children slowly and gently). I watch to see if there is any communication that develops between them, or if any glimmer of interest exists within the child to relate to my dogs, even if cloaked by a veil of fear.

And what if there isn't? What if the child we hope to help pays no attention to my dogs, either in the past or to the present canine invitations to relate?

Unfortunately, this is when you may need to reconsider the concept of obtaining an assistance dog for your child. Animal-assisted therapy only works with children who are drawn to and made happy by the animal in question. Being certain that the animal you have chosen for your child is appropriate is crucial to consider, along with knowing that if it is you that wants a dog for your own psychological purposes, then this is reason enough to purchase one if you are in a position to do so. Your children, challenged or not, depend on you to provide a healthy emotional climate for them. All things being equal, what is good for you emotionally tends to be good for your children. No matter how old we are, we all need to have our hearts' hungers satiated.

Although I love my North Star dogs, I am quite aware that these dogs are just golden tools for animal-assisted therapy. There are other dogs, and even other animals, which can work just as effectively with children who face special challenges. There is nothing magic about North Star dogs; they are simply well-bred, beautiful, social, and intelligent creatures that are trained specifically to work with children. Personally, I glean more comfort from a relationship I have with a calico cat named Pitu than any of the four golden retrievers that live with us. Pitu finds me whenever I am lonely, she touches my tears with her paw when I cry, curls up next to my pillow every night and never asks me to play fetch. I relax at the mere sight of her stepping delicately toward me across the comforter.

I once gave a canary to an older woman, who proceeded to call me once a month for a year, just to thank me yet again for the happiness that Sunny gave her. Her depression had lifted and her life was clearly enriched by this little yellow bird with its joyous song. A friend of mine recalls a rat that gave her great solace during a rough patch in her childhood; she wouldn't even let me tease her about this relationship, standing firm by the genuine feelings this animal sparked within her young soul.

Last summer I observed people swimming with a group of dolphins, including a person who was suffering from a serious illness. I watched this exchange carefully, straining to find any traces of the magic some recent articles in woman's magazines attribute to interactions with these mythical creatures. I saw nothing magic, however, only radiant expressions on the faces of the people in the water and rather bored bottle-nosed creatures who worked for fish much the way I train my goldens with cubed pieces of hot dog. The dolphins were clearly working, and yet the people were thoroughly fooled into thinking they were expressing human emotions. This cemented what I had already suspected: the beneficial effects of animal-assisted therapy come from inside us. It is not something given to us by magical creatures; it is born of our perception of the animal, along with our own response to their actions and overtures. It is our appreciation of the animal and our bond that grants us the positive physical and psychological effects that we crave.

But before we get too cynical, consider this: when the dolphins swam to their trainers to get rewarded for performing for the charmed swimmers, the trainers did more than just chuck fish at them. The trainers leaned forward; they established eye contact and spoke with warm enthusiasm. I asked the head trainer why they did this; why not save their energy and just drop the fish into their opened mouths? She replied that the dolphins would not work without a warm and engaging relationship with the trainers. The eye contact, the vibrant tones and warm social contact are as critical to a successful training relationship with the dolphins as it is between my goldens and me. The trainers paved the way for the charmed swimmers to enjoy their perceived bond, perhaps to even elicit true healing. If so, this healing will not come from any dolphin aura or magical connection; it will come from a person convinced this creature could help him. (Don't ever sell the placebo effect short, for it speaks to the power of the mind.)

From the moment they are chosen for service work, the puppies we raise know the joy of sharing enriched relationships with both children and adults. They greet a variety of people, animals, and obstacles on a daily basis. Gentle handling allows pups to overcome their fears, which strengthens their confidence; training a young puppy is really just a matter of communicating your desire for its behavior. Understanding the pup's stages of development is important, as each phase presents a series of risks that can undermine or support the dog-human relationship. Stress should be avoided at all turns; signs of stress in the child should be recognized and respected, along with similar signs of stress in the puppy or dog. Knowing how both the dogs as well as the children I serve communicate and what they tend to communicate about helps me greatly in attempting to increase the interactions that flow between puppy and child.

Dogs, like the wolves that they descended from, are social animals. They are comfortable in a hierarchy and long for company as well as a leader. The day might come when your young dog will try to hopscotch over your child in its mistaken shakeup of the hierarchy of your family; your job is to convince this young canine upstart that he is mistaken. There are several signs that your dog is becoming too big for his britches; among them is growling (never good when directed at anyone), refusal to take commands from your child, and a lack of desire to please. This stage can happen at approximately six to seven months of age, although it can reemerge any time the conditions in your home lead the dog to perceive himself as more dominant than your child.

To remedy this misperception, you can do several things. The most important is to carefully supervise the interactions between your child and his or her dog and be ready to physically back up your child's authority. Starting with simple commands, have your child train the dog in many short segments throughout the day. The act of obeying a child's commands is a powerful message to your dog about where it exists in the hierarchy of your family. Having your child control treats dispensed as well as dole out the evening meal (only after the pup watches your family finish yours) will also encourage him to treat your child with deference. Any growling, even in play, should be actively discouraged with a stern "no!" followed by a very short period of purposeful ignoring. Some people use a crate for this purpose; if you choose to do this be certain this particular crate is not the one that is used for sleeping, as dogs are associative creatures.

Time is the only thing needed to cement a placement. Give yourself a lot of it, and allow the child and puppy a mixture of privacy and proper supervision to bond with trust. Careful observation from a distance is the best way to enjoy watching an assistance dog with a child with autism in action. I can guarantee you that the best moments will be ones you witness rather than create.

Part 2

Raising Your North Star

6

Choosing Your Companion

The dog was created specially for children.
He is the god of frolic.—Henry Ward Beecher

Before we begin to discuss how to select and train a dog for a child with autism, we need to first understand what an assistance dog can and can't do for a particular child. If we don't have a good grasp of our mutual expectations we run the risk of disappointment; this can be dangerous, even if it's just in the danger of missing the point. I often tell families that come to me to first make a list of what their hopes and dreams are for their placement, and going over this list together is a valuable way to be sure we're on the same page.

The first question I pose to families that come to me for advice is to ask if their child truly desires to have a dog. This seems a simple question, but it speaks to the heart of the matter: children who like dogs and have had some success bonding with them in the past are clearly the best candidates for an assistance dog placement. The second most important question to ask is whether or not the parents and siblings of the child like dogs, as the comfort level of everyone in the family needs to be taken into consideration before inviting a dog to join them.

Next I ask questions about the parents' and older children's available time to care for a young dog as well as their inclination to partner up with us to complete his or her training. This question is important to help us discover whether our method of placement is appropriate for the family in question. If it is not, then several organizations exist around the country that place older, more trained dogs with children with challenges, and I am happy to help families to find them.

When North Star creates a placement with a child, our primary emphasis is on selecting a puppy with the proper temperamental fit to meet the needs of the child in question. This temperamental fit begins with proper selection of puppy, and so I would urge anyone thinking of purchasing a puppy for this purpose to go slowly. Several organizations exist to help with this process, including North Star, and although much of early intervention tends to give the illusion of a window of opportunity quickly slamming shut, selecting an appropriate puppy is so important when pairing a potential assistance dog with a child that we are wise to take our time with this part of the process.

Selecting a puppy to serve as a partner to a child is still more art than science. When I began North Star's breeding program, I began with the premise that certain breeds were genetically predisposed to interact socially with people in a manner that dovetails with our need for them, that within these breeds existed genetic lines that tended to produce puppies that displayed this social orientation more than others, and that even within a specific litter certain puppies were more inclined to peer over the side of the whelping box to catch my eye rather than wrestle or cuddle with their littermates.

Your knowledge of the specific genetics of the breeding that will produce your puppy will impact you in two different ways: the first and most obvious has to do with the soundness of his hips, eyes, and heart. A pedigree takes knowledge and time to read; having many relatives cleared for the above tests is a good sign that the pup's odds of developing expensive and heartbreaking future maladies will be greatly reduced. Some potential genetic pitfalls such as cancer and epilepsy can only be deduced through word of mouth and can't be spotted on a pedigree, which is why gold standards for breeding assistance dogs are so necessary to maintain.

The second way the genetics of breeding might influence a potential assistance dog placement has to do with canine temperament. I am just another link in the chain of people who have been breeding dogs selectively for temperament for a very long time: Peter Savolainen of Stockholm's Royal Institute of Technology, who has been conducting experiments based on samples of mitochondrial DNA (or MTDNA) from living and deceased dogs from around the world, has concluded that genetic branching from wolf to dog began between 15,000 and 40,000 years ago. He believes the "Eve" wolf we seek may actually be several wolves, most likely originating from a wolf pack somewhere in eastern Asia. The particular population of East Asian wolves identified in Savolainen's studies may have had some genetic feature that made them easier to train or more desirable as a companion.

The settlers who reached North America via Beringia, the land bridge that used to span the Bering Strait, originally brought dogs along. Once dogs had been domesticated, they may have been important to hunter-gatherer societies, although we can only speculate on their perceived value. A dog may have been prized for its ability to guard the cave, for instance, but this same dog may have also kept the children warm and secure while parents foraged and cooked the food.

When two species live together for a long time, they influence each other's genetic evolution. Wild dogs with an innate talent for understanding how to communicate with people would have had a decided advantage in living long enough to raise a litter to maturity; puppies who inherited this talent and were also raised to be socialized with people stood an even greater chance of ensuring their genetic contribution to the gene pool. Over time, the combined influences of nature and nurture domesticated wild dogs and caused them to become intrinsically motivated to interact with people.

During the past 500 years, conscious and selective breeding of dogs has been evolving in organized and specific ways. We now have dogs bred to herd, to hunt, to guard and protect, to search and rescue, to assist the physically impaired and to lead the blind; dogs bred specifically to meet children's social, emotional and educational goals is a continuation of the discovery of dogs' ability and inclination to work with us.

Recent research described in the journal *Science* is shedding light on fascinating ways this evolution has unfolded. Using a series of experiments, most of which involved finding food hidden in scent-camouflaged boxes, anthropologist Brian Hare of Harvard University compared the ability of wolves, chimpanzees, adult dogs and puppies to pick up subtle cues in human behavior. Both puppies and dogs showed a talent for locating the food using nonverbal signals as subtle as a simple gaze from the researchers; they far outshone the more intellectually gifted chimp or their ancestor wolf. The researchers surmised that the ability to read our social cues has developed since dogs became domesticated, in a slow process of our two species becoming biologically entwined.

Once we find a puppy with the right genetic potential to work with a child we can nurture this potential as early as possible. However, there are some traits that are desired in assistance dog work that you cannot train, but must spot and develop to their potential. The term "intelligent disobedience" refers to the quality that would motivate a dog to lie down in front of an open manhole rather than obey his blind master's urging to press forward. Like seizure alerting, you can't specifically train a dog to possess this rare ability, but you can set the stage for its appearance and reinforce its continued existence.

Even after spotting the correct puppy for you in a well-bred litter, your work has just begun. Early and effective bonding between the puppy and the child he will end up serving is also key to a successful North Star placement. The earlier we can select a puppy with the right genetic potential for communicating with children and responding to their social cues, the better we can design an appropriate early training program, and the sooner we can pair this puppy with his child to begin their life together.

Resist the urge to rescue a puppy or dog from a shelter, not only because it may be impossible to know the genetics of the puppy or dog but also because we cannot know the prior experiences that may shape his future behavior. Dogs are associative creatures, and if a child in a previous home has treated a puppy too roughly, especially during its first few months of life, that pup will more than likely retain a degree of suspicion and perhaps even aggression toward children. During times of stress the dog may display the defensiveness and/or aggression that at other times will lurk quietly beneath the surface.

Remember that our standards for this puppy search are much higher than in purchasing your average family pet. Children on the spectrum can occasionally be inadvertently rough with puppies due to their difficulties in distinguishing the animate from the inanimate. (This is why proper supervision between child and puppy/dog is essential.) In fact, providing this supervision is the main way we have to realize our goals for the placement, as joint attention paid to the pup helps a child socially by keeping his focal point the same as others in the room. Reminders to be gentle, along with specific recommendations for how to do so, will help a child to develop empathy for all living creatures. Ensuring that the puppy uses restraint in play as well as encouraging the child to develop gentle hands is equally important. Respect flowing in both directions is the cornerstone of all North Star placements.

My strict policy of breeding the pups I place or selecting them from equally high-quality breeding programs was formed from the unpleasant experience of North Star's very first and very ill-fated placement. While we were still securing our nonprofit status a family approached me for help training a nine-month-old Labrador retriever puppy named Toby for their teenage daughter, who was in a wheelchair and suffered from seizures. I had not bred or selected Toby for her; the family had located this puppy from a haphazard breeding on their own. My initial impression was that Toby was much too active and impulsive for public access, but she had several qualities that intrigued me. Toby was very bonded to this young lady and had developed the ability to detect her impending seizures, actually climbing into her wheelchair and plastering herself against her minutes before they would occur. (I have since come to believe that this dog's hypersensitive temperament is part of the profile of a dog that tends to alert.) We were not able to focus on expanding this ability to alert into creating a valuable response, as the family in question had rigid predetermined goals for public access, which North Star decided not to pursue due to temperament concerns. I kept working with this dog, waiting for her to settle down enough to offer her public access; unfortunately, this never happened and we parted on a very sour note.

In retrospect, I felt this dog's training was compromised, as the family insisted on using a shock collar despite my pleas to train with only positive methods. They also kenneled her much too frequently, keeping her for many lonely hours at a time in a crate in the basement. This may well have contributed to her sky-high level of anxiety. The lesson I learned here was twofold: first, that not every family is capable of becoming a partner in their dog's training according to our philosophy of positive training, and second, that a dog's temperament and future health are too important to leave to chance, especially when working with children.

It is difficult to predict the potential soundness of a puppy's future health or temperament when you pick it up at the pound, the pet store or from a neighbor's accidental litter. One benefit of purchasing a purebred from a quality breeder is the knowledge you can obtain about the breed in general as well as its specific pedigree. Although it is impossible to predict the future of any eight-week-old puppy, trying to whittle down the odds that your particular pup will develop hip dysplasia, heart malfunctions or eye problems involves a thorough shaking down of the family tree. Talking to breeders about genetic problems not reflected on the pedigree, such as epilepsy or cancer, is wise. Getting breeders to talk about other breeders' practices as well as their own can give you an education about both the general and the specific things you need to know about buying your pup. Solid knowledge of a puppy's genetic characteristics will help to lower the risk of physical or temperament problems interfering with the placement.

Most quality breeders are happy to talk about their dogs as well as the specific goal of each and every breeding, but proper clearances of both parents that are appropriate to the breed in question is the simple bottom line.

I once attended a seminar at Tufts University where I listened to a behavioral geneticist speak of the characteristics of different breeds of dogs. She spoke quite cautiously, uncomfortable about appearing a breed-ist. I feel none of her caution when discussing the implications of canine behavioral genetics, or the morality of selective breeding of dogs. We have been consciously shaping various canine breeds to suit our needs or our whims for a long time now; we have worked with dogs since they gathered hungrily around the edges of the campfires we built. They watched us closely as they waited for our discarded bones, for they are intelligent and social animals that want to fit into our pack's hierarchy. Domesticated dogs seem to long to make themselves useful to us and to crave our approval. Tapping into these instincts is the goal of North Star's breeding program, and to recognize and nurture these qualities in the tiniest of puppies is my challenge.

For several hundred years we have been consciously manipulating breeds for various purposes, and it remains important to consider the qualities that were sought when a breed was initially created. Some breeds were created to herd sheep, others to catch rats, others still to serve as gentlemen's hunting companions. An insider's knowledge of canine behavioral genetics can give you an edge in creating a truly therapeutic placement, for it is infinitely easier to ride a horse when you are going in the same direction.

Toy dogs and smaller breeds are not usually good choices for assistance dogs for young children with developmental differences, as they are quite delicate (especially as puppies). These smaller dogs are often quite smart and social, and I have heard of many successful wheelchair placements with smaller breeds such as papillons. But I personally would discourage use of a smaller dog in placements with most other challenges children face.

Dogs bred to guard or protect are also not appropriate assistance dogs for children with physical or mental challenges; a dog that is hard-wired to serve and protect can be a double-edged sword in terms of keeping people safe. Here the danger may not be to the child with a challenge but to those around him or her, for children with autism may suddenly become quite alarmed and a dog bred to protect might be unable to correctly perceive the danger to be abstract or nonexistent.

Herding dogs can also be problematic. We once owned a wonderful border collie named Britty, whom we adored. Unfortunately, she was compelled to herd my 18-month-old daughter; if she tried to toddle away, Britty would leap and nip to stop her flight. Nothing I did to dissuade her worked, and the professionals who helped me to try to extinguish this behavior were equally unsuccessful; this stimulus/response sequence seemed woven into the very strands of Britty's doggie DNA. One day when she knocked Kelsey down yet again, this time splitting her lip, I had to come to the painful decision to place her with another family with older children (the dog, not the child). This time I purchased a golden retriever, Juliet, who has the perfect temperament for working with children, along with a pedigree packed with both clearances and legendary temperaments.

I have personally found that the water dogs (golden and Labrador retrievers, springer spaniels, and standard poodles are all good examples of this category) work well with children. Water dogs have been bred primarily to provide companionship and assistance to hunters. They tend to have qualities such as intense loyalty, good work ethic, ability to communicate with people, and a strong desire to please. It would just not do to have a hunter's dog take off with the fallen duck to enjoy a tasty and private lunch. If a dog made a habit of this, he or she would certainly not be bred to produce the next generation of companions in the field. Canine personality traits such as intelligence (along with the capacity for intelligent disobedience), deep loyalty and people orientation can be passed down from one generation to the next, along with some more subtle but important characteristics, such as impulse control and reactivity to stress.

Some people believe that goldens are "softer," perhaps more sensitive, than Labs, which may or may not be a good thing, depending upon a particular child's needs. (I have heard Labs were created to be more hardscrabble, rummaging for food they would bring back for their families, while goldens were shaped by the tendency to be gentlemen's companions in the field.) Certain genetic lines of Labs as well as goldens are much calmer than others, with much better impulse control, and I feel these are breeds you need to approach carefully when working with children, as young and energetic Labs or goldens might inadvertently hurt a vulnerable child due to their size and developing strength.

Once you have selected a breed you need to educate yourself on the proper clearances the parents of the litters you will research will need to receive. Every breed has its genetic frailties; at the very minimum, both parents of your intended puppy should be tested for that breed's specific weaknesses. (For instance, a Lab or golden puppy should have passed the hip, eye and heart clearances, and ideally the pup's pedigree should be populated with dogs that have earned these three clearances.) There are also other traits that might not appear on a pedigree, such as the tendency to develop epilepsy or cancer in certain genetic lines. Currently about the only way to discover a "clean" line is to communicate with breeders. I personally have culled a precious handful of breeders I rely on for puppies and studs.

The field of canine behavioral genetics is still in its infancy, with the field of human genetics not that far behind; in this newly born area politics can shape what research is designed as well as the theories that the studies are meant to support or reject. I am not qualified to properly interpret the results of most of the studies I have researched over the years, both about dogs as well as children, but I have learned a thing or two about posing the right questions. The shifting sands of public perception can bury potential research, skew results or put a misleading spin on facts, but the power of observation and honest collection and interpretation of evidence (including anecdotal evidence for areas not well studied) can help to keep us on the path to the truth.

Years ago there was a woman who received a bit of publicity about her book's assertion that parents took a decided back seat in their kids' development; she based her assertions on misinterpreted studies, and decided that who our kids ended up being was all about genetics. Magazine covers began to trumpet her claims as though they were gospel truth.

I saw one of these magazine covers with a title blatantly asserting that parents didn't matter on a particularly bad day, with all four of my small children surrounding me in a narrow checkout line, whining for candy as they kept me from realizing my own personal potential. I managed to purchase my groceries and wheel both the kids and the cart to the car without incident, but by the time I had them all strapped in, every single one of them had asked me what was wrong, even though I had not said a word about my state of mind. By the time I had driven home I realized what this woman didn't: that while nature might seem to rule the day, nurture creates the finer points of our existence, such as love, connection and compassion. My children might have grown to adulthood with the exactly same I.Q. whether I'd chosen to be there for them or not, but they might not have ever noticed if I was upset, or even cared if I was; it's the relationship we form between us that is the point of parenting them and shapes their potential for a happy life. Results that can be measured in a lab or pinned down by surveys can be deceiving, and even genetics can steer us wrong if we pay it too much attention. What any puppy or child is born with is genetic potential, but it is clearly up to us to determine how this potential will be realized.

When searching for an assistance dog to help a child socially, emotionally, or educationally, it is wise to choose not only an outstanding litter from the breed that is most appropriate for your child's specific challenge, but also to handpick the particular puppy within the litter that stands the best chance of fulfilling its intended role. Some people believe that females tend to be more trainable and males more restless, but I have personally found that pups neutered or spayed by six months have very few, if any, behavioral differences. I feel that if dogs and bitches are neutered or spayed by six months, the effects of hormones are negligible and personality differences you see are not gender-specific. Such considerations as the individual breeding line and the individual personality traits of the dog are bigger factors to consider.

The law of natural selection is on our side here, for nature likes variety. In nearly every high-quality litter we look at, we can probably find at least one puppy with the temperament we seek. Having a clear idea of the desired temperament is necessary in order to recognize this special pup upon sight.

In my most recent litter between North Star's Juliet and CCI's Kitteridge, only one pup out of a litter of ten proved incompatible for working with a child. (The longer you specifically breed for a particular temperament, the more success you will have in producing it.) I worked with Nicky for a full six months because he had such great potential in the areas of intelligence and problem-solving ability, but whenever Nicky was outdoors he thought with his nose, not his heart. He followed trails with intense interest, pointed when he caught a scent even though he never had a bird-hunting lesson in his life, and threw me apologetic glances when I tried to call him over to interact with me. I kept detailed records of Nicky and his littermates, so I was able to see I had spotted him even as a little guy, wandering to the edges of my woods instead of clambering onto my lap like most of his siblings.

Breeding for the show ring or for fieldwork—which often boils down to selecting mating pairs primarily for specific physical characteristics or for qualities such as speed or endurance or scenting ability—can compromise puppies' temperaments for working with children. Most good breeders will keep temperament in mind when selecting breeding pairs, but it is best to inquire what attention has been paid to this important consideration. At North Star, temperament is paramount when considering any potential mating.

One avenue to try in your search is to contact high-quality breeders and inquire what kind of temperament they breed for, and if they have any puppies in the litter that are unusually gentle and people-oriented. This is not the temperament that is valued in the show ring or the field, and if luck is on your side this people-oriented pup will have a physical flaw or two, thereby making her available to you ("pet quality"). You may have to spend some time on a waiting list to acquire this pup, but the time it takes to find the right dog is well spent. Resist the impulse to buy the flashiest or most "correct" golden puppy. If a perfect temperament is what you desire, then qualities such as shade of coat or shape of head could distract you from your quest for the true golden grail. In the absence of the ability to read between the lines of the pedigree the breeder will offer you to inspect, talk to the breeder about the bitch as well as the stud, and ask about why the breeding took place.

Following these guidelines in choosing your puppy is smart as well as practical. Unfortunately, it is also expensive, but the quality of your pup's pedigree is well worth the price tag. Raising a litter of puppies correctly is an expensive and time-consuming activity; but in my experience people tend to be penny-wise and pound-foolish when purchasing a puppy, for mistakes made in breeding can end up being quite costly in the long run.

Now that you've swallowed hard and decided to spend the money to buy the right dog, you will be faced with entire litters of well-bred pups. Which pup do you choose? A temperament test is a valuable tool in the tricky business of trying to decide which pup has the appropriate temperament for your child, but I believe these test can be easily misinterpreted by the general public; the best guide to discovering this tricky blend of temperament is the quality breeder. Breeders know their puppies best and can help you make this important decision. In general you want a pup that is people-oriented but not overly dependent, confident but not brash, brave but not impulsive. Be prepared to spend a good amount of time on the floor with the litter, observing the behavior of the puppies as well as your child's reactions to individual puppy styles. Choosing an appropriate match between puppy and child with autism is something that requires a great deal of thought, patience and creativity. Chemistry matters, and quiet personal observations can be the most valuable tool of all to help you decide.

One thing to pay attention to as you sit and watch your child discovering the puppies is where the pups are being raised and what kind of nurturing they are receiving. One way to determine how the pups are being raised is to investigate where the pups are kept. If they are tucked away in a dark basement or a distant shed then they are probably not receiving an appropriate amount of stimulation and nurturing. The environment should also be conducive to good development: is it well-lit, clean, and spacious? Are there cool new puppy toys, appropriate to their level of development? A quality litter is worth waiting for; this is not an area for compromise. Puppies raised without being socialized the first eight weeks of life are at a disadvantage compared to the lucky pups that are raised with care and attention. For service work, paying attention to the environment and socializing the puppies when young is critical; wariness or aggressiveness toward strangers can develop if pups are not properly socialized during critical early weeks of life. Puppies pass through stages of development much like children, and there are periods of readiness to learn along with vulnerable windows where bad experiences can permanently alter a young dog's temperament. Young animals need continual reinforcement to keep optimal socialization abilities; it is not enough to peek at them once in awhile. At our home we keep our young pups in a whelping box in a corner of my kitchen as long as possible to give them exposure to the stream of kids that come for a snack and stay for a cuddle.

Intraspecific sociability is also important; resist the urge to take possession of your puppy earlier than eight weeks. Since most pups stop nursing at 5–6 weeks, the temptation might be to take a pup too early, perhaps to get a jump on socializing the puppy, but this would be a mistake. Puppies teach each other many things during these weeks, including what it feels like to be bitten too hard in play or pinned down too roughly in a struggle for dominance. Ideally, we would like our puppy to learn the majority of these lessons from its siblings, not from you or your child.

Once you have found an excellent breeder with an eye for temperament and waited the requisite time for your name to come up on some mysterious list (a bit like adoption), you are ready to actually choose your puppy. You may then find yourself sitting on someone's kitchen floor—hopefully cleaner than mine—clutching a wrinkled copy of a temperament test. You are surrounded by a litter of golden puppies leaping up to eat it. So now what do you do?

The answer is blissfully simple: do nothing. Just observe the puppies playing with each other, watch the roles they take in their play, notice which puppy tries to make eye contact with you instead of romping around, which pup looks up and comes when you clap your hands. If your children are there, bring them in one at a time and encourage them to play with the puppies. In a minute, you can gradually add communicative gestures and vocalization to see which pups respond. Share observations and reactions with the litter owner for his or her responses and insights.

Once you have narrowed the field to two pups, I would suggest leaving your special child alone with them, with only one trusted adult there to observe and intervene if the pups invade the child's comfort zone or the if the child's attempts to interact cause discomfort to the puppies. This is the moment your endeavor would seem to become more of an art than a science, though you could probably videotape the encounter and boil down the decision to the pup that makes the most successful and sensitive approaches to your particular child.

The puppy we kept from our last litter actually responded at a mediocre level to most components of the test the examiner performed. She administered a temperament test used by Guiding Eyes for the Blind, and when the puppy we picked as having the best temperament had such middling scores, I wondered about the criteria of the test and what it was created to measure and judge. When I reviewed the scores of the test, it became apparent why our puppy, Suzy, did so poorly.

The Guiding Eyes organization requires an extremely confident dog with alpha tendencies, one that is not easily upset and not terribly sensitive. These qualities are not high on our list of an ideal candidate for a North Star dog, because guiding blind adults in public-access situations and helping a child with autism relax and relate to the animate world are two completely different job descriptions. In fact, North Star Foundation is occasionally offered puppies that wash out of the Guiding Eyes breeding program due to their soft and sensitive nature. For North Star's purposes, a softer, more sensitive and a bit more submissive temperament is needed so the child can be accepted as leader; the younger the child in question, the truer this is. However, an overly submissive temperament is to be avoided. The danger in pairing a very sensitive and overly submissive dog with a child who has meltdowns or erratic movements is a phenomenon called "fear biting." The heightened fear that an extremely sensitive dog experiences in a stressful environment might lead it to defend itself in a dangerous manner. Consistent and even-tempered patience and tolerance are the cornerstones of an ideal North Star temperament.

A certain level of curiosity in the environment is desirable, but I have found the best candidates to work with children with developmental differences are the puppies that are oriented more toward people than to the environment or their siblings. Watch for good eye contact in your potential puppy, and pay special attention to the pup that is the most consistent in greeting you and your child.

Visit the pup you intend to adopt regularly, to establish a bond right from the earliest weeks of life. If the breeder of the litter you have chosen doesn't mind, taking the young pup on short field trips between the ages of six and eight weeks is advisable. The more novel experiences they have during this fertile time, the better. It is worth mentioning that if everyone, including and especially the puppy, is not having fun during these supported excursions, nothing is gained and much is at risk of becoming lost.

Keeping trauma and discomfort to a minimum for both puppy and household during the transition is the goal; achieving this requires solid planning. Setting up a space where child and puppy can get acquainted without a lot of rules being enforced would go a long way toward helping to create a relaxing and welcoming environment. Purchasing a crate will aid with housebreaking your puppy and keep bad habits at bay, as it will prevent your pup from roaming the house unsupervised. Crating pups occasionally also gives them an opportunity for some important down time; a chewy toy to keep them company in the crate will make this a pleasant experience they will come to enjoy.

Now that you have the correct puppy, a nice crate with interesting chew toys, excited children, and high hopes, get ready for the requisite crash of thunder when fantasy meets reality. Any puppy you choose will whine, make mistakes, chew horrifying things, wake you up from a sound sleep, soil a rug or two and—finally!—settle down to curl up in the softest place to be found inside your family's heart.

7

Charting Your Course

*Every moment offers the potential for
constructive learning and adaptation or
the reverse, especially in the case of an
impressionable puppy.—Steven R. Lindsay*

It is not simply nature or nurture that creates an assistance dog, but rather the interplay between the two that matters the most. Once we have selected our assistance dog candidate for a child at North Star, we stress appropriate early socialization for the puppy, and a supervised and supported transition of the pup to the child's home. Setting the stage for this success takes more than a bit of work, but the truth is that raising a puppy to be an assistance dog is fun, for you can't teach a puppy or a dog outside the context of play. If puppies or dogs can't find the play in an activity, they will not willingly perform it for any length of time. Nothing is more motivationally important in dog training than to develop the skill of becoming a good playmate with your dog. As luck would have it, learning proper ways to play is also a high priority for a child with autism and many related challenges. Children who are grieving or recovering from a trauma need to play with abandon to allow them to briefly lay down their burden; in this case a puppy can be a touchstone to the innocence of happier times. When creating any training program for a puppy slated to work with a child, having fun has to be kept uppermost in mind. If the child and pup are not having fun together as they learn how to communicate with each other, you should go back to the drawing board.

Proper and specific training is essential in the creation of any assistance dog placement, along with close supervision until you are certain the interactions between dog and child are appropriate and gentle. Intelligent guidance in forming this budding relationship is crucial; initially it may be the puppy that will need protection from a child still learning how to be gentle and nurturing. In fact, I think this is perhaps the most important lesson any child can learn from forming a relationship with a dog. Later, it may well be the young dog that needs firm reminding to be gentle in all its interactions with your child.

We try to help our dogs out by understanding them, and so we buy them appropriate items to chew and carry about in their mouths, such as a kong or nylabone. Our goldens tend to frantically grab something—anything!—to put in their mouths when they greet us at the end of a long day, and it helps to understand their need to do this and have appropriate items available for them to keep them out of trouble.

I prefer to think of training a puppy as simple communicating; I use my voice and body language to get my messages across. Suddenly standing up and turning sideways, with no eye contact and just a moment or two of cold silence is often enough to convey your displeasure to a misbehaving puppy, especially if it follows a quick scold. (Bear in mind a puppy has a short-term memory of less than a minute, so any scolding or silences are useless if they last longer than this time frame.) Likewise, if you discover a puddle on the kitchen floor after the fact, your best bet is to simply clean it up and try to keep a closer eye on the puppy. Catching the puppy in the act of a transgression is the only effective time to communicate your displeasure.

At North Star, all our training is positive, and physical corrections are never employed. Personal integrity aside, I am being practical in setting this standard for North Star dogs. A child can't depend on having the strength needed to dominate a rapidly growing puppy or adult dog. Your puppy will need to cooperate in any training program you design, but luckily most well-bred and well-raised puppies generally want to please you. We may as well capitalize on this fact.

How can we communicate with this puppy when his behavior pleases us? If you watch your pup closely you will probably see him offering you many behaviors, and watching you for a clear reaction. One way to mark good behavior is with a positive social reaction paired with an immediate treat. Although some people choose to mark this desired behavior with only their voice, others prefer to use a small devise called a clicker specifically designed for this purpose. Karen Pryor, author of *Don't Shoot the Dog,* has championed the use of the clicker in videos, lectures and books that are easy to follow.

Karen Pryor and others have explored the possible relationship between clicker training and the amygdala, which is in the limbic system (one of the oldest parts of the brain). Research in neurophysiology has identified the kinds of stimuli, such as bright lights and sharp sounds, that bypass other parts of the brain to reach the amygdala first. This particular pathway is accompanied by rapid learning, often on a single exposure. North Star dogs are clicked from birth during nursing sessions; by the time they are eight weeks old they have already mastered the concept of click = treat on a primal level and are ready to participate fully in their training program.

Because clicker training does not rely on force, the stress level during training is lower and the atmosphere remains playful and spontaneous. This is the best climate for animal-assisted therapy, as dogs that are corrected physically and harshly often become paralyzed with fear of making mistakes. Social and outgoing puppies are more apt to be creative and spontaneous in their overtures to a child when they are trained in a positive and relaxed manner, thereby playing a more valuable role in a child's life.

Morgan Spector, attorney-turned-clicker-training expert, identifies three basic elements that can shape a dog's behavior:

- Set criteria reasonably.
- Consistently deliver a timely click to mark a desirable behavior.
- Maintain a high rate of reinforcement.

His book, *Clicker Training for Obedience,* is a bit more advanced in theory than Karen Pryor's materials, but retains at its heart both simplicity and integrity. (These books, as well as clickers, can be purchased from Sunshine Books, Inc. by logging onto www.clickertraining.com or calling 1-800-47CLICK.)

But clicker training is often not appropriate for many children with developmental differences, especially when they are young. Just the hand-eye coordination and seeking the correct timing for clicks can be overwhelming to some children, or just plain boring. Having a relationship that is as free from stress and boredom as possible will set up a child and a pup for success, so the clicker as a training tool is not for everyone.

It is best to focus on creating good habits right from the beginning, and so our work with North Star puppies begins at birth, with frequent and gentle handling long before our puppies can see or hear (they can still smell, feel, and taste us). Research suggests that mild stresses are good for a litter of very young pups in developing such qualities as resiliency and confidence. Overprotected pups tend to startle more easily and are more prone to fear responses later in life; based on these findings we handle our litters carefully from birth. Several times a day we place the tiny pups on the cool linoleum floor of our kitchen for a minute (cuddling them close when this nasty experience has finally come to an end). When they are older, enriched environments with equipment available to help practice emerging motor skills are offered to the puppies. This serves the dual purpose of helping the puppy to develop physically, as well as psychologically. An emotionally stable and confident pup is crucial to the successful development of a dog to be used for any assistance dog partnership. For children with autism, who may make sudden loud noises or quick movements, a dog that will not overreact to stress is absolutely vital. It also helps to cultivate a dog who is intelligent enough to problem-solve and courageous enough to feel comfortable thinking for him- or herself. This quality of understanding between dog and trainer is the richest soil to nurture intelligent disobedience.

I find that by the age of six weeks North Star puppies pay great attention to what pleases me, especially if I mark this time with a click and a treat. (Treats don't have to be edible; a back scratch is rewarding enough.) I would rather create good habits than spend time breaking them in the future, and even the youngest member of our family knows never to let a puppy jump up on us, even when their front legs feel as soft as a tickle. There are few sights more charming than a four-week-old puppy jumping up for attention, but it seems quite unfair to permit this, only to begin to scold months later when it becomes annoying.

Goldens and Labs are mouthy creatures in general due to their genetic inclination to retrieve, and if not properly trained they may nip your child with their needle-sharp teeth. There is generally no malice in this nipping; in fact, it is a twisted compliment, as they have grown used to spending a fair amount of time mouthing their beloved siblings inside the whelping box. It can be very hard for them to break this habit when they try to relate to you or your child. Their expressions of love and desire to play, while inconvenient, should be seen in proper context.

But I am particularly careful to work on North Star puppies' ability to inhibit the strength of their developing jaws, for in short order puppy nibbles become needle-sharp nips, and by then it is difficult to break the puppies' understanding of how we feel about their mouthing behavior.

The bonding experience of mouthing, which puppies use to interact and connect with their siblings, is a tough one to break; they are trying to express love and connection, and great care should be taken not to hurt their feelings when you attempt to correct this behavior. When I interact with young pups I let them mouth me, but I communicate to them when their playful nips hurt (yelping as their siblings would to express this) and I try to gradually decrease the amount of pressure that they are allowed to put on my hand when they bite. My goal is to have a pup possess a very soft mouth by the time it is six months old. When I interact with puppies, I stay low to the ground (to discourage jumping), issue a sit command (my default position) and give an abundance of physical affection, especially concentrating on the scruff of the neck, where my hand is not in nipping distance. Avoid lying on the ground, as this will kick their puppy play instincts into the mix; any training past this point will be like rowing upstream.

Rather than considering formal training for your young puppy, I think it is best to simply observe the pup at play, both alone and with your special child, clicking and treating actions you would like the puppy to repeat. For instance, if the puppy sits spontaneously, you can click and treat this behavior, saying, "Good sit!" to put it on cue. I stand behind the child during these training sessions, both to lend my authority over the puppy to the child as well as to help the child gain the puppy's attention. Some early commands that are valuable in a relationship conducive to animal-assisted therapy are sit, down, stay, and fetch, along with a really reliable recall. Children can be enlisted as much as possible to deliver the commands and the treats; we have one 10-year-old client who is becoming a master at clicker training. In fact, some children who have faced special challenges take up clicker training quite easily, as the method has a great deal of overlap with the behavioral modification that may have shaped their own behavior.

Successfully issuing commands to their puppies is often empowering for children with developmental differences, who have frequently been on the receiving end of many commands. In particular, children on the autism spectrum must frequently endure being told what to do, what to say, and even how to say it; this is a necessary part of educating them, but it must still feel burdensome. It has always struck me as refreshing for these children to be able to shift gears and be the teacher for a while, especially if the pupil is a willing and responsive participant in the training. The fact that this responsiveness must be voluntary makes it a valuable interactive experience for the child, who must elicit the puppy's cooperation along with his obedience.

An added bonus of including your child on the ground floor of your training is to elevate his or her status in the eyes of the puppy or dog. Issuing commands with confidence and clicking and/or treating compliance are ways to enhance your child's authority over the dog. Some formerly feisty puppies may grow too big for their britches around adolescence (for a dog this is about nine months). They may begin testing their power in the pack (i.e., your family), and increased supervision is called for if trouble seems to be brewing; often just standing behind your child ready to reaffirm his or her authority is enough to keep your canine ruffian in line. Growling is a bad sign, even when this growling occurs in play such as tug-of-war. I see it as an indication that the play has become too serious, and I divert the game to something with less at stake.

Games that a child with autism can play with a dog that reinforce the reciprocal nature of social interaction, such as fetch and peek-a-boo, are fun and valuable to play. (One North Star dog independently taught his young master with autism how to play fetch, rather than the other way around!) Another North Star dog essentially made up his own version of this game by hiding the tennis ball every time I threw it to him, actually training me to play his game of fetch and throw until I finally got wise. Dogs can also be taught to play hide-and-seek, preferably from a young age. I use an unwashed pillowcase of the child's so the puppy has a chance to smell before he begins to seek, and at first the child "hides" in plain sight.

No games will fly without a dog's understanding that he or she is playing by established rules. This is why the first step to creating a successful assistance dog is the dog's willingness to work at knowing and following the rules specific to your family. But before you can even begin to train a dog, the relationship must be conducive to training. There is no room in a working training relationship for a power struggle, so we have no need for electric shocks or choke chains. By raising a well-bred puppy right from the start you are able to reap what you sow: a dog who cooperates with you because he wants to, not because he wants to avoid pain.

North Star dogs have knowledge of a series of basic commands, such as sit, stay, down, come, go to bed, and leave it. Having the child be able to issue these commands will ensure that the developing relationship between your dog and your child will remain respectful. Until you are certain that such trust exists, please be on hand to supervise all interactions, and be ready to intervene delicately but swiftly upon the first sign that either party is uncomfortable with the interactions. It takes a bit of work to help facilitate the first year in the life of this important relationship, but I can guarantee it will be well worth the effort.

Your local library or bookstore has shelves full of books written on the subject of dog training, but before you crack any of them open I advise you to be aware of the philosophical underpinnings that will shape any advice offered to you. Is the author into control or a slave to permissiveness? Are positive or punitive methods of training used? A well-behaved puppy or dog placed carefully for a child with a challenge can be a joy, but an unruly or poorly trained puppy can grow up to be a danger to the child you had hoped it would serve. I recommend professional local guidance in shaping a training plan for a puppy that is going to live with a child with developmental differences, but you must be careful that this trainer works with a positive and respectful approach. I am happy to help support anyone who contacts me seeking advice on this matter, or to give help seeking a talented local trainer, as education is an important part of North Star's mission.

To communicate with a puppy, or a child without language, you need to come to the table humble and hungry for a relationship free of our own ego and communication style. Tossing out preconceived notions or a deep need for control can be an incredibly difficult and painful process, and I think this is why having a newborn or young pup is so daunting to many first-timers, while old-timers can raise them with the proverbial hand tied behind their backs. It isn't that the task itself is difficult, it is the work of shifting your paradigms that you need to do before you can form a healthy and intuitive relationship. You need to take the perspective of the child or pup you are communicating with, and understand how he learns in general and how he is feeling at that particular moment in time. It helps greatly to understand how you learn as well, and how you are feeling, for this will greatly influence your day-to-day decisions and communication techniques. Nonverbal creatures are often incredibly perceptive and pick up very subtle nuances in our body language and tone of voice, which can easily set off a chain of negative interactions. Catching a child or a pup in the middle of this negative spiral and punishing him to gain control is very counterproductive. I think it is also cruel.

I've already told you how Madison came to us from Canine Companions for Independence fully trained and uncomfortably robotic. Shortly after Madison's arrival we purchased a golden puppy named Pennie, whom we trained from scratch. In training Pennie, and the many puppies that I've trained since her arrival, I used the instincts I had honed when raising Danny and took my cues from the pup in front of me rather than experts. This was how I discovered that the best dog training, like the best parenting, is a dynamic process, springing from a relationship that is free from punishment and control. I wanted Pennie to cooperate with me, and as luck would have it she wanted to cooperate right back; communication was the only thing that stood in our way of understanding the specifics.

The first thing I teach my puppies is to sit, and they all master this skill quite early. It amazes people to see a tiny six-week-old pup sit on command, but it is actually very simple to accomplish this; the only thing it takes—in abundance—is consistent and enthusiastic praise. Every time I see them spontaneously sit in my presence I sing their praises to the skies, put a label on this desired behavior ("Good sit!") and offer them a tidbit of food. Before my pups leave my side they all melt into a default sit when in the presence of people, for I have communicated to them that this is the behavior I value the most from them. The reason I value this sit is that a sitting dog by definition is not a jumping dog, and a jumping dog can easily sent a child sprawling to the ground or back inside a shell.

If a pup does jump up on me, I simply step back so that he or she is once again on all fours; I then wait patiently to be offered a nice sit before delivering the reinforcement of praise or food. I am communicating what I want the pup to offer me by way of behavior with my attention and my food, and even the tiniest of pups responds to this.

I control the pups' environment for a long time to be certain they are properly socialized to the role I want them to take in the family they will come to serve. This sounds more complicated than it is, and I have become very good at entwining the threads of training into the tapestry of my day. Recently I brought a nine-month-old North Star golden retriever named Monty back to my home to complete training for a young girl named Sarah, who is on the autism spectrum and suffers from extreme anxiety. Monty's puppy raiser did an excellent job with him, but she reported that he tended to bark when he was alarmed, which was especially problematic because loud noises startled Sarah. The first morning after Monty arrived I saw this in action when he fiercely warned my lawn mower to back off; I had never raised a dog before with this strong a tendency to bark when alarmed, and for a moment I was unclear how to respond. When in doubt I have learned to observe, and so I saw how Monty looked back to me when he took a breath from his barking tear, and how his hackles stood on end. I decided to walk over to the lawn mower slowly, speaking soothingly, holding the handle and moving the mower gently back and forth while I met Monty's eyes; he stopped barking and the hackles slowly fell back into place. The next few days I moved the lawn mower around to various spots on the lawn and eventually turned it on and pushed it, with Monty having the freedom to retreat or approach at will. Within days of this full-blown alert, Monty was prancing past the lawn mower, whether it was running or not.

This process is called desensitization, and it is part of behaviorism rather than simple dog training. A trainer might have advised me to put Monty's bark on cue so that he could then understand the "Quiet!" command, but this technique would not scratch beneath the surface of Monty's behavior to pull out the barking weed by the roots. The desire for immediate control often sends the offending behavior underground, where it will spring to the surface in a different and sometimes more dangerous context. Fear biting is a very real danger with dogs that are on the submissive and sensitive side.

Monty communicated to me about some deer that lurked at the edges of my property one morning, and on several occasions I came to stand beside him and murmur that they meant him no harm as he swung his head back and forth between me and the scary deer: did I really see what he saw? By the time I had turned my back he had turned his as well on the delicate creatures that merely wanted to munch on my garden undisturbed. I gradually discovered that touching Monty's nose when he was faced with any new and potentially frightening stimuli could nip his arousal in the bud; it was our signal that I understood what he saw and had it covered. So while technically I was desensitizing Monty to frightening stimuli, pairing his perception of these events with my soothing attention, I was also simply letting him know I did indeed have it covered. It was this trust that allowed Monty to relax and not bark, and this is quite different from achieving this feat by shouting "Quiet!" when he was in full-blown alert mode. By delving deeper into the reasons Monty barked (fear) and responding in a way that took advantage of the bond we had developed to cash in on the trust I deserved, I was able to sooth Monty and have him move through his day both quiet and relaxed. I could have achieved his silence by virtue of my ability to exert control over him, but I would have then left him afraid even if fully compliant.

I once heard a frightening example of how some well-meaning parents employed this kind of "outside-in" thinking with their children with autism. A group of mothers in a very wealthy and educated part of my state got together on a weekly basis to all hold their children with autism close on cue until all the screaming stopped. I believe this chilling activity sprang from the false belief that refrigerator mothers were responsible for their children's autism, the thinking being that these mothers could thaw their children by the heat of their tightly wrapped arms, especially with the power of numbers on their side. To me, forcing eye contact with a child with autism is equally misguided, but coaxing this eye contact with rewards, especially the reward of a hug or smile, is the way to go. It seems clear to me that with children or with dogs you can't begin by forcing the end result: you need to work up to a goal like eye contact or a hug or a peaceful walk together, respect flowing consistently in both directions.

A well-trained dog is a joy to live with, but training has to be individually crafted for each particular child-and-dog team. Training in the "right way" isn't nearly as much trouble as training the "wrong way," so time spent doing research and reading good books about positive training methods are well worth the effort.

8

Raising a Dog for Search and Rescue

We are all travelers in the wilderness of this world, and the best we can find in our travels is an honest friend.—Robert Louis Stevenson

Families who request my help to select and train a North Star dog to help them to keep track of a wandering child often approach me after presentations or by email; I have mixed feelings when I advise them, as the risks are great that I will be misunderstood.

The most important thing for me to communicate to them is that a dog, by virtue of its limited intellect, should never be in charge of any child, and especially not in charge of a child with autism. I am personally against the concept of tethering a child with autism to his or her dog for this same reason, although I am aware of other, highly regarded organizations that recommend this method under specific and controlled circumstances.

I believe the first line of defense to take in keeping a child who wanders safe isn't even a dog at all, but a technology. It is called a global positioning device, and it works with your home computer to locate a child who wanders. One can conceivably be attached to a dog's collar as well as on the child him- or herself for extra safety (in case the child wanders without his own device on.) I am happy to send anyone who emails me my recommendations for the best devices on the market.

Other products that can help us keep track of a child include state-of-the-art locks for the home and a bell that rings when a door is opened. Proper education of the child can also go a long way toward helping him to be responsible for his own safety as soon as he is developmentally ready to do so.

In the meantime, there is another potential safety net to put underneath a child who wanders, and this is a trained assistance dog. An assistance dog organization in Canada called National Service Dogs (www.nsd.on.ca) has pioneered a concept of tethering a dog to a child with autism who wanders, thereby helping to keep him or her safe, but our goals at North Star are primarily social, emotional, and educational. However, our method of socializing and training North Star dogs has also helped to keep kids who wander safe, without a tether to connect them. Dogs have evolved by our sides for thousands of years, and they are genetically programmed to seek out their role in the pack (i.e., your family). Surprising benefits accrue and dovetail when assistance dogs grow up familiar with their children, with an appropriate temperament handpicked and a training program created specifically to meet this child's particular needs.

One of the first puppies we placed at North Star (named, appropriately enough, Star) went to two brothers on the autism spectrum. One of the boys, Danny, was very high-functioning, and his younger brother, David, was on the lower end of the spectrum. From the start, Star seemed to understand that his job was to relate to the boys, and he went from one to the other with a remarkable ability to shift his demeanor. With the older boy, Danny, playfulness and a bit of rowdiness was noted, but with David he was much more sedate and careful in his overtures. In his work with David, Star would merely accept a dog toy being handed to him and drop it as soon as he received it, clearly understanding that his reward would come from David's parents, not from the intrinsic value of the toy itself. With Danny he would take the toy and run, inviting him to play catch-me-if-you-can. I have also witnessed Star teach David to play fetch, and not the other way around, but clearly the most impressive skill Star developed with David was to be able to warn his family when he wandered away.

Like many young children on the autism spectrum, David often took off on his own, despite his parents' vigilant attempts to keep track of him. This was alarming, as this family lived on the edge of dozens of acres of woods. In creating this placement we incorporated games such as hide-and-seek into this pup's training in preparation for the terrifying day that Star's help in a search might be needed. So far, this has not happened, but twice Star has alerted the family to David's wanderings by barking frantically and circling him. While growing up with David,

Star picked up on the intense focus that his parents shared to keep him in sight, and quickly responded to their rewards and praise helping them with this task. This barking/circling alert was not specifically trained, but happened as a result of good breeding as well as an excellent communicative relationship between Star and the boys' parents. It takes a high degree of intelligence, communicative ability, and motivation for a dog to even recognize that a vulnerable child has wandered away, much less to alert to it, and while the potential for these qualities is in the genes, realizing this potential takes conscious effort.

The ideal candidate for a puppy for search and rescue work would be a puppy genetically inclined to use his nose to explore his environment, along with a rather high energy level. For working with children with autism, however, these qualities may work against our need for a people-oriented, mellow-tempered pup, and so we find ourselves conflicted from the start when we seek to add search and rescue to the job description of a dog meant to help serve your child's social and emotional needs. The temperament of a search and rescue dog, along with the recommended training protocol, is different from the temperament and training required to work with most children with challenges. An ideal search and rescue candidate is just too aware of the scents in his environment and has too much energy to be comfortable with the slower-paced life of working with a child.

However, we can select an intelligent puppy that has the potential to alert along with a sensitive and mellow disposition; we can then pair him up with a child as early as possible, and reward the pup's attempts to follow this child around and keep track of his or her whereabouts.

As with any other training offered to a pup in its first year of life, the context of the training should be an enjoyable game. Examples of simple games to play to encourage a puppy to follow a child who wanders include "go to" games (where a family sits in a circle around a pup and rewards successful attempts to "go to" particular members) and "follow the leader" games (where a dog is rewarded for following a child wherever he may roam). After these games have been played successfully for a while, you can ask your dog to find your autistic child by playing hide-and-seek. At first have your child hide in plain sight, and say, "Find Timmy!" in a cheerful voice. If your dog knows who Timmy is and that he has something like a yummy treat or high-value toy, he will be highly motivated to find Timmy. To increase the likelihood that your pup will enjoy this game, trail after him and make a big fuss over him when he finds your child. Play the "find Timmy" game as often as you can, as long as it holds your dog's interest.

Eventually you will be able to encourage your dog to find your child out of doors. This skill may prove invaluable some day if you have a child who wanders, but keep this skill set specific to your child and don't have your dog attempt to find anyone else. It will also be helpful to socialize your dog to allow strangers to peek at her name tag, so that she will be comfortable having a stranger read this tag to find out where you live in the event that your dog has followed your wandering child.

You do not have to teach your dog to trail and track; most dogs have exceptional noses and learn very young how to follow whatever interests them by scent. What you will want to do is to teach your dog to follow the scent of your particular child. It's not hard or even complicated to do this. As with all training, it should be fun for you and fun for the dog.

A helpful book you may want to read is *Following Ghosts: Developing the Tracking Relationship* by Suzanne Clothier and John Rice. In addition, the Southwest Tracking Association is a great resource on the Internet for articles and leads to books on tracking. Unless you are also preparing your dog for competition and tracking titles, you will want a relaxed and natural approach to trailing and tracking. A dog should not be trained to keep track of your child within an inch of anybody's life.

That said, on four separate occasions to date children have been kept safe from their inclinations to wander by their North Star dogs. Two barked to alert to their children's attempted wanderings, and one North Star dog named Buddy followed his young and nonverbal girl with autism out the mistakenly open front door and down the block, staying by her side and allowing a distant neighbor to read the number engraved on his collar. The most recent story I heard concerning this important subject was from the mother of a boy with autism named Gavin, who told me a remarkable story about their North Star dog, Bailey. During a vacation at the ocean she came downstairs to find the locked sliding glass door wide open, with both Gavin and Bailey nowhere in sight. She stood on the deck with her heart in her throat and above the noise of the waves heard a faint but familiar bark. From down the other end of the beach she then saw Bailey coaxing Gavin back to the beach house with a mixture of barks and gentle nips at his heels. I could not have taught him this skill specifically if I had tried, but I believe I know why Bailey acted this way. I believe he understood Gavin's vulnerability as he wandered away alone, and that Bailey's overriding inclination was to bring him home again. This level of creative concern is our goal with all our North Star placements.

9

Raising a Dog for Seizure Alert and Response

To accomplish great things, we must
not only act, but also dream; not only
plan, but also believe.—Anatole France

Despite any claims you may have heard to the contrary, no one is currently able to train a dog to alert to impending seizures. A canine alert to a human's impending seizure is something that naturally and occasionally occurs; it is the seizure response that can be trained in a dog that has first displayed this spontaneous alert. The first recognition of this phenomenon was by people whose pet dogs began to communicate their knowledge of their owners' impending seizures. Often this alert was quite similar to Lassie's urgent attempts to communicate that Timmy was in danger (yet again!); whimpering, pawing, nose catapulting. Epileptic pet owners report being initially confused by these anxious attempts to communicate with them immediately before they were swept up by their seizure.

The fact that some dogs have the capability to alert to people's seizures has been proven, but we are still at the stage of forming theories to explain how this is done. Most scientists speculate the alert is due to a dog's heightened sense of smell, and the stories I have heard support this idea. (Many people to whom I have personally spoken relate their dogs' smelling their palms as part of the alerting process.) Although anecdotal evidence is inferior compared to proof gleaned from the scientific meth-od, the lack of scientific inquiry into this phenomenon currently leaves us at the mercy of anecdotes. Part of the scientific method is to gather and sort evidence, but we have finally turned the tide in recognizing that this ability exists in dogs, even without being able to prove exactly how this is done. (It is important to remember that just because you can't prove something doesn't necessarily mean it isn't true.)

I believe that many more dogs are physically capable of alerting to seizures than actually display this remarkable ability, and that there are other physical conditions to which dogs are capable of alerting. Besides alerting to seizures, there have been many reports of dogs alerting to other dangerous physical states, such as the low blood sugar dip that can be quite dangerous for diabetics (especially at dawn, when help would be difficult to summon). I have even heard that dogs are able to smell the difference between normal cells in a petri dish and cancerous ones. To facilitate the existence of a canine alert to a physical condition (and, more importantly, to the communication of this alert as a recognized response), I believe there are several things you can try.

Many assistance dog trainers believe the ability to alert to human sei-zures is heightened by the dog and human developing a very close bond. I think that a dog that believes a particular human is a fully realized part of his pack will do whatever he can to alert that person to any danger that exists, from the outside threat of approaching intruders to the inward dan-gers of chemical imbalances. In order to properly perceive the approach-ing seizure as a stimulus that it is a dog's job to communicate, a high de-gree of intelligence is required. Dogs as well as people continually perceive vast amounts of information from the senses; it is up to us to sort through this information and determine what is dangerous and what is benign, what needs to be recognized and what can pass by without a response.

Three of my four golden retrievers could care less if anyone comes to our door. My fourth golden, Pennie, considers it her main reason for living to warn me of any stranger that even wanders by our property. The fact that this alerting behavior exists is a marriage of Pennie's biological inclination and ability to sense approaching intruders (nature) and my ten-dency to encourage her to communicate her knowledge to me (nurture). This happened because my husband used to travel for weeks at a time when our children were small; for years I would consciously reward and encourage Pennie's natural watchdog inclinations. (I have fond memories of feeding newborn babies with Pennie perched on the back of our living room couch, her nose pressed to the window, diligently waiting for nasty intruders she could alert me to.) To this day Pennie greatly enjoys her important job, and she will come to me for praise anytime she warns me of those potentially dangerous strangers. Although nearly every warning she has ever given related to benign visitors and innocent hikers, I still reinforce Pennie's warnings; the casual "thanks!" I throw her like a bone is now enough to relax her from her heightened state of arousal.

Once a dog has developed the ability to alert and respond to seizures, it appears this close bond is no longer necessary for this remarkable ability to surface. Dogs have been known to alert and respond to strangers' seizures, but normally this alert and response has already been established with someone close to the dog. As a dog trainer, this makes sense to me. You train a dog to respond to a command (i.e., "sit"), and this paves the way for others to successfully issue this command to the dog. As sitting on command is a learned behavior, someone first has to teach the dog this skill, and pulling him or her up the learning curve works best within the context of a trusting relationship.

The first client North Star had was a girl who suffered numerous seizures per week. Her dog would climb into her wheelchair several minutes before these seizures would occur; she was nearly impossible to pry off or discourage with a scolding. (Of course, this behavior was reinforced when its meaning became clear, as anyone with a seizure disorder will tell you advance notice is quite valuable.) Once the seizure alert is noted and encouraged, the appropriate seizure response can be trained as a chain of behaviors that leads to communicating possible danger to the appropriate people. The telephone company has a specialized piece of equipment with a footpad that can be used to get outside help should no one be available in the home. It is a relatively easy matter to train a dog to press this footpad when alerting to impending seizures; this would then activate an intercom where verbal communication can take place between a disabled person and someone trained to help. (Obviously, the lack of response from the disabled person would indicate a need for emergency vehicles to be sent to the home.)

Another client of North Star's was a two year-old boy named Adam who suffered from tonic/clonic seizures. These seizures required medical intervention, and naturally his parents were desperate for several safety nets to exist beneath their son. (Along with calling North Star for a possible seizure alert dog, they located a state-of-the-art mattress designed to trigger an alarm when a seizure took place.) The availability of dogs that already have proven ability to alert to seizures is understandably low, with long waiting lists where the family couldn't afford to linger.

When they came to me with their dilemma, I was initially at a loss to know how to locate and train a puppy that would have a higher-than-average chance of developing this important alert to Adam's potentially life-threatening seizures. I was tempted to sidestep these desperate parents for lack of solid knowledge and firm guarantees, but I knew of no one to refer them to. I also did not want to back away, because I believe there is untapped power here, and hope for helping people with a variety of medical conditions. (Dr. Tadeusz Jesierski of the Polish Academy of Sciences is currently consulting on a research project in California to study cancer detection in humans by trained dogs on the basis of emitted scent, and several organizations in the country are now focusing on training dog to respond to low blood sugar levels in diabetics.)

In my search for a puppy or dog that might have a better chance of developing a seizure alert than the one-in-ten odds currently cited in the population of pet dogs of epileptics, I located a breeder with a line of golden retrievers that had several members reliably alerting to their owners' impending seizures. Lines that contain more than average amounts of seizure alerting dogs probably reflect greater than average biological tendencies toward high intelligence, along with unusual inclination and ability to communicate with people. In my experience, dogs that alert to seizures tend to be, by nature, intelligent, sensitive and people-oriented. Exactly why these dogs are able to alert to a seizure, typically from 15 to 30 minutes before a seizure strikes, is still a mystery. Theories abound, but my belief is that the dogs are reacting to different sights, sounds and smells put forth by the person about to seize, and of these perceptions I believe smell is probably the strongest indicator. The dog's sense of smell is estimated to be nearly 300 times more powerful than ours, and before a seizure takes place the abnormal activity in the human brain may create an odor that certain dogs can perceive (there may be other factors at work, such as subtle behavioral or body posture changes that occur in a human before a seizure strikes that dogs may perceive as well.) But it is not enough for dogs to stop at these perceptions, for we also need to train the dog to then deliver a recognizable and predictable response in order to communicate this knowledge to others, thereby alerting them to the impending seizure.

This is the seizure response, and before it can be created it has to first be conceived. To do this I wondered what I as a parent would want my dog to do with the knowledge that my child was about to have a seizure; this is when technology entered the picture, for a dog can be trained to use a telephone footpad that to call for help with the simple press of a paw. At North Star we have rigged up a much simpler but no less effective "warning box" that a dog can start with a press of a paw to alert parents to a child engaged in a potentially dangerous activity. Noticing that a child is wandering away from a crowd is not really different from noticing that he is about to seize in terms of training; we want our dog to communicate his alert to us so that together we can take action to prevent danger.

"When it comes to identifying a dog who might alert, we can only say, 'We think he has the right characteristics to do this,'" says Darlene Sullivan, founder and executive director of Canine Partners for Life in Cochranville, Pennsylvania. The signs to me include a puppy that is more interested in life outside the whelping box walls, attempting to make eye contact and communicate with people more than with other dogs or animate objects in his or her environment. Most breeders will tell you that in nearly every litter there is one pup that will follow them around, ignoring even their mother in favor of human attention. Other desirable attributes in a puppy you hope may develop a seizure alert are heightened sensitivity to smells and sounds, and an unusual ability to tune into human moods. The seizure alert dogs I have personally had contact with were rather high-strung, craving approval, with a close bond with people in general, and their special person in particular.

Deciding what organization you should apply to with an educated and discerning eye is a critical first step in locating the perfect dog to work with a child with seizures. For Adam, I located a breeder in Texas whose line had contained several dogs that alerted to their owners' impending seizures at young ages. Many of this breeder's puppies went to assistance dog homes, which increased the odds of having owners with medical conditions that included epilepsy; in fact, this is how this line's genetic ability to detect seizures was inadvertently discovered.

North Star purchased a puppy named Abby from this particular line to work with Adam, in hopes that she would develop this valuable seizure alert, which we could then lengthen into a response to help predict Adam's seizures. We chose a middle-of-the-road puppy in terms of temperament, since an overly submissive dog might not have the courage to break training to alert to a seizure, and a dominant dog would be too much for a two-year-old to handle. We also chose the puppy in the litter most interested in people, as opposed to her environment or her siblings.

Abby was initially brought to my house for training of impeccable house manners, as Adam and his baby brother were both obviously delicate. Although my training methods are always positive, I was especially careful to reprimand Abby sparingly and gently, for two reasons. One was the fact that she was quite a sensitive girl and needed nothing more than soft-spoken direction for learning proper behavior. It is my observation that dogs that alert to seizure are quite sensitive to social cues from people and generally quite eager to please, and I wanted to nurture this quality.

The other reason for a gentle and positive focus when relating to Abby was the possibility of her needing to disregard prior commands in order to communicate her knowledge of Adam's impending seizure. For instance, if she had already been given the command to down/stay, she would need to break this in order to attempt to communicate. Initially, her restless pacing instead of obeying the down/stay might be rebuked. To minimize chances of this occurring, Adam's family had been instructed to be more concerned about possible beginnings of an alert as opposed to insisting on Abby's immediate and unquestioning obedience.

Another instruction given to Adam's family was to keep hot dogs in the refrigerator to be given to Abby, along with profuse praise, at the first sign of Adam seizing. (They were only to feed Abby the hot dogs if a seizure was actually taking place.) Pieces of these hot dogs, along with praise, were offered even if Abby had given no prior alert to a seizure; we were merely creating a positive association for her with Adam's seizures so that she would understand they were important events. The tone should be as calm and relaxed as possible under the circumstances. I am naturally aware of how difficult it is to speak this way in the midst of attending to a child's seizure, but my hope is that when Adam's family acts calm and in control of the situation, Abby will also feel calm and in control, which is obviously the best way to approach communication. Following this procedure can also be used to absorb some of the helpless anxiety that parents are apt to feel at this moment in time, and any brothers or sisters within the home can also feel comforted if they are present. Tasks such as fetching hot dogs and delivering praise to the dog can help them to cope with their sibling's seizure by giving them something helpful to do.

Dogs are associative creatures, and the next time Abby smells the chemical changes in Adam's brain that precede his seizing, she will become aroused (hopefully thinking something like: "The last time I smelled this smell I got that yummy treat and lots of praise and reinforcement; I think I'll nudge, whine, and travel between Adam and the refrigerator hoping to get this anticipated treat"). If Adam's parents noticed any unusual behavior on Abby's part, especially if it was directed either toward Adam or the refrigerator, they were to give low-key praise in case it was the beginning of a seizure alert.

It is actually important to follow these steps when any child or adult has a seizure in front of any dog, even if training a seizure alert and response dog is not the goal. This is because dogs take their cues of how to interpret events from us, and if they see us panic or if a dog gets kicked aside when a child is seizing, the dog will be a nuisance in this situation at best, and a hazard at worst. A highly reactive dog (which we naturally don't want for North Star's work) may be overcharged in this situation, especially if medical personnel end up coming into the home.

Streaming treats to the pup, petting him or her and talking softly and reassuringly will have a positive effect on all concerned, including the child when he or she comes around. We want to communicate to the dog the importance of the event of the seizure, along with the understanding that alerting to an impending seizure is a good thing to do. This is a more complicated process intellectually than you might think, and this is probably why only one pet dog in ten alerts to his or her owner's seizures naturally; the desire to communicate with us, along with the knowledge of how to communicate this message to us, is key.

Developing an appropriate alert response should be an important part of this dog's training program before he or she is placed with a child. It is not enough to just encourage an alert; the dog should then be required to follow a chain of behavior that is considered appropriate responses to the child's seizing. This is usually best served by training the dog to stay with his or her child in a down/stay until given the "release" command. The presence of a calm dog in a down/stay next to a child who is seizing will make an immediate impression on whoever approaches the pair. The seizure alert dog should always have a vest on in public that clearly identifies its purpose along with the fact that information is contained in the zippered pouch on the side of the vest. This pouch should contain information regarding the child and necessary and crucial next steps to take and telephone numbers to call in the event the child has a seizure when he is unattended.

In further training a seizure response, after a period of time with the dog in a down/stay, someone should check the dog's identification tag and zip open the vest the dog is wearing and remove any paperwork inside, to socialize the dog to expect this to occur. It is very important that this step be followed in this process of training for seizure alert work. The thinking behind this training exercise is that it may someday be a stranger that will unzip this pouch on the dog's saddle to get information, and we want the dog to allow the person to do this without flinching or growling. The person playing the role of unzipping the pouch in the training scenario should stand and bend over the dog, matter-of-factly unzipping the pouch, not speaking, and all the while streaming treats to the dog. This helps the dog we are training to look forward to someone bending down at a certain point after the seizure has occurred to unzip his pouch and remove the papers inside. For our important purposes it doesn't matter that the dog that looks up and wags his tail in happy expectation will be disappointed. The child or adult in the throes of a seizure in public will have the necessary information available to whoever is first on the scene, courtesy of our canine companion.

It is a relatively short distance from a dog's anticipating the hot dogs that have become associated with a child's seizures to having the dog deliberately communicate to someone that this important event is about to take place. As a dog matures, I believe it will not be the food that motivates him as much as his understanding of the important job he is performing in his pack and his desire to gain the approval of those he considers his superiors. This is why I feel the bond is so important in developing a dependable seizure alert and response dog; we wouldn't want a dog to only alert when he was hungry. I recommended that Abby spend as much time as possible bonding with Adam, even sleeping in his room, so that she could remain available to detect any impending seizures in order to alert his parents to them.

Ironically, Abby has not been able to develop a seizure alert for the happy reason that Adam has not had a seizure since her arrival at his house, so it is impossible to know if an alert would have preceded it. His medication is working to keep his seizures at bay, and Abby is on hand as the safety net she is happy to provide. We do know that Abby is greatly loved by both Adam and his baby brother; we also know she is a comfort to both of Adam's parents. We are quite certain she is worth the price we paid to find her and train her for this young family. And while we trust that some day Abby's ability to detect seizures will be there if needed, she is currently just a beautiful and well-trained pet for Adam and his brother.

We all hope she gets to stay this way.

10

Raising a Dog to Help a
Child Who Suffers a Loss

Sorrow makes us all children again.
—Ralph Waldo Emerson

These words of Emerson express the devastating effect that losing someone you love can have on your life. Grief, like love, knows no bounds. Grief is indiscriminate in selecting its victims, striking young and old, rich and poor alike. It can punch gaping holes into a life, allowing the winds of depression to whip through with frightening speed. This is especially true in cases involving young children, since many do not comprehend the full meaning of death and are often puzzled by the state of mourning they feel and observe around them.

A properly bred and trained puppy or dog can be a valuable tool for animal-assisted therapy and can help to comfort a child following a devastating loss. The presence of this puppy or dog can have many potential benefits to help children deal with their grief.

Death is not the only event that can deal a painful blow to a child; the loss of a parent to divorce, a late-in-life adoption or a move to foster care can seriously impact a child's developing emotional life. Children suffer loss in a different way from adults, as magical thinking influences the expression of their sorrow. While adults are normally wrapped up in the details of death or divorce and grounded in its reality, children are usually preoccupied with a mixture of fantasy and fear when struggling to comprehend their devastating loss. The child who has a weak grasp on concrete reasoning due to immature age or cognitive level is more vulnerable to the influence of illogical thinking. Knowing the cognitive stage of the child who suffers a loss is helpful in dispelling common fears (such as a child's belief that he or she caused the traumatic event in some unexplained way). These unconscious and unexamined thought processes, if left to multiply outside the light of logic, can wreak havoc on a young life by fueling destructive anger, guilt or depression.

Dogs can play a part in recovery by helping to lift a child's battered self-esteem and make him or her feel safe and loved. It is this comfort that allows children to open the floodgates to painful thoughts and experiences, especially in the presence of a delicate guide. Sometimes thoughts too painful to express to an adult may find expression by being whispered into the ear of a dog, who can be simply trained to place a head on a child's lap, helping him or her to feel understood.

Dr. Barry G. Lewis, a psychologist who specializes in grief counseling, has this to say about the concept of assistance dogs being employed to help children to recover from a traumatic loss:

> Trained dogs provide a connection to life; they are there for you and give meaning to the present, which helps to restore unity and peace. Their unconditional love and support helps foster and promote the resiliency that is within most children . . . [this] raises self-esteem and confidence in children and renews a grieving child's sense of normalcy. Trained dogs bring a wealth of love, attention, consistency, relaxation, and fun that promotes a feeling of belonging and provides a sense of safety, protection, security and comfort, helping to positively nourish a child's identity.

Long ago I realized that in any school presentation I gave, the children that gathered around would eventually start talking to me about painful and confusing experiences. They often told me sad stories of lost puppies, lonely tales of dogs dying or running away, heartbreaking descriptions of pain mitigated by their pets or heightened by their peers' intolerance. Sometimes I heard stories of violence or shame. Recently a young girl told me about a parent beating her dog as she tried to stop him; she was all of six years old, much too innocent to notice teachers exchanging glances or my own carefully frozen expression. I ceased indulging my own thoughts, I stopped paying attention to the room full of other children and nervous teachers and I took the puppy on my lap to sit next to this little girl. I took the time to simply bear witness to a hurt this child had both witnessed and suffered. I believe this simple act of bearing witness is at the very heart of the power of animal-assisted therapy, for dogs never attempt to fix their children; they only try to comfort, and therein lies their power.

Psychologists have used dogs for years to help children soften their defenses and allow them to speak of their sorrow and confusion. Relating to dogs and their simple emotions can also form the first step in a chain of insights that lead to understanding the complicated world of human emotions. The selfless and nonthreatening nature of a well-bred and trained dog can act as a springboard to help children to dive into the sometimes cold and roiling water of social interactions with other people.

Often the only action that needs to be taken with animal-assisted therapy is this commitment to listen with your whole heart. Children lean in when they tell me their stories, touching the dog that lies between us with trusting fingers. They are visibly happy to leave their story at my feet and relieved to be reassured about the innocent role they play in the unfolding drama of their lives.

Flight was North Star's first placement with the goal of working through a loss; two young girls coming to terms with being adopted acquired Flight to help them on this journey. The girls' adoptive family was extremely supportive, birth families were on the scene, and the girls were both animal lovers; this was the perfect climate for a North Star placement, and this particular placement went as smooth as silk. Flight proved so therapeutic with these girls that their adoptive father, an oncologist, began to take her with him to keep his patients company when they received chemotherapy.

It was in his waiting room that Flight met and greatly helped Courtney and Justin, the children of a cancer patient named Sharon. The children would accompany their mother to her treatments and found great solace in Flight's company as they waited with their father, Mike, for Sharon to return.

Months later, when Sharon died, we placed a North Star puppy named Angel with this grieving family. This was our first grief placement, though Flight's placement was a natural stepping-stone for Angel's. It proved much sadder and more difficult to make this placement than any other we have made to date, but Angel ended up becoming a very valuable lifeline for this family. They visited Angel nearly every week while she was in training, and Mike reported it was a help just to have a structured activity in the lonely months that followed his wife's death. One night he called me and gently asked if they could speed up the timetable for Angel's placement, and I immediately agreed. I had been confused about what Angel's specific training goals would be beyond simple housetraining and basic commands. That night it became quite clear to me that Angel's true task was just to be her lovely and lively self for these children.

One of the greatest difficulties for a child is the death of a parent. The world will never be as secure as it once was, the pain will be softened but not erased by time, and it is absolutely crucial that a child be supported through this devastating loss. One of the ways an assistance dog can be helpful in supporting a child's grieving process is simply to give unconditional love and comfort. Knowing that an animal will always love you despite your transgressions is invaluable to a child in turmoil. This helps children cope with lingering feelings of irrational guilt and fear that they may have caused their parent's death or are responsible for the surviving parent's sorrow. This fear and guilt is common in young children, who tend to think in an egocentric manner. Contact with a trained dog provides these children with a stable force at a time of intense disarray by providing them with physical comfort as well as emotional support. Children, especially when they are very young, crave close contact when they suffer a loss, and a dog trained to stay by their side can be a source of invaluable comfort by their very presence. It was observed that after Sharon's death, Courtney initially had trouble leaving her father's side and became anxious when he was out of her immediate sight. Angel's purpose was to help her feel safe again in the frightening world on the other side of losing her mother.

Animals act as an ally for the child in his or her struggle through what has been called the "journey of grief." According to Dr. John Bowlby of London's Tavistock Clinic, children may experience three phases of a normal grieving process. The first is protest, when they cannot believe that the person is dead and they attempt, sometimes angrily, to regain him or her. The next is pain, despair, disorganization, which comes when the youngsters begin to accept the fact that their loved one is gone. Finally, there is hope, when they successfully reorganize their lives without the person they have lost. The length and severity of this process varies with each individual and his or her particular set of circumstances.

An animal's role in the first difficult stage is mainly to support the children through their sense of shock. This stage has different effects on children, but whether their reaction is to withdraw or act up, certain dogs are intelligent and bonded enough with their children to comfort and calm them.

Turid Rugaas, a canine behaviorist from Norway, pioneered the concept of dogs as pack animals that are deeply invested in maintaining peace in their pack. She believes that "dogs have the same ability and the same social skills to avoid conflicts as the wolves have . . . these signals are used to make the others involved feel safer and understand the goodwill the signals tell about." Rugaas studied calming signals that dogs send to each other, and observed these signals being sent to their human owners. A dog that is well-trained behaviorally, genetically sound, and close to children can be surprisingly prepared and motivated to comfort them.

The next stage of grief for the child after the initial shock is of pain, despair and disorganization. It involves restlessness, preoccupation, family dissonance and lower self-esteem. A dog can help during this stage by satisfying some of the restlessness and helping to raise depleted self-esteem. Simply having an animal to care for and nurture allows the child to have some sense of normalcy in this confusing time.

From despair, one usually rises into a state of reorganization, to a place where life begins to make sense again. It involves bursts of energy and hope mixed with indifference, fatigue, detachment and apathy. An animal can be of significance during this stage of mood swings by serving as a steady focal point. A companion that provides unconditional love, non-judgmental listening (for children often talk to their dogs) and consistent feedback is welcome on this difficult road to recovery.

The final stage of this "journey of grief" is reinvestment and emergence from the shadow of intense grief with a new identity. The child's life is forever altered by the loss he has experienced but he has been able to move forward. In the end I felt that Angel's true purpose as a North Star dog was to comfort and provide good company to these two young children, as well as to their lonely father, as they move on with their lives without their cherished mother and wife by their side.

Animals can also serve as a means of support for the surviving parent. A child's grief at losing a mother or father can be made more painful when he or she sees the surviving parent having difficulty dealing with the loss as well. Children often suffer as much from the loss of parental support as from the death experience itself. Therefore, adults must recognize the importance of creating or sustaining a caring relationship with children when death is experienced. It is often difficult for the parent to connect with the children during this fragile time, as emotional isolation is usually part of the grieving process. An animal can be a liaison between the parent and child here, a way of reconnecting and sharing the grieving process. In a time when every day seems to bring a new struggle, a quiet walk with a dog can be welcome relief. It can be a way for a child and parent to invest their love in something together and enjoy the love they receive in return.

In this particular case, the children's father, Mike, was over the moon about Angel. I saw this as the luck of the draw (he might have been someone who merely tolerated the puppy for the sake of his children). Mike came up frequently with the children to bond with Angel and watch her grow. He later reported that this consistent visiting schedule gave them a focus that pulled them into a future that seemed so uninviting. There are times following a loss when the most difficult aspect of life is deciding what to do, since so little about life makes sense in the emotional wreckage following death. Mike and his children now play soccer with Angel every night; they are creating new traditions and routines that incorporate Angel as they struggle to rebuild their lives. Losing a parent is an experience that forever alters a child's future. For these children, having Angel could never make up for the loss of their mother at such an early age. This is not the goal of animal-assisted therapy. Angel's mission is simply to give the children comfort and support as they weather the tough times that lie ahead.

Loss through the death of a parent is not the only way that a North Star dog can help a child. We have several young children with North Star dogs that are moving through the stages of loss and eventual acceptance that adopted children often experience. The adoptive parents' roles are especially challenging because they have to introduce very complex truths to a child who may still be in a developmental stage where thinking is very concrete. A dog can help a child to process the weight of the words in a way where language is not needed. Very young children may also be impressed with the fact that their dog was, in fact, also adopted, which doesn't lessen his value in anybody's eyes.

Parents and even professionals sometimes assume that if a child is quiet about the issue of his or her adoption, there is nothing to work out. In truth, it may be that at certain times in a child's life giving a voice to a fear by expressing it in language may be too threatening. This is the reason why I believe adopted children need extra support throughout all the stages of their early lives: they face a challenge that will be revisited many times over the course of their childhood. Although you want to grant a child the time and space he or she needs to work through these feelings, you don't want the child to deal with this alone. Having the unconditional love of a canine companion can be invaluable during troubling times.

There is a great deal of loss in children facing adoption later in life, especially if they have spent time in foster care. These feelings of loss often manifest themselves as anger. The best gift we can give a child facing this appropriate anger is to teach him or her constructive ways to deal with it. Setting limits is reassuring to children, as their own anger can feel overwhelming to them. Control is an important issue for adopted or foster children. It is quite understandable that children who have had their lives change irrevocably in one terrible day will have concerns over their lack of control. I have worked with children who have dealt with the worst hand that life can deal out: the death of a parent, the removal from a home, and the discovery of a brain tumor. For these children issues of abandonment and feelings of loss and separation take on more than the usual tone. For them, a dog is much more than a typical family pet. Having a dog that is within the child's control (i.e., well-trained and ready to take the child's commands) can help a child to regain his feelings of confidence on his darkest days.

At North Star, one way we have helped children to gain better control of their negative emotions is to suggest that their dog is frightened by their loud voices, stomping feet, or flying objects thrown in anger; encouraging children to comfort their dog and explain why they are feeling so angry and out of control can act like a balm to help to heal their unexpressed feelings of loss. Younger children think magically, and an invitation to them to whisper their troubles in their dog's ear can help them to express thoughts they might feel too uncomfortable to express to an adult, or even to themselves out loud. I believe the simple verbal expression of a fear alone is a powerful release.

Older children may be more private with their feelings, especially as they approach adolescence. As much as parents want to be there for these children, they are sometimes shut out behind a closed, or slammed, bedroom door. It can be much easier for a trusted dog to gain admittance, due to the simple nature of their communication and the lack of pressure for them to communicate with words and expectations. Our hope is that a canine companion can travel to these children with the love and support their parents want to offer them without the expectations that can make them uncomfortable. For parents, it can help greatly to know there is a golden ambassador under their roof that can travel back and forth with immunity.

A sensitive and intuitive assistance dog can be an invaluable companion to a child who must journey through grief. It is territory that few of us can comfortably travel ourselves, let alone guide a child through. Occasionally in my own life I have let my dogs take the lead when our family has suffered a painful loss, for there are times when my intellect is just no match for my dogs' gentle acceptance of fate.

Part 3

The Possibilities of Partnership

11

From Puppy with Potential to Autism Assistance Dog

The following chapters have been written for this book by parents and professionals who have worked with us over the years to create North Star placements. All contributors to *The Golden Bridge* have offered us their writing without compensation, and for this I am extremely grateful. They are a talented bunch and our work is truly a collaborative effort.

Shari Dehouwer has been helpful in creating North Star's high public access standards. Her organization, Discovery Dogs, has worked with us on a North Star placement that included training a North Star dog named Max for public access in his child's California community.

Trainers Dee Ganley, Renee Premaza, and Michelle Goldner have contributed chapters on training assistance dogs to work with children at different stages of their development. These talented women write about selecting a correct puppy for assistance dog work with children, along with how to create a pup's early socialization program and training plan for the second year of life. They have all worked with me on creating North Star placements in their respective states and have helped to form much of North Star's training guidelines.

Rachel Friedman began her association with North Star as a puppy raiser who came to us as a talented dog trainer and licensed social worker; she ended up serving as director of North Star for several of our early years of development, and she helped us to shape some of our policies her with intelligence, insight and humor.

Sue Bulanda is an award-winning author and lecturer on dog training as well as a certified dog behavior consultant. She is has been a search and rescue dog trainer since 1981, and is currently head trainer of the Phoenixville Fire Department's K-9 Search and Rescue Unit.

Kris Butler brings 100 hours of experience in educational programs and 900 hours of professional experience in an in-patient rehabilitation hospital when she writes her chapter. Her workshops have taught healthcare providers, educators, and volunteers throughout the country the best ways to include visiting dogs in programs that enhance human healing, learning, and self-awareness.

Diane Rampelberg is a teacher in California, where for the past six years she has served as an animal-enhanced learning and therapy specialist in three special schools with her CCI dogs, Dustin, Ovelle, and Geralyn (a CCI Change of Career Dog). I consider her a true expert in the field of assistance dogs within the classroom, and I have long considered her a role model because of her ability to turn challenges into miracles. Her nonprofit, Dustin's Paw, can be found on the website www.DustinsPaw.org.

Kathy Vranos has included a letter she has written to her son Jake, who has received a North Star dog named Nomar. Kathy is one of the most sensitive mothers I have ever met, and her words reflect the level of love and care that she puts into her role as Jake's mom. Jake has made great strides by the use of facilitated communication, with Nomar as catalyst for this work.

I want to thank all these contributors for the generosity of their written words. Education has always been important to us at North Star, and we gratefully accept help toward fulfilling this important mission. Raising puppies and training dogs to serve children is a more time-consuming and delicate affair than you might imagine. By cooperating to help children reach their goals through the use of well-bred and well-trained dogs, we are setting up these children for success. By combining with other organizations and trainers in a nonprofit spirit, we have the chance to make important differences in the lives of the children we collectively serve.

We will start with an essay written by my friend Riggan Shilstone, president of Olympic Assistance Dogs, who has generously offered us her words to contribute to our understanding of the evolving assistance dog field from a dog's perspective. Before any assistance dog placement is made, it's important that families come to understand just what it costs both them and the dog to create an assistance dog partnership, and to appreciate the ethics that should govern assistance dog placements to keep them safe and fair to all concerned. It is not just the needs of all the members of a child's family that must be factored in when we set out to create a placement; the dog's needs must be factored in as well to keep the placement safe and effective.

Riggan's chapter will be followed by others written by breeders, trainers, therapists, and educators considered important in the emerging field of selecting and training assistance dogs to work with children. All these contributors have inspired me to create placements around the country that are helping children with challenges to meet their social, emotional, and educational goals through the use of well-bred, well-socialized, and well-trained North Star dogs.

I trust they will also inspire you.

12

Ethical Use of Assistance Dogs

Riggan Shilstone

Compassion, in which all ethics must take
root, can only attain its full breadth and depth
if it embraces all living creatures and does not
limit itself to mankind.—Albert Schweitzer

Many people are expressing a growing concern about the assistance dog movement—are we being fair to the dogs we ask to take on this demanding role? Veterinarians and dog trainers are reporting physical and behavioral problems associated with stress in some assistance dogs. Digestive problems, skin disorders, lameness, obsessive/compulsive disorders and severe separation anxiety are just a few of the problems seen. There is no question that assistance dogs are expected to function at an extremely high level of reliability in surroundings that are very abnormal from a canine perspective. We ask them to disregard their genetic and evolutionary wiring: don't touch food within easy reach; don't run away from new or scary things; ignore enticing smells; don't chase birds or squirrels; don't bark or growl at someone who appears threatening. We place them in stressful environments foreign to the average dog—crowded shopping malls, noisy restaurants or concert halls, medical facilities filled with odors that must be overwhelming to sensitive canine noses.

Yet I truly believe that some dogs can live a happy and fulfilling life in the role of assistance animal. Wouldn't most of our dogs love to be with us 24 hours a day, rather than home alone in the back yard? No one who has seen the joy with which a retriever proudly delivers a toy to his owner or who has watched an agility dog on course can doubt that many dogs revel in working with their human partners. The big question is: how can we nurture this enjoyment of the job and minimize the stress we place on assistance dogs?

I believe that there are three major components that need to be addressed to maintain a healthy, happy working dog. These are careful selection of assistance dog candidates, proper training for their future role, and appropriate education and training of the assistance dog partner.

Assistance Dog Selection

Selecting an assistance dog candidate, whether as a puppy or mature dog, is more art than science. There are several factors that need to be considered. The first question is whether the dog has a suitable temperament for public access work. Any obvious issues such as aggression (to people or animals), timidity or noise shyness should immediately preclude the dog from further consideration. While a skilled handler may be able to manage these issues, neither the dog nor the handler will ever really be able to relax in public. Another factor to look for is resiliency, often called "bounce-back." When the dog is startled, frightened or experiences a mild hurt, how does he deal with it? Is there a moment of alarm, and then he gets over it, or does the dog shut down and act fearful for an extended period of time? There will always be surprises and unexpected occurrences in public work. A dog that recovers easily and quickly from these moments will be much happier than one who is less forgiving. The cumulative effects of stress will also likely be less in dogs with good "bounce-back."

It is also important to consider the tasks the dog will be asked to perform. Does he have the physical characteristics to be able to do the job? To ask a dachshund to do balance/support work would be ludicrous. In less obvious situations, we must be brutally honest with ourselves—is this task in the dog's best interest? For example, asking any dog to regularly pull a wheelchair can be extremely hard on the dog's body. Typical assistance dog harnesses do not provide the same pulling mechanics that a sled dog harness provides. In some cases, there might be other ways to accomplish the same objectives (e.g., buy a power wheelchair). In other cases, it might be time to look for a different dog. For example, due to the structure of the nose and jaw, a pug might not be the best choice for someone who requires a lot of retrieval work. If there is any doubt about a dog's ability to perform a specific function, seek out a veterinarian, canine physiologist, or working dog trainer for an assessment.

Assistance dog selection procedures should also include a standard veterinary assessment. Dogs who already have skin, digestive, or obsessive/compulsive problems are poor assistance dog candidates. It is quite likely that the demands of the job will exacerbate the problems. It is also unfair to ask a dog with itchy skin to refrain from scratching in public. Proper health screening requires more than just a visual inspection. Any dog expected to do support work or occasionally pull a wheelchair should have both hips and elbows x-rayed to ensure that the dog is structurally sound for the job.

By seriously evaluating temperament, structure and health, we have reduced the pool of possible assistance dog candidates dramatically. Now that we have a dog that has passed all of these hurdles, it is time to focus on how our training methods can set the dog up for a lifetime of success. Many assistance dog trainers have switched to positive reinforcement techniques such as clicker training and lure-reward for task training. In these techniques, the focus is on rewarding desired behavior rather than punishing incorrect behavior. Criteria for correct responses are raised very slowly so that the dog always has a high probability of success and can be rewarded. If the dog's success rate drops, it is a failing on the part of the trainer—not the dog. It is up to the trainer to figure out why the dog is no longer able to respond correctly. Did the trainer go too fast, skip a step, or add too many distractions? The dog learns to enjoy working, because working brings the good things in life—treats, toys, praise and affection.

The best, most reliable assistance dogs will often go a step beyond working for rewards once they are placed with their partners. There seems to be a point where the assistance dog transitions from being in training to being part of a team. It is as if a light bulb turns on, and the dog understands why he has been asked to do all those silly things. The dog seems to understand that there is a reason to walk at an unnaturally slow speed, or respond to a ringing phone, or roll an unconscious person over. The behaviors become self-rewarding. These are the dogs that can be counted on to respond reliably even when the person is unconscious or otherwise unable to reward the dog for a job well done. Rewards always have a place in reinforcing desired behavior, but they are no longer the sole reason for the dog to do the task.

Punishment and correction-based training can be very effective when done by an experienced trainer, but it is inherently stressful for the dog. Also, timing is critical when administering corrections. Most assistance dog partners don't have the coordination or dog training expertise to be able to effectively administer corrections. The results of poorly applied corrections can include refusal to work, increased stress, fear and behavior problems such as aggression. (Timing is also very important in positive reinforcement techniques, but in that case poor timing does not tend to be as damaging to the dog or the relationship. Slow learning, frustration, and learning unexpected behaviors are common results of poor timing with reward-based training.) While occasional corrections are not unreasonable, the vast majority of interactions with the dog should be positive. This will result in a dog that responds eagerly, knowing that he is fulfilling his role in the partnership.

In order to be comfortable working in public, there are certain basic skills that all assistance dogs must master, regardless of their partner's disability. While it is tempting to focus training on the amazingly complex tasks that assistance dogs are often taught, a primary focus of training should be on the more mundane foundation skills. Is the dog really comfortable doing a one-hour down/stay? Is walking quietly by his partner's side a well-entrenched habit for the dog? Has "leave it" been so thoroughly trained that the dog doesn't give a second thought to that french fry on the ground? Can the dog pass by another dog or a cat without becoming aroused? Fluency in these skills enables a dog to relax in public. Lack of attention to these skills will produce a dog who may be able to do impressive things, but who will always be somewhat on edge and tense in public.

Assistance dogs must also be taught to accept a wide variety of situations and circumstances. Dogs do not generalize well. Just because a dog seems unflappable in the mall does not mean that he will be comfortable at the airport. The dog should be systematically acclimatized to many different settings, including malls, grocery stores, medical facilities, airports, stadiums, restaurants, and any other place that their future partner might decide to go. Initial exposure should be to relatively calm, quiet places. As the dog gains confidence he can be taken to noisier, more crowded locations. It is important to recognize and prepare for new situations that might be stressful to the dog. Be prepared with plenty of treats to reward the dog for calmness and acceptance of new situations. As the dog gains experience in a variety of settings, his confidence and comfort level with new situations will increase.

An area that is frequently overlooked when training assistance dogs is preparing the dog to be separated from his partner. While assistance dogs are often with their partner 24 hours a day, occasional separations are inevitable. For many assistance dogs, separation provokes some of the most severe stress the dog will ever experience. It doesn't have to be this way. Dogs can learn to be comfortable and even happy when left alone or in someone else's care. This is easiest to teach when the dog is young, preferably still a puppy. By pairing separation with pleasurable experiences such as scrumptious treats, playtime or the opportunity to socialize with another dog, the dog learns that if the partner leaves, it is not the end of the world.

Stress can be physical as well as emotional. We must always keep this in mind when we decide what tasks we are going to train the dog to do. The question is not "Can we teach the dog to do this?" but "Should we teach the dog to do this?" Some tasks such as bracing, wheelchair pulling, or carrying heavy packs place physical strains on the dog. Some otherwise safe tasks can be dangerous under certain circumstances (e.g., asking the dog to turn on a light switch when he is standing on a slippery floor). Other tasks such as seizure alerting can be emotionally stressful for the dog. We must not sacrifice the welfare of the dog for the welfare of the person with a disability.

Throughout the training period, we should be constantly reassessing the dog's suitability for service work. Does the dog adapt well to all the different environments he has been exposed to? Does he seem happy performing the tasks expected of him? Are there significant signs of stress on a regular basis? After investing several months in a dog's training, it can be tempting to overlook warning signs. This is not fair to the dog or the dog's future partner. Dogs who are not assistance dog material might be able to work very happily in other roles. If public access is too stressful, the dog may be a perfect candidate for someone who only needs an in-home assistance dog. Other dogs may make wonderful therapy animals visiting hospitals and nursing homes. Many dogs that have been too intense or hyperactive for assistance dog work have gone on to successful careers as drug and arson detection dogs. We must always consider what role in life will be the best choice for this particular dog.

Selection and Education of Assistance Dog Partners

The final, and in many aspects the most important, factor in minimizing stress on an assistance dog is proper selection and education of the assistance dog partner. While an assistance dog candidate might be in training for 1–2 years, the assistance dog partner will hopefully be working with the dog for 10–12 years. For everyone's sake, it is critical to match the dog and person with great care. There are several questions to consider when deciding whether to accept an assistance dog applicant in the first place.

Can the person benefit from the use of an assistance dog? Are there realistic expectations of what an assistance dog can do for him or her? Does the person truly understand the amount of time, money and effort required in caring for a dog? Are there adequate financial resources to provide for the physical needs of the dog? For some people, setting proper expectations and education can resolve these questions. Other people will need guidance to realize that an assistance dog might not be the best option for them (or the dog!).

If a person is a suitable candidate for an assistance dog, it is then necessary to select the right dog for the person. Will their temperaments work well together? Placing a strong-willed, high-energy dog with a soft-spoken person whose major activity is going to doctors' appointments once or twice a month would be disastrous. Yet this same dog might be an ideal candidate for an on-the-go business executive. Do the person's assistance needs and the dog's task skills match? Most assistance dogs are taught a wide variety of skills, but each dog will have strengths and weaknesses—tasks he loves performing and others he just accepts. Whenever possible, the primary task that a person requires should be the task that really lights up the dog's eyes, whether it be retrieving everything in sight, racing along pulling a wheelchair, or curling up for another long nap under a table. A dog that truly enjoys his duties will tend to be a happy dog. Once the assistance dog partnership is made, the major education effort can begin.

Most assistance dog partners are not experienced dog trainers. Many have never even owned a dog before. As a result, topics such as learning theory, canine psychology, training techniques and nutrition are brand-new to them. If the team hopes to have a healthy, long-term relationship, there is a lot to learn!

The importance of proper nutrition and exercise is easily understood by people, but often extremely difficult to put into practice. The assistance dog partner needs to not only understand what is appropriate, but also why it is important. An overweight dog is putting a lot of unnecessary physical stress on his joints and organs. Overweight animals tend to be less able to adapt to changing environments and the demands of service work. This leads to additional emotional stress for the animal. The same is true for dogs that are out of shape. Assistance dogs tend to have long periods of idleness, followed by short spurts of exertion. The dog may be sleeping under a desk for a couple of hours, and then need to get up and pull a wheelchair. This would be like asking a human athlete to run a 50-yard dash when he first wakes up in the morning. It is even harder if the athlete is out of shape to begin with. Assistance dog partners can be taught ways to help the dog with stretching and warm-up exercises before asking for exertion. Since many assistance dog partners are physically incapable of large amounts of physical exercise, it can be a real challenge to find ways to provide this for the dog. The use of treats as rewards can also further complicate issues related to weight control and proper nutrition.

We have already mentioned the importance of only asking dogs to perform tasks that are safe for them. The assistance dog partners need to be educated on what types of situations are unsafe for their dogs. What things they should look out for? For example, if a dog is being used for brace work, the person needs to be taught the importance of putting the weight over the strongest part of the dog's structure and the damage that can result from putting weight on the dog's back, neck or head; guidelines for determining how much weight the dog should be expected to support; how to maneuver from chair to bed; the impact different floor surfaces can have on the dog's ability to brace; and so on. Even such a seemingly simple activity as getting on an elevator can be hazardous if the dog is caught on one side with the handler on the other. The importance of proper and complete task training cannot be overemphasized.

Along with task safety, the assistance dog partner must learn to assess situational safety from a canine perspective. What might be an enjoyable musical experience for us could be a noisy nightmare to a dog unused to loud noises and crowds. A sporting event with raucous crowds stomping their feet could be terrifying to a dog when the floor starts shaking under his feet. This does not mean that assistance dog partners should not go to concerts or ball games, but that they must be aware that what they experience is different from what their partner experiences. They must consider the dog's temperament, prior experiences and training level to decide whether it is appropriate to take the dog along, or whether the dog deserves a night off. Being educated on the world from a "dog's-eye view" can help partners avoid putting their dogs in a stressful situation due to ignorance.

Assistance dog partners must also understand canine psychology. Dogs are not little people in furry coats. They are pack animals and they expect one animal in the pack to be the leader. The pack leader is responsible for assessing new situations and determining the response to perceived threats (fight or flight). All packs must have a leader—even if it is a pack of two. In the absence of a confident, dominant leader, a timid or submissive dog may assume the leadership role. This will be an extremely stressful role for a dog temperamentally unsuited to the task, but the pack must have a leader!

Let's now take this knowledge and look at what can happen in an assistance dog partnership. The very nature of the assistance dog role indicates that the person has some degree of dependence on the dog. In some cases, such as with medical alert dogs, we are even asking the dog to be watching out for potential dangers that the human partner may be confronted with. This combination of circumstances makes it all too easy for the dog to perceive that it is the leader of the team. If the dog is basically a submissive animal, being placed in the leadership role can create anything from mild to severe stress. Even with a confident, dominant dog, being the leader in an assistance dog partnership can produce unhealthy stress. Most of what we regularly encounter in society could legitimately be considered a threat to a dog. A dog has two normal reactions to perceived danger—fight or flight. With our assistance dogs, we ask them to suppress both of these reactions. The dog is on leash, so flight is not an option. We frown on assistance dogs' growling, barking or otherwise showing aggressive behavior, so fight is also ruled out. From the canine view, what is left? Even a confident dog normally quite comfortable in a pack leader role can justifiably feel stressed out. Over time, this constant stress level can cause many of the emotional and physical symptoms mentioned at the beginning of this chapter.

The solution is that all assistance dogs should clearly perceive their human partner as the leader of the pack. This does not imply the use of force, or doing alpha rolls, or other aggressive means of dominating dogs. Rather, it is the development of a relationship of trust and confidence where the human is looked to for guidance in all issues of importance or decisions about safety and danger. Even with guide, hearing and other alert dogs, the dogs should be trained to respond to certain environmental cues and take specific actions such as alerting the owner. They should not be deciding on their own which environmental cues are important or how they should respond. With confidence in his leader, the assistance dog is free to relax and let the human partner make the decisions about how to respond to events.

Conversely, a confident human leader can trust that the assistance dog understands his role and will be there when needed. There are many leadership programs in use today. Whatever tool is used, the assistance dog partner should understand how to earn the leadership role with his or her assistance dog.

The final area that assistance dog partners need to be educated on is how to prevent, recognize and respond to stress in their dog. Everyone would agree that it is best to prevent stress when possible. There are several ways to accomplish this. Ensuring that the dog is healthy and fit helps prevent stress. Maintaining the dog's training through regular practice sessions helps the dog be confident in responding to commands and situations. It is also a great way to reinforce the leadership role of the assistance dog partner. Providing regular "vacations" for the dog enables him to unwind, similar to the way we do on a vacation or the weekend. Vacations can last anywhere from a few minutes to several days. Activities such as agility, swimming and fetch can be great stress relievers. Sending the dog off with a friend (and a dog friend!) for a couple of days can provide a great vacation. Many assistance dogs are "on duty" whenever they are with the handler. Even if they are not in heel position or in harness, they must still be vigilant in case their partner needs them. The only way for them to truly relax is to get away. In order for them to enjoy this time, however, they must be comfortable being separated from their partner! This is a great way to practice those separation skills.

Prevention is great, but it is not always possible. What happens when the dog is faced with something scary and gets frightened? A natural reaction for most of us when we see an animal in acute stress is to reassure and comfort it. Generally this has the opposite effect in dogs. It is as if we have confirmed for them that there is something to fear. If we can't reassure the dog, how can we react to stress? The assistance dog partner needs to learn a variety of tools to help the fearful dog. Desensitization, redirection of focus, rewarding lack of fear response, and removal from the situation are all possibilities. Part of team training should provide opportunities for the team to practice as many tools as possible.

The partner should also be on the lookout for symptoms of chronic stress—lack of enthusiasm, physical or behavioral problems, and refusal to obey are just some warning signs. The first step in dealing with chronic stress is to recognize that it exists. Once it is recognized, a plan can be put in place to deal with it. Regular follow-up should be provided to answer any questions, make sure the plan is being followed and to update it where necessary. With proper selection, training and care, there is no reason why assistance dogs should be victims of stress and burnout. We ask a lot of these dogs. It is our responsibility to make sure that it is not too much.

Riggan Shilstone is president of Olympic Assistance Dogs, which is a nonprofit organization that provides trained assistance dogs to people in the Pacific Northwest who cope with mobility impairments such as spinal cord injuries, severe arthritis, multiple sclerosis and conditions that result in balance problems.

13

Selecting a Puppy to Work with a Child

Dee Ganley

*Not only is another world possible, she
is on her way. On a quiet day, I can
hear her breathing.*—*Arundhati Roy*

Selecting a puppy to work with a child with developmental differences requires a large amount of thought and consideration. It should not a spur-of-the-moment decision made because the puppy in the window looks so cute or because you feel bad for his or her situation.

When you bring a puppy home, you have taken on a responsibility for the next ten or fifteen years, and you should think carefully about what type of home you can provide. Do you have time to walk, train, and play with a puppy? Can you afford to pay for food, vaccinations and veterinary bills to keep your dog in good health?

Once you are certain that you are ready for the responsibility of dog ownership, you should give thought to the type of breed and canine temperament that would work best with your child. Libraries, bookstores, and pet supply stores are all places you can go to find books with information about different breeds. Make a list of breeds that interest you and then call your local dog club to locate breeders in your area. You should meet some adult dogs of the breed you are interested in to be sure that the breed is a good match. Find out how much grooming the dog requires. If it is a longhaired breed that may require professional grooming, find out how much this will cost in your area.

Obedience trainers are a good resource and can give you information about the temperament of varying breeds. While a good breeder should give you honest information, some may be more interested in selling you a puppy than in meeting your needs.

Temperament Evaluation

While different breeds have different characteristic temperaments, individual dogs within a breed can also have very different personalities. How can you choose a puppy who will best meet your child's special needs? There is a series of tests that can help predict the type of dog your puppy will become—aggressive and dominant, confident and eager to please, or shy and submissive.

If you aren't experienced with puppies, ask a friend who is to go with you. Some dog trainers are happy to help you select an appropriate puppy. Here are a few simple tests that you can do to get a better sense of a puppy's temperament:

(Try to do these tests in an area that is new to the puppy.)

1. Attraction to people—Place puppy on the floor and walk away. Turn and kneel down, then clap your hands and call the puppy to you in a happy voice.

   a. Puppy comes readily, jumps up on you and bites or mouths your hands.
   b. Puppy comes readily, tail up and happy, and may climb up on you.
   c. Comes quickly, with tail held level or slightly down.
   d. Comes hesitantly, low to the ground.
   e. Doesn't come—sits and looks afraid.

2. Following—Put puppy on the floor and walk away, without talking to or encouraging the puppy. Watch to see what he does.

   a. Follows closely, tail up, nipping at shoes or shoelaces.
   b. Follows closely, tail up.
   c. Follows hesitantly.
   d. Follows with tail level or down; may crawl.
   e. Doesn't follow—sits and may start to cry.

3. Retrieval—Crumple up a small piece of paper or have a small toy ready. Toss it so that the puppy can see it.

   a. Chases it, brings it back to you but won't let you get it back.

b. Chases it and brings it back to you.

c. Chases it slowly and brings it back to you, letting you take it.

d. Doesn't chase it.

e. Gets it and runs away with it.

4. Trainability—Crumple a small piece of paper into a ball or a piece of kibble and hold it just above the puppy's head, making a crinkling noise to get the puppy's attention. Tell him to sit and move the paper slowly back over his head towards his back. If he sits, give lots of praise and let him have the paper for a couple of seconds. Repeat this three or four times and check his response.

    a. Jumps up on you to get the paper.

    b. Jumps the first time, but then sits quickly and is obviously happy to do it.

    c. Sits the second or third time.

    d. Sits, then lies down.

    e. Walks away—doesn't want to do it.

5. Social handling—Squat down next to the puppy and rub or stroke his head, neck, back, face, and then feet. Stop and wait for puppy's response.

    a. Jumps on you, bites at your hands or growls.

    b. Paws at you, wiggles and squirms, tries to climb on you.

    c. Wiggles and licks your hands.

    d. Rolls over and exposes his belly.

    e. Struggles to get away from you.

6. Tolerance to human intervention—Put the puppy in a down position or invert the puppy in your lap and hold it gently in this position while you count to 60. If the puppy struggles, don't let it up until you have finished your count. Repeat this test three times; you are looking to see if the puppy struggles less each time. Circle the letter that reflects his last reaction to the test.

    a. Struggles hard, tries to bite your hands, cries or growls.

    b. Struggles—may cry.

    c. Struggles, then settles down.

    d. Little or no struggling, licks your hands.

    e. No struggling, but whimpers or urinates.

Remember, this is just an evaluation! You are just getting a small picture of who the puppy is, and these test results should be added to the breeder's knowledge of the pup along with your own observations.

Scoring Puppies

3 or more A's—This puppy is very dominant and has aggressive tendencies. He could become a biter later on—he is not a good choice for families with children or first-time dog owners. He will need non-physical but firm training from an experienced owner.

3 or more B's, or combination of A's and B's—This puppy will tend to be outgoing and dominant, and he should go to an experienced owner. While he should not be in a family with young children, he might be okay with older children.

3 or more C's—This puppy will adapt to most households and should do well with children if he is properly socialized. He is a good choice for an older couple or first-time owners.

3 or more D's—This puppy will be submissive, and will need lots of positive, gentle handling. He would be a good companion for a senior citizen or quiet adult. Socialization will be very important.

3 or more E's, or combination of D's and E's—This puppy will be very shy and antisocial. If he has an A in his scoring, he may also bite out of fear. He should not be placed with children or inexperienced owners. He will require lots of love and work, and may never be reliable in crowds.

If you are not sure of your scoring, try again in a new location or ask a friend to help you. Some breeders do temperament testing on their litters as a routine practice. If the litter you are looking at has already been tested, ask to see only those puppies whose temperaments are appropriate for your child. Don't risk falling for a cute little fellow who isn't a good choice in the long run.

Also remember that this test is only a guide, and any puppy can have a bad day. Ask the owners lots of questions to see what they have noticed about the puppies' behavior.

If you have a child with special needs, you should look for a dog that will be tolerant and mildly submissive, not dominant and aggressive or shy and antisocial. Avoid both the rambunctious puppy as well as the shy pup who hides in the corner. Search instead for a puppy who follows you around the room in a happy and alert manner: head up, eyes bright, and tail wagging.

If you have already brought home a puppy that is either very aggressive or very shy, think seriously about exchanging him for another before you get too attached. The risk of a dog biting your child due to poor temperamental fit is just too great to take.

Applying Temperament Evaluation Scores for a Potential Assistance Dog Placement

Temperament testing gives us a picture of a puppy/dog's emotional view of the world. Even with a young puppy, some of what we see is genetic and some of it is learned. Some of it can be modified with positive reinforcement training while some of it will always require management. How a puppy scores is critical to successful client matchmaking. These scores will allow us to objectively divide the pups into three basic categories. Some puppies/dogs will sit between categories. Usually this means the puppy/dog has some good behaviors and some less easy to live with behaviors that which can be modified with smart management and positive training. But the categories definitely tell us what kind of home environment and training commitment will be needed for this puppy/dog to be successful.

A & B puppies: "Make it worth my while"

Puppies or dogs with these scores will be assertive, mouthy, and pushy and will need an experienced, dog-savvy home. Puppies falling under this category would not be appropriate candidates for assistance work with any child.

Note: If this A/B puppy's confidence includes being antisocial (not caring how other dogs or people react to him), then this puppy will probably grow to be dangerous. Its pack members in the wild would very likely kill this puppy.

C puppies: "Whatever you want me to do, I'll do"

The "whatever you want me to do" dog accepts human leadership naturally. This is the easiest dog to train and to live with. This dog should be successful with children of all ages. This is a low-maintenance dog. Puppies with 3 or more C's will fit nicely into most homes.

D & E puppies: "Lions and tigers and bears, oh my!"

Puppies with fear issues are either:

- Fearfully submissive/shut down and often unresponsive to reinforcement so they are really difficult to retrain, or
- Fearfully aggressive. Again the fear may be so strong that the dog has no reinforcers that can be used to change his emotional point of view. Sharp/shy dogs are very unpredictable and require 100% management for their whole life.

This puppy will succeed only with careful training to learn to work cooperatively with people. He will require lots of training time and skillful management for his entire lifespan; he will also be likely to push young children around and be quite destructive when left alone. This is a high-maintenance dog and should not be placed with children, especially not with a child with special needs.

Mostly A & B Scores

Adults and 12+ kids—Jumpy/mouthy, will be destructive if left alone. Able to learn and like working with humans who make it worth their while. Adopters must be willing to take training classes (and/or agility). Will need good management until two or three years old while learning self-control.

Mostly B & C Scores

Adults and 6+ kids—May be active, busy, a little mouthy/jumpy, but looking to kids and adults to be petted. Pesky, but wants to be with people. Will take about a year of good management and training and will become an easy-to-care-for dog.

These are puppies that can live in any situation, including children under five years old. These dogs have sweet manners. They come readily to all people for attention—they like being touched, but don't get over-stimulated. They follow people around, sleep at their feet, and rest comfortably wherever they are. They have self-control and are easily trained. Some of these puppies/dogs may seem "soft" but are not submissive or fearful; they are just letting you know people are in charge.

Puppies with 3 or more E's

Very, very shy—need lots of socialization and easy hand. These puppies will not thrive in a loud, lively family home. Need a quiet home where they don't have to warm up to everyone.

Puppies with 3 or more D's & E's

Are on the shyer side and will need TLC and a quiet home with folks willing to spend extra time socializing the puppy. This dog may never like everyone.

Adolescent or adult dogs with D's & E's

Quiet homes, no children. These dogs did not learn to feel safe with people as puppies and it will take a tremendous amount of effort to make them less fearful. If they are sharp/shy they will require 100% management for their lifetime.

In summary, the puppy we are seeking as an assistance dog to work with a child is one that receives mostly B and C scores from this evaluation. When young, these puppies may be active and a bit mouthy and jumpy in their attempts to receive the human attention they crave, but with a year of good management and training, they are likely to become a terrific companion to a child. These puppies will come readily to your child and greet him or her politely with proper socialization; they will tend to follow your child around, curl up to nap contentedly at the child's feet, and quickly develop the self-control and intuition necessary to work successfully with a child with a challenge.

Dee Ganley is a professional dog trainer who has partnered with North Star to create several successful placements. Since 1999 she has been the training and behavior manager for the Upper Valley Humane Society in Enfield, New Hampshire, where she works with the staff, volunteers, and the public.

14

Right from the Start

Sue Bulanda

Whoever said you can't buy happiness
forgot little puppies.—Gene Hill

If a person wishes to find a dog that meets special needs, it is important to select the right breeder, the right breed, and the specific puppy within a particular litter. Even if a potential dog owner finds the perfect breed, selecting a breeder who is not ethical can result in disaster.

If a person is interested in a dog that will be a good pet or working dog, the important qualities are intelligence, temperament and health. These are the things that make a good companion dog. Some people feel that the best dogs are mixed-breed dogs or the new fad breeds. Some of these dogs can be excellent dogs, but there is no way to tell until the dog is fully mature. The potential dog owner should realize that mixed-breed dogs and the new exotic breeds are a very high risk because they are not established breeds. There is no consistency in what the breeder produces. For example, consider the common "poo" breeds. If a potential puppy buyer compares all of the cock-a-poos, it will become evident that they are not alike. Some act and look more like poodles, some more like cocker spaniels. The differences can be vast in terms of health, size, coat, temperament, and personality.

Typically a breeder of quality purebred dogs is not going to take his best dogs and create a mixed breed of dog. The people who create the mixed-breed dogs usually do not have a large selection of dogs to outcross what they produce; therefore they either breed the same parents over and over or inbreed the puppies. In many cases, these mixes cost as much or more than a purebred dog and the potential puppy buyer does not get the benefit of the health tests and the selection process that a breeder gives the quality purebred. The buyer also does not get the benefits that a registry offers nor does the buyer know how the dog will turn out when it is grown. Most of the mixes are a fad, and people often pay double the price of a good purebred. So in essence they do not get what they pay for.

To avoid miscommunication, it is necessary to understand the terminology that people who are involved with dogs often use; therefore most of the common terms are outlined below.

Breeder: A breeder is anyone who breeds dogs. The term breeder does not mean that the person is ethical or has quality animals.

Backyard Breeder: A person who breeds any dog to any dog just to make the dog pay for itself. The term originated because many of these breeders chain or kennel their dogs in their backyards and whelp the puppies outside. The term now refers to those people who decide to breed their pet and do not give any thought to what they are doing or the quality of the puppies. On a larger scale, this type of breeder is called a puppy mill.

Commercial Breeder: This term often refers to the person who makes a living or a profitable hobby breeding dogs. The dogs are not kept as pets but usually kenneled and bred continuously. These dogs are treated a bit better than the backyard dogs; however, in order to make a profit this type of breeder will cut corners. These breeders often do not care which dogs are bred together because their main goal is money. This can cause a genetic mess in terms of inherited defects.

Papers: People often think that if a dog is registered, it means that it is a quality dog. This is not true. There are many organizations that will register anything if you fill out the papers. Even the big registries do not check to determine if the dog and papers represent each other. Without DNA testing, there is no way to determine for sure if the dog represented on the papers is the correct dog. This will depend entirely on the honesty of the breeder.

Registered: When a dog is referred to as "registered," it means that the dog has papers. The benefit of having a registered dog is that the dog owner can enter the various competitions that the registry recognizes. The only competition that requires a dog to be intact is the conformation show. All of the rest allow spayed or neutered dogs to compete. Initially many potential puppy owners may feel that they are not interested in the sport activities, but change their mind a year or so later. It is always nice to have the option available.

Bitch: The correct term for a female dog.

Dog: The correct term for a male dog.

Intact: Either a bitch or dog who has not been altered. Spayed—female, Neutered—male.

Show Quality: A term used by breeders for puppies that they feel have the potential for winning dog shows for conformation.

Conformation: Usually refers to the type of dog show that judges the dog for looks and movement. This term can also refer to the dog's physical qualities. Example, "This dog has nice conformation."

Temperament: Refers to the dog's mental ability to react to life situations. The dog's breed will determine a large part of the dog's temperament. Some people refer to it as the dog's personality.

Personality: This is usually the individual traits that make the dog unique. They are not necessarily inherited and vary with each individual dog.

Breeding Quality: Breeders will often claim that all of their puppies or some of their puppies are breeding quality. This is often a ploy to get more money for a puppy. A breeder with high standards will not make this claim because puppies cannot be tested for the inherited problems which are associated with the breed. Also, puppies that look nice when they are young can grow up with faults that make them ineligible for breeding. Even though some young dogs will earn a championship before they are two, it does not mean that they will mature into the best specimen of the breed. It is fair for a breeder to say that he feels a puppy will have breeding or show potential, based upon how the puppy tests and develops. For certain breeds, inherited faults are obvious in the first weeks of life, and those puppies can be ruled out as showing and breeding prospects.

Breeding Contract: Breeders sometimes have puppy buyers agree to a future breeding arrangement with the puppy. Some breeders will even give away a female puppy with the condition that you let them breed the bitch two or three times. This arrangement is typically offered by a breeder who is interested in producing a lot of puppies, but does not want the expense and bother of doing it correctly. However, a breeder cannot tell if a dog is going to be worth breeding when it is a puppy.

This is not a good arrangement for the puppy owner or the puppy. Breeding contracts can get complicated, and it is usually not wise to sign on the dotted line. If a dog turns out to be an exceptional dog, the dog owner can always make breeding arrangements with the breeder at a later date. However, breeding contracts always prevent the puppy owner from having the dog altered. That means that the puppy owner will have to live with the problems associated with owning an intact dog. As life situations change, the breeding agreement may no longer be suitable. The breeder may want to breed the bitch when she is too young and cause permanent health problems. Also, breeding a dog can cause the behavior of the dog to change, and the dog owner is left with a dog that is not what he or she wanted. Dogs should not be bred without being proven first. These contracts typically do not benefit the owner of the bitch. The puppy buyer must question the breeder carefully to fully understand the breeder's motivation for making this type of arrangement.

Proven: In order to properly breed a dog it should be proven as worthy of breeding. This means that the dog will have been tested for congenital (inherited) defects. It should also mean that the temperament and breed instincts have been verified. For example, a pointing dog should show that it can point by either winning hunting competitions or working the field. The dog should also demonstrate that it has the proper conformation. The total dog should be breeding quality.

Pedigree: This term is often used when discussing the ancestors of a dog. For example: "The dog's pedigree shows . . ."

Champion: Breeders will often refer to the championships represented in a pedigree. The titles that appear before the dog's name are the conformation titles, or the awards that a dog has earned for its looks. The titles after the dog's name represent the working titles. These are the awards the dog has earned in competitions that judge a job that the dog has to perform. They can be sporting events, obedience, or other events. Miscellaneous titles are also placed after a dog's name if they are recognized by the registering organization. This would be tests such as the Canine Good Citizenship (CGC), temperament tests or herding instinct tests. Often these miscellaneous tests only indicate that the dog shows an ability to perform the sport but not that the dog will succeed at this sport. Such is the case with the herding instinct test. It can only determine if the dog has inherited instinct, not whether or not it actually can herd livestock.

Keep in mind when considering champions in a puppy's pedigree that the most important to consider are the ones the puppy's parents have obtained. The rest are not going to influence the puppy that much. What the history does represent is that the odds are good for the puppy to have the abilities documented. This is often referred to as a proven line.

Finding the Right Dog and Breeder

Step One: Determine which breed or type of dog is best for you.

To do this, get a copy of the book *Simon and Schuster's Guide to Dogs*. Have all adult members of the family go through the book independently and make a list of ten dogs they like, no matter what kind. When this is completed, have everyone compare their lists. Select five dogs from the compiled family lists. To do this, pick the breeds that are common on each list, or everyone's first choice. List the pros and cons of each of the five breeds selected.

Consult with someone who is experienced with dogs but who does not sell them. The best choice is a dog trainer or canine behaviorist. Do not depend on the Internet for information, as it can be unreliable. Ask the professional what his experiences have been with the selected breeds. He will know what these dogs are like in your area. Do not be afraid to look out of state for a dog.

Step Two: Get the names of breeders.

There are a number of ways to do this. (1) Contact the American Kennel Club (AKC) and ask for a list of the Federation of Dog Clubs. Contact the one nearest to you for a list of breeders. (2) Get a list of breed clubs from the AKC and United Kennel Club (UKC). Before calling any of the breeders, get a pad of lined paper and write their names, phone numbers and any other information about the breeders at the top of the sheet. This will serve as a reference sheet to write down the breeders' answers to the following questions. It is courteous when first talking to the breeders to explain the purpose of the call and ask if it is a good time to talk.

Using the lined pad, write down the answers to the following questions:

1. Q—How long have they been breeding this breed of dog?

   A—The longer the better. If they have just started, are they being mentored by an experienced person? Breeding is complicated and should not be done by someone who is inexperienced.

2. Q—Do they breed more than one breed of dog. If so what breeds?

   A—Good, dedicated breeders will only concentrate on one or two breeds. It takes too much time to do it right to manage more than that.

3. Q—Do they belong to a breed club?

   A—If they do not, be suspect. A breeder with goals needs the support and help of a breed club.

4. Q—Why do they breed dogs?

   A—The best answer should be a variation of the thought "to better the breed."

5. Q—What is their goal when they breed a litter? (This applies to their current litter, planned litter or past litters).

   A—Every breeder should have a goal that improves the breed in a specific way. No vague terms here. The more detailed the answer, the more it shows that the breeder knows their dogs. This is essential in order to better the breed.

6. Q—How many litters have they bred and in what time period? (Years, months, etc.)

   A—Someone who has bred multiple litters at once and who produces many litters through arrangements is one to be avoided. (See Breeding Contract, above) Four litters in six years are not bad. Four litters in one year would need further exploration about the circumstances.

7. Q—How many litters do they have at one time? Where are the litters whelped and raised.

   A—You want to pinpoint this information. A breeder who puts his all into a litter cannot do so with many litters at once. If the breeder tells you that the puppies are home raised, you do not want to see puppies in raised crates housed in a room by themselves. Some backyard breeders move their operation into their homes.

8. Q—What genetic testing do they do to the parents?

A—The tests vary from breed to breed. Check with a veterinarian or breed club to see what is necessary for that breed and how likely the breed is to have that defect.

9. Q—How do they prove or justify that a bitch or dog should be bred?

A—Every dog that is bred should be worthy to breed. Breeding candidates should possess the ability to pass onto their offspring a sound mind and body. The intelligence and temperament are what makes a good pet. The physical soundness means that the dog will be healthy and have less of a chance to incur vet bills for inherited illnesses. These qualities are demonstrated by temperament tests, working competitions, and testing for conditions such as hip dysplasia. Conformation show wins do not prove anything except that the dog looks good and physically meets the breed's standard as determined by the parent club and registry. Therefore the titles that come after the dog's name (working titles) are important when considering a pet dog or a working dog, not the titles before it (conformation). This does not mean that breeders who breed for the show ring do not produce temperamentally sound dogs. It means that the conformation of their dogs is their main goal, not its mental condition. Unfortunately too many show breeders sacrifice everything else for the ring. This means that the show dog breeder's puppies need to be evaluated as carefully as any other breeder's dogs.

10. Q—How do they choose the mate for their dog?

A—The mate for a litter should be based on the points raised in the answer to question nine. What you don't want to hear is something like, "My neighbor had a male from the same breed as my female and we decided to get them together."

11. Q—How often do they stud their dog (if they have a stud dog)?

A—The dog should not be indiscriminately bred to any bitch that will pay for the service. This shows the owner may not care about the quality that they produce. Thus, the owner of the bitch may not care either.

12. Q—What guarantees do they give with a puppy or dog that they sell?

A—All breeders should give a potential puppy buyer some form of guarantee. At the least, the new puppy owner should be allowed to take the dog to a veterinarian of his choice, and return the puppy if it is not healthy. Many breeders will guarantee the temperament of the puppy for life. This guarantee should not require that the dog be returned. Any terms mentioned in a contract should be made fully clear in writing as to what they mean. For example, how will a breeder determine if a faulty temperament is due to breeding or the way the dog was handled by its owner? Be sure to have any contract reviewed by a lawyer.

13.   Q—Do they have a puppy buyer's contract?

A—If they do, the breeder should be willing to let the potential puppy buyer review it before discussing the purchase of a puppy. Many needless problems and lawsuits arise over verbal guarantees or contracts that have been signed without being fully understood.

14.   Q—What age do they let the puppies go to the new home?

A—All breeds are different. Most puppies should not be released before 12 weeks if the breeder is going to give the puppy the proper socialization during that time. Many let the puppies go at eight weeks. Never earlier. A puppy taken from the litter younger than eight weeks is a high risk of developing behavioral problems.

15.   Q—How do they raise the puppy until it goes to their new home?

A—This requires details about the socialization methods that the breeder uses. Be wary of generalizations and statements such as, "We have a lot of kids around to handle the puppies." Or, "We have lots of people in and out of the house." Or, "This is a busy household." Comments like these imply that the puppies sit and watch the world go by. The breeder should outline specific handling and activities for each week of the puppy's life. If the potential puppy buyer has doubts about the socialization program, consult with a good canine behaviorist or trainer.

16   Q—How many puppies were in the last litter?

A—Be wary if the breeder refuses disclose this information. They may refuse on the grounds of confidentially. However, in many cases, happy customers are delighted to talk about their experience and the breeder will have references available. This question is important to act on the next question.

17.   Q—Ask them to list the names and phone numbers of the people who bought puppies from their last litter. This information is necessary for step 3.

Step Three: Call the people who own puppies from their last litter.

Ask them what life is like with their dog. Listen for statements such as, "He's a great dog except that he barks a lot." Or, "This is a great dog but he eats paper." While these idiosyncrasies are not something that the breeder will breed for, they can be inherited tendencies. If five out of seven people say this, then there is a chance that this line of dog has these types of idiosyncrasies.

Step Four: Visit the breeder, see the dogs.

Sometimes a potential puppy owner may think that they like a breed of dog until they see it in person. There can be wide variations between different breeds of dogs as well as within the same breed of dog. Therefore it is wise to be sure that the breeder has what the puppy buyer likes. Visiting the breeder and seeing the breeder's dogs will also reveal the way the breeder takes care of the dogs and the amount of time the breeder spends with the dogs. The potential puppy buyer should avoid breeders who don't work with their litters, or who raise their pups in a kennel or outbuilding.

Step Five: Call the breed club and ask about the breeder(s) being considered.

A good breeder should be well thought of by most of the people in the club. If not, find out why. Always get a general consensus instead of one person's opinion.

Step Six: Wait for the puppy!

Once a good breeder has been located, be patient and willing to wait for the puppy to become available. When a person starts to look for a puppy, they can get lucky and find one right away or have to wait a year or more. The wait is well worth it. Most good breeders have a waiting list for a good reason.

When the pup is born, picking it out is easy. With a good breeder, a good line and a consistent litter, the actual puppy selection is not as critical as it was to select the right breeder. Often the breeder can guide the puppy buyer as to which pup will best match what they are looking for. This is because the breeder has watched the puppies grow and develop. The breeder should have asked the puppy buyer as many questions as they have asked the breeder.

Selecting a Puppy When Children Are Involved

This can be a genuine challenge. Parents want their children to be involved in this process. However, the selection process is far too important and difficult to allow children to be involved during the early stages. It is difficult enough for an adult to walk away from a litter of puppies without having to deal with pleading children. This is one of the reasons why it is better not to see the breeder and their dogs until the breeder has become a candidate to consider as a source for a puppy.

The best way to allow a child of any age to become involved is to wait until the breed and breeder have been selected. Then after the litter is born and the breeder is ready to let the puppy buyer select a puppy, the adult should go alone. Usually there will be a number of puppies that meet the puppy buyer's criteria. The adult should pre-select a number of puppies, and then bring the child to choose from those. This will keep everyone happy and allow the puppy buyer to make a safe selection.

If the puppy buyer gives in to the child at any other stage of the selection process, the family could find that they have a dog that is not suitable. The family may find that they are in a position where they have to get rid of the dog at a later time. This is much more traumatic for the child than being told to wait until the proper time to make a selection.

Selecting the correct puppy to live with a typical family is difficult enough, but choosing a puppy to work with a child with a challenge raises the stakes even higher. The best guide you will have in this important process is a dog trainer or behaviorist, as these people know different breeds' characteristics and potential pitfalls the best. The breeders you meet will be understandably partial to their breeds of choice and specific lines. I advise you to be sure to do your homework when considering purchasing a puppy. It will be well worth your time!

Sue Bulanda is an award-winning author and lecturer who has been training search and rescue dogs since 1981. She is a certified Animal Behavior Consultant and Senior Conformation Judge for the United Kennel Club. She also developed and teaches a dog-training program at Kutztown University.

15

Puppy Socialization

Dee Ganley

*Properly trained, a man can be
a dog's best friend.—Corey Field*

Socialization is most critical for young dogs from four weeks to four months, when windows of opportunity will gradually close, taking with it a puppy's opportunity to develop to its full potential. Despite the importance of these early months, maintaining your dog's socialization is actually a life-long process. Your dog needs to be exposed to all sorts of people and environments with a confident handler that the dog trusts at the other end of the leash. Socialization is accomplished by gradually allowing a dog to investigate different looking people, children, environments, objects, and other dogs. It is critical that the dog is exposed to new stimuli on a voluntary basis and not forced to interact with beings or objects he is afraid of.

In the book *Dogs—A Startling New Understanding of Canine Origin, Behavior, and Evolution,* Ray and Lorna Coppinger discuss how 80 percent of a dog's brain is fully formed by 4 months of age, and that from 4 months to a year the remaining 20 percent of the brain develops. Most of a dog's brain growth occurs between the ages of 4 weeks to 4 months; therefore this is the most critical time for a puppy to receive proper socialization.

Once the brain's growth stops, it becomes far more challenging to, "change the wiring." During this time a puppy's wiring pattern of the nerve cells takes place, and the Coppingers make it clear that consistent and appropriate socialization during these early months is critical to a pup's healthy brain development.

Of all the brain cells present at birth, a huge number are not connected or wired together. What takes place during puppy development is the wiring pattern of the nerve cells. The Coppinger's writing makes it clear that consistent socialization from 4 weeks to 4 months is critical for healthy brain development.

Proper puppy socialization is more than just exposing your pup to your children, other dogs, and some friendly neighbors; it means taking your puppy many places with you during his first year of life. You want your pup to be exposed to many different environments, to meet and greet people of all shapes and sizes, and to develop good social skills with a variety of other dogs. This socialization is vitally important to the young assistance dog who is slated to work with children, for an undersocialized dog is more likely to bite or become stressed in unfamiliar environments or situations.

Rules of Socialization for Potential Assistance Dogs

Make sure all experiences are safe and positive for the puppy. Each encounter should include treats and lots of praise. Slow down and add distance if your puppy is scared!

By the time a puppy is 12 weeks old, he should have:

- Experienced many daily different surfaces: wood, woodchips, carpet, tile, cement, linoleum, grass, wet grass, dirt, mud, puddles, deep pea gravel, grates, uneven surfaces, etc.

- Played with many different objects: fuzzy toys, big and small balls, hard toys, funny sounding toys, wooden items, paper or cardboard items, milk jugs, metal items, car keys, etc.

- Experienced many different locations: front yard (daily), other people's homes, school yard, lake, pond, river, boat, basement, elevator, car, moving car, garage, laundry room, kennel, veterinarian hospital (just to say hi and visit, lots of cookies, no vaccinations), grooming salon (just to say hi), etc.

- Met and played with many new people (outside of family): include children, adults, elderly adults, people in wheelchairs or with walkers, people with canes, crutches, hats, sunglasses, etc.

- Exposed to many different noises (always keep positive and watch puppy's comfort level—we don't want the puppy scared): garage door opening, doorbell ringing, children playing, babies screaming, horse neighing, shopping cart rolling, pan dropping, truck roaring by, loud singing, clapping, vacuuming, etc.

- Exposed to many fast-moving objects (don't allow the pup to chase): skateboards, roller-skates, bicycles, motorcycles, cars, people running, children playing soccer, squirrels zipping by, etc.

- Experienced many different challenges: climb on, in, off and around a box, go through a cardboard tunnel, climb up and down steps, climb over obstacles, play hide-and-seek, go in and out a doorway with a step up or down, be exposed to an electric sliding door, an umbrella, balloons, walk on a wobbly table (plank of wood with a small rock and underneath), jump over a broom, climb over a log, etc.

- Handled by owner (and family) many times a week: hold under arm (like a football), hold to chest, hold on floor near owner, hold head, look in ears, mouth, in-between toes, hold like a baby, trim toe nails, hold in lap, etc.

- Eaten in many different locations: back yard, front yard, crate, kitchen, basement, laundry room, bathroom, friend's house, car, schoolyard, bathtub, up high (on work bench), under umbrella, etc.

- Played with many different puppies (or safe adult dogs) as much as possible.

- Left alone safely, away from family and other animals (five-fortyfive minutes) many times a week.

- Experienced a leash and collar many different times in lots of different locations.

These recommendations are minimums, as the more people and places your puppy is comfortably exposed to, the better adjusted he'll be as an adult.

By following these suggestions you will be rewarded with a competent dog who is relaxed in almost any situation and less inclined to be fearful or insecure. Whether socializing, training, or just playing with your puppy, remember to be consistent and gentle in your responses to his behavior. This early and kind attention to your pup with help you to shape a confident and intelligent canine partner for your special child.

The following game is designed to help a puppy to develop safe and appropriate social skills:

The Food Bowl Game

Resource guarding is natural behavior. Sharing is a learned behavior. You will have to teach your dog that if he "shares" he will get what he wants. There are two places that resource guarding is likely to happen: eating meals and bones, and playing with treasured toys (which may include your stolen sock or telephone bill).

If your puppy guards his food bowl, you can help to discourage this unfortunate tendency by playing the following training game.

This is a self-control exercise that is easy to teach because your dog is so motivated to get what is in his food bowl. To play this game you'll need your pup's food bowl with at least ten yummy treats inside. The goal is for your dog to stay sitting while you lower his dish onto the floor and to wait until you release him to eat.

1. Start by standing up while facing your dog with his food bowl in hand.

2. Ask your dog to sit then start to lower his food bowl. If your dog stands up and/or moves toward the bowl stop lowering it—lift it up so the dog can't get it. Have your dog sit again. If he sits, give a treat from the bowl so he knows he can earn a reward for cooperating.

3. Lower again, stop and give a treat just before your dog moves. If he gets up, stand up straight and say "too bad," and then ask your dog to sit again. Once again start to lower the dish and make sure you reinforce him for staying in a sit. You reinforce from the dish with your free hand (take piece from the dish).

4. By the sixth or seventh time your dog should be waiting while you are lowering the food dish and not diving into it. What a wonderful way to link good manners to something your dog wants without any scolding, pushing, pulling or correcting by you. Your dog is learning that he can control what he earns by exercising self-control.

Once your dog remains sitting when you take your hand away from the dish, you can give the command "OK" (or whatever phrase you choose to denote that your dog is now free to eat). You can stretch the time your dog will wait until you are able to walk around the room before releasing him to eat.

To expand this game and its effectiveness in combating resource guarding, when you get to the point where you can put your dog's dish on the floor with food still in his bowl, start to reach forward to add more food while he is still working on the last few remaining treats. As you reach to add food to his bowl, your dog should back up to let you put the food in. If he dives for the bowl remove your hand and put no pieces in the dish. Each time you move your hand to drop in food, pull it back as soon as your dog moves forward instead of staying back. As before he doesn't get more until he is polite and waits for you to release him.

Self-control cannot be imposed on any animal. It develops when the individual (dog or human) sees a positive benefit coming to them by waiting rather than acting on impulse. Dogs can quickly learn to look up to us for leadership without using force, intimidation, or coercion. All we have to do is "pay" them for good behavior with what they need—food, shelter, exercise that is fun and loving social contact. Because we can provide all these needed resources for our wonderful friends, we have everything we need to help our dogs feel secure, guided, confident and content. The trick is learning how to "pay" only for good behavior. You already know that nagging or being overbearing toward your dog doesn't work. It isn't any fun and it certainly doesn't produce a harmonious loving relationship. And more important—you don't need to use emotional (shouting) or physical (correcting) force to have a "good dog." Positive reinforcement training and good management will mean you won't need to worry about your dog taking over the world or your household—you can throw out your concerns about preventing doggy dominance by learning how to be a fair, attentive, positively reinforcing leader.

Here are some important pointers to help you create and maintain harmony in your daily relationship with your dog:

- Feed your dog on a schedule (it can be once or twice a day) depending on your own personal schedule, and/or the dog's age or medical conditions. Avoid self-feeding or free feeding your dog (i.e., leaving a large amount of food always present in his/her food bowl). When you feed on a schedule, you know how much food your dog is eating and also see when your dog is off his food. Realizing when a dog is off his food may help determine if there is a medical condition brewing. By allowing your child with special needs to be in charge of feeding your dog, you increase the status of your child in your dog's eyes and deepen the bond between them. This responsibility will also raise your child's self-esteem.

- Teach your dog to have polite meet-and-greet manners. Jumping up is almost always about the dog wanting to gain attention, so make it clear that greeting behavior such as offering a nice steady sit will be rewarded with praise and people's attention. (Hint: keep your dog attached to a short leash when you are expecting exciting guests and step on this leash to prevent your dog from jumping on them if this is problematic for your pup. If your pup jumps on your children, advise them merely to step back, as children's gentle scolds are sometimes mistaken for positive attention by a young pup.)

- Focus on what your canine friend is doing correctly and develop this into larger chains of good behavior in small increments. Take undesirable behavior and redirect it into desirable behavior (i.e., if a dog jumps up, step back and then tell the dog to sit).

- Play with your dog frequently and allow your dog to occasionally initiate the game. Allowing a dog to initiate a game or offer you behaviors for your approval allows the pup to become a confident and spontaneous playmate, which is a highly desirable trait for a dog partnered with a child to possess.

- Always supervise young children and dogs when they are together. If something happens to a child when left unsupervised it is not the fault of the dog or child, it is your fault!

- Don't put unrealistic demands on your dog. Train new behaviors the way you would like to be trained. Be supportive, respectful and let your dog know when he has done a great job and/or tried really hard.

- Teach your dog that he can be away from you (left home alone) and still be a confident and happy dog. Remember to crate the dog for short periods of time when you are home too!

- Share quiet times with your dog, and encourage your child to join you. Reward these calm interactions with your relaxed presence and don't be surprised if you enjoy these times as much as your dog and your child. Building quiet moments in your day to simply relax together will allow you to slow down a hectic pace that can drive up the stress level in your home.

- Don't be angry when your dog is just being a dog; appreciate your differences and allow yourself to marvel at how well you are able to communicate with another species.

- Enjoy watching the relationship develop between your child and your dog, and know that you have given them both an amazing gift.

Dee Ganley is a professional dog trainer who has partnered with North Star to create several successful placements. Since 1999 she has been the training and behavior manager for the Upper Valley Humane Society in Enfield, New Hampshire, where she works with the staff, volunteers, and the public.

16

Puppies 101

Renee Premaza

*Puppies are nature's remedy for feeling unloved . . . plus
numerous other ailments of life.—Richard Allan Palm*

Puppies are cute and cuddly. They may not require taking a college course
to learn how to care for them as pets, but when you understand the dynamics of an assistance dog placement for a child with social, emotional
or educational goals you know how important it is to get a pup off to an
excellent start in life. For a puppy destined to work with a child in public,
the stakes and necessary precursors to training are even more crucial. I've
tried to list the most important training and management techniques here
that you should be implementing as soon as you can with a dog slated to
work with a child. If you follow the advice given, your relationship with
your dog will begin on the right "paw." Remember that you want your
pup to trust you and to view you as a good leader. You never want to ag-
gressively punish your puppy or to use scare tactics to train him. Not only
is this cruel, it is counterproductive.

It is vitally important that you begin socializing your puppies now!
Long before your pup's three-month birthday you want to gradually introduce your puppy to all sorts of people from all different races and walks of
life: tall people, short people, fat people, skinny people; people dressed in

uniforms or decorated with tattoos; men with beards, women in hats, girls in pigtails, boys in baseball caps, and little ones strapped into their strollers. When you are socializing your puppy with children, it is very important that you provide constant supervision for the safety of both the pup and the child. On the first sign of your puppy being stressed (i.e., tail hanging down, soft whimpering, yawning), you should remove him from the situation and either cuddle or crate the pup (providing a nice bone or favorite toy so this isn't viewed as punishment).

Try to take your puppy to five new places per week. Put your puppy in the car and take him/her for rides in traffic. Speak to your dog along the way in a happy voice. Go and get gas at the gas station so your puppy gets used to someone reaching into the car to give you change. Ask the attendant if he'd mind offering your dog a treat through the window.

Expose your puppy to many different novel stimuli. Let him see the hose outside, or the rake, or your feather duster. Familiarize him with all different sights and sounds. Let him walk on all sorts of surfaces, such as concrete, grass, tile, and asphalt. Purchase a CD that has the sound of thunder on it, and gradually let him hear this recording at louder and louder volumes. Have some toys and treats, and play with him while he's listening to your thunder CD. If there is a real thunderstorm, play with your puppy and feed him delicious treats during the storm. Even if there is a loud, scary clap of thunder, clap your hands and laugh about it. Expose him to other sounds, like the vacuum cleaner, the dishwasher and clothes washer and dryer. Turn on the food processor and let him get used to that. If your dog shows any fear or discomfort from hearing those sounds, don't console him because he'll think you're rewarding his behavior. Just speak to him in a happy tone of voice, as he will be very affected by your own emotions. Your puppy will be very affected by your feelings about all things in general. If your puppy suspects that you're nervous or upset about something, he will respond in kind. This is because training a dog is actually forming a give and take relationship with them, not simply getting a small creature to take our commands.

Once your dog has had its first set of shots, try to arrange play-dates with other vaccinated puppies of similar age and size. Make sure you know and trust the owners of these dogs when they tell you their dogs are healthy and friendly! Be careful not to overwhelm your dog at first. Do this very gradually. Most vets recommend that you keep your puppy off of any surface that might have been soiled by unknown dogs.

If, at any time, you see your puppy begin to look stressed or anxious, please give him a break. Puppies can become ill if they are feeling overwhelmed. If you notice that your puppy is acting afraid of something, don't console him with cooing and coddling, as this will only reinforce the behavior. Instead, speak confidently and offer treats to desensitize your pup to the frightening object.

Some puppies don't like being restrained, handled or being picked up. You can work on these problems by using food rewards to encourage him to like these things. Pair up being handled or restrained with being given very tasty morsels of food so that the dog will learn to associate being handled as a good thing. If you pick your puppy up and he squirms, don't put him right down. Hold him gently, but firmly, until he stops fussing, and only then put him down.

Here are some handling exercises you should begin doing to accustom your puppy to being handled and restrained. Bring your left arm around the front of your puppy's chest while your right hand and arm supports him under his chest and belly. Gently restrain him with just a tad of pressure and then release him. Praise and reward him with a nice treat if he remains unaffected. Reward him each time he accepts what you're doing. Little by little begin to lift him up while you support him against your body. For each step you take, praise and reward your dog. You will be shaping behavior that you may need in the future for veterinary exams, lifting him onto a vet or groomer's table, and in general, getting him used to being held, picked up and moved around. Touch your puppy all over his body, including his ears, paws and belly. Get him used to your putting your finger in his mouth to brush his teeth and stroke his gums. Touch him around his collar and do gentle collar-tugs. The more gentle handling you do now, the more your dog will come to accept your child's touch, which may consist of unusual petting, such as stroking against the grain of the fur. Even though you want to educate your child about how a pup likes to be handled, it is still very important to raise your dog to be tolerant of all types of physical contact.

A word of caution here: Please do not take anyone's advice when they tell you to flip your puppy on its back and restrain him to settle him down if he becomes overly excited. This will scare your puppy, and he will learn that you can't be trusted. A puppy will feel very vulnerable to being attacked while he's got his belly exposed. This is instinct here. If you try to flip an adult dog on its back, be prepared to get bitten!

Many people like to pet puppies and dogs by reaching over their heads. Desensitize your pup to this now so he won't feel afraid when a stranger decides to extend a hand and place it over his head. So, pet your puppy by placing your hand over his head and patting him, and then give him a tasty treat for a reward.

When your puppy becomes overactive or obnoxious (and they all will on occasion!), here is an exercise to help him learn to settle down. Sit in a chair in a quiet room with your dog. Watch what your dog is doing, and any time he behaves calmly, tell him, "Good boy!" and toss him a treat. If he gets all excited again, and starts jumping on you or pawing at your clothing, ignore him or get up and walk out of the room leaving him alone. The instant he stops this behavior say, "Good boy" and give him some very tasty tidbits of food. He will learn that a good default behavior is being calm and quiet. Set these training sessions up a couple times each day. Just sit there and wait for behaviors to reward him for. Remember to always ignore your dog when he's demanding your attention. If you put your puppy in his crate, and he immediately starts to whine or bark, put cotton in your ears and don't run back to him. Otherwise, you'll have a dog that knows he can get out of his crate by barking and whining. If, however, you've put your pup in his crate for the night, and later you hear him whining or barking, you'd better check to see if he needs to go out and to relieve himself.

Practice putting your puppy on a high surface, like on top of your washer. This will help him get used to being on a vet's table. While he's up there, do a physical examination of him, much like the vet would, checking his ears, feet and teeth. Begin cleaning your puppy's teeth using special doggy toothpaste—not human toothpaste. Good dental care is important, especially for the small breeds of dogs that are prone to dental disease. Dental problems can lead to other physical problems.

If you have young children in the family, please teach your children safe and proper handling of your puppy. Do not allow very young children to pick your puppy up while they're standing. Dropping the puppy can cause his death or serious injury. Many puppies do not like being picked up because they feel vulnerable to being dropped. Have your child sit on a chair and then place puppy in the child's lap to pet gently. Do not allow children to pull your dog's ears or tails. Do not allow children to lie all over your dog and jump on him. Some dogs will not tolerate this childish behavior and will snap or bite children for doing this. An excellent website to visit to learn about how to avoid dog bites with children is: www. doggonesafe.com.

Do not allow your young children to lie on the floor with your dog. Make sure you supervise both kids and dogs whenever they're together. All too often, kids and dogs get into trouble with each other because the dog gets overly excited around the child, or he misinterprets the child's behavior, and then bites the child on the face. When children play with puppies or dogs, the children should be standing up or sitting on a chair or sofa and the dog should be on the floor. This eliminates all possibilities of child and dog being at face level. If you cannot be there to supervise, then your dog should be in another room behind a baby gate with a toy or chewy to occupy him.

If your children are mature enough, you can allow them to take turns training the puppy; stand behind the child issuing commands to lend your authority to this process and echo your child's command to the pup if needed. The "sit" command is a good place to start, and this command should be given by all family members in all rooms of your house (and various spots outside your house), because a young pup does not generalize very well. Place a treat in your child's hand to offer the puppy for successfully following the command, while your own hand initially helps to guide the process. Many children inadvertently tease dogs by offering a treat and then pulling it back before the puppy gets the food, tempting the pup to nip the child's hand.

All puppies bite, both because they're teething as well as because that's how they've played with their littermates. It's important to teach your dog to have a soft mouth. To teach bite inhibition, communicate to your puppy when those sharp puppy teeth have hurt you with a loud squeal, and then cease playing for a minute, standing up and ignoring your puppy to deliver the message that you will not play if your pup isn't gentle with his mouth. If the puppy keeps biting too hard, stop playing altogether, and instead offer your pup a chewy toy or bone in his crate (puppies often get nippy when teething or overtired, and this technique will help in either case). Your pup should gradually learn to inhibit the strength of his developing jaws with you and your children if you are consistent with this process. If your dog has been taught good bite inhibition, if he is ever provoked to bite in his lifetime, he will not do any damage because you have taught him to bite without pressure.

I once knew a man who owned three Pomeranians and enjoyed teasing his dogs; he thought it was funny when they would come back and try to bite him. Two of the three Poms in this household have since shown serious aggression toward their owners as well as toward each other. Always think about what behaviors you are reinforcing! Again, use good common sense when you're raising a puppy. Whatever behaviors you reinforce now will follow through into his adult life.

When the mailman comes or the UPS driver pulls up to your house, give him a treat to give to your puppy. Let your puppy know right from the get-go that the mailman is a good thing because he represents treats. Take your puppy for a walk around the neighborhood and let him meet anyone who is willing to politely greet your pup, holding back their reinforcement until your pup is sitting nicely. Have treats on you so you can give your neighbors and/or their children treats to offer the puppy. If you see a patrol car or fire truck anywhere, seize the opportunity to introduce your puppy to a police officer or fireman.

If you don't want your puppy to learn to chew on or steal socks or other laundry items, do not make them available! Keep laundry items in a closed hamper. Keep all food items off the kitchen countertops from the very beginning, so your puppy won't want to "countersurf." If you start out doing the right things, you won't have to "fix" these training problems later on. Use common sense when training and interacting with your puppy. Keep tight lids on all trash containers. Puppies love toilet paper, paper towel and used tissues.

Dogs who guard their food bowls, bones, or toys are resource guarding; sometimes this behavior is instinctual, but other times dogs learn to do this because cherished objects have been frequently and forcefully taken away from them when young. I usually see this type of behavior develop in puppies at the beginning of adolescence, which for dogs is about six months of age. A dog who guards his resources is especially dangerous around young children, who may get bitten if they take a cherished object away from a dog or wander too close to the dog's food bowl. To prevent resource guarding from developing with your puppy, I suggest you work on training your pup to obey a "drop it" cue, so that he'll gladly relinquish anything you or your child requests. To do this, learn to make food or toy exchanges with your dog. If you need to take something away from your pup, put a treat right on his nose; when the pup opens his mouth to take the treat, say "drop it!" and praise lavishly. You can do this exercise with your pup's toys as well, and the "drop it" command should be given in this manner by all the members of your family. In this way you are not only creating a safe canine companion for your children; you are also building a trusting relationship between your dog and all the members of your family.

Get your puppy accustomed to being lightly stroked during mealtimes, and occasionally toss something yummy into his bowl when you do, so that your pup will look forward to your presence when he is eating. When your puppy is enjoying a nice bone, occasionally pick up the bone for a moment, praising his calm acceptance of this temporary loss. Have your pup watch you and your family enjoy your own dinner before your pup gets to enjoy his own meal. All these activities will firmly establish your role as benevolent leader with your pup. Carefully include all members of your family in this process, standing behind your children to back up their authority when you do.

Please remember that your puppy is not human! If your puppy doesn't learn your house rules he will behave with typical dog behaviors; this includes biting, chewing objects, eliminating at will, and jumping up for attention. Puppies don't intrinsically view any of these activities as wrong, and they need our kind guidance to learn the rules of our households. If your puppy has a housebreaking accident, don't this he feels guilty when you act horrified. Your pup may look guilty, but he is actually responding to your own change in demeanor. The lowered head and body is your pup's attempt to calm you down and avoid possible punishment, not an expression of guilt over soiling your new rug.

With proper management, housebreaking your puppy should be a rather simple process. Your pup will be more easily housetrained if you feed 2–3 distinct meals per day, rather than keeping food in his bowl at all times. Puppies that are fed freely tend to lose their appetites because they have been nibbling all day long, and their elimination patterns are more erratic. It is much more difficult to establish a regular pattern of elimination when a puppy is not eating on a schedule. Below are some other housetraining tips to follow:

Housetraining Procedures

Take your dog out:

1. First thing in the morning.

2. Within 5–10 minutes after every meal.

3. Immediately after every nap.

4. Take your dog out after being played with for awhile. This is very stimulating to many dogs and they will need to eliminate soon after something exciting happens.

5. Take the dog out on an average of every half-hour to an hour. You might want to keep a log on this to determine just how often he needs to go from how many times you can get him to eliminate when you take him outside. Set a timer to remind you to take him out.

6. Before taking the dog outside, say to him, "Want to go potty?" and bring him outside on leash to your designated spot. (It helps to keep treats on you 24 hours a day.) Use special treats for housetraining

and use them only for this purpose. You should use good things, like cheese, liver, bits of hotdogs, leftover chicken, etc. Within a half second after your dog pees or poops in the right spot, immediately give him a treat and praise him to the skies. You can reward good house training behaviors by then letting him run around outside with you or taking a walk. Throw him a puppy party any time he eliminates in his spot.

7. When you've established a fair amount of success in getting the dog to go in this spot, begin putting a command word on the behavior. For example, when you bring the dog to his spot, as he starts to eliminate, say your phrase, like "Go potty." Then reward him with a treat when he's finished. Don't rush giving him the treat because he might interrupt what he's doing in order to get that treat!

8. If you can't keep your eye on him at all times, put him in his crate or tether him to your waist with his leash or long-line.

9. Watch him for certain signals that he may have to go: (1) sniffing the floor, (2) looking a bit anxious or worried, (3) coming to you and just staring at you, (4) preparing to squat or lift leg, (5) behaving like a lunatic or being unusually obnoxious. Don't expect your puppy to give you a clear signal that he has to go out until he is older, but do reinforce increments to this desired communication, such as moving close to the door and whining softly, with praise and treats.

10. Take your puppy's food and water away one hour before bedtime. Otherwise, your dog should have free access to water all day. If he's crated for any length of time, arrange to have someone let him out to eliminate and have a drink of water.

11. Take your puppy out right before bedtime.

Remember, the success of teaching a puppy to eliminate outside your home depends upon correct management of the situation.

Teaching Your Puppy to Have a Soft Mouth (Teaching Bite Inhibition)

Have you ever watched how puppies play with each other while they're still with their littermates? They love to bite each other, often on the face. If one puppy bites another puppy too hard, the "victim" will yelp and run away to play with a different pup. In essence, the biter gets a time-out for applying too much pressure with those needle-sharp puppy teeth. Gradually the puppies learn from each other to bite with less pressure to keep their beloved playmates. This is one reason that you should not purchase a puppy before he or she is eight weeks old. When puppies don't learn to inhibit their bite from their siblings, they will come into our homes and play-bite us, leaving us with bruised and sore arms.

We need to teach our puppies to inhibit their bites to protect ourselves from their sharp puppy teeth, but there is another, more critical reason why we need to work on developing this skill. Adult dogs are capable of inflicting considerable damage on people or other dogs, and dogs that have been raised to inhibit their bite will do minimal damage if they are ever provoked to use their teeth to defend themselves. As children may occasionally be inadvertently rough with a puppy or dog, this is an especially important skill to teach your puppy when young.

After you bring your puppy home, you will begin to see play-biting behavior once he grows comfortable with you and your children. I find that puppies bite with harder pressure when (1) they become overly excited about something, (2) someone, particularly a child, plays on the floor at their facial level, (3) someone roughhouses with them, or (4) they are just plain tired and need a nap. We can avoid having the puppy bite too hard in the first place if we avoid these situations, and situation 2 should always be avoided to avoid facial bites. Your children should always be sitting or standing tall when they play with their puppy.

If your puppy bites you and it hurts, yelp "ouch!" in a high-pitched voice, and then immediately walk out of the room and leave your puppy alone for 30 seconds. If he remains quiet during this time period, you can return to him and resume your play (if not, wait until he is silent for 30 seconds). If your puppy bites you with hard pressure again, repeat this 30-second time-out. After you have established this training exercise with your pup, instruct all your family members to give your puppy this feedback to his hard bite, and be careful that all your children are consistent in their response. As autism and related developmental disorders obviously impact communication, it is very important to be certain your puppy understands that he is to use a gentle mouth with everyone at all times. As your puppy responds to this work, up the ante and squeal at increasingly smaller amounts of pressure from his teeth. The end result of successfully teaching bite inhibition will be a dog that has learned that teeth on skin is never allowed.

Your work to raise your puppy correctly will be time-consuming, but you will be greatly rewarded by the gentle canine companion you will have helped to create for your child.

Renee Premaza is a professional member of the Association of Pet Dog Trainers as well as a Clinical Member of the International Association of Dog Behavior Consultants. In addition she volunteers her time at a local shelter helping dogs to be safe companions and has helped to train several North Star dogs in her home state of New Jersey.

17

Raising Piper

Training an Assistance Dog for a Child with a Developmental Disability

Rachel Friedman

When a dog runs at you, whistle for him.—Henry David Thoreau

This chapter is about raising and training a puppy for a role of assistance dog for a child with a developmental disability, from the selection process through the first sixteen weeks of the pup's life. This chapter is not designed to cover in detail the critical preselection process, which is often overlooked by many people and organizations that wish to locate a puppy to train for assistance work.

In the case of Piper, the golden puppy we raised for North Star, this prior research was done. North Star Foundation had carefully bred Piper and her littermates to possess temperaments conducive to working with children with a variety of challenges. From the moment Piper was born, her socialization process had begun; she was carefully nurtured and socialized with lots of gentle handling from a large variety of people. Piper was handpicked from this golden litter to work for a young boy named Devin, who has Down's syndrome, due to her intelligence, sociability and exceedingly calm nature. The most important point to consider when pairing a puppy with a child with a developmental disability is the concept of temperamental fit: in this case, although Devin was very attracted to dogs in general, he was extremely sensitive to sensory input and quite fearful of quick or sudden movements. A dog that is loud and active would hurt Devin more than help him, and so a calm and sensitive puppy was found who had the intelligence and desire to pay close attention to Devin's cues. (Conversely, a child who is loud and active would not necessarily do well with a timid, sedate pup.) The other members of the family also need to be considered, especially the siblings. Although every member of the family can potentially benefit from the arrival of an assistance dog, each member also has the potential to cause a placement to go south. Parents must consider themselves partners with puppy raisers and trainers in order to create the most valuable and safe placement possible.

We're going to presuppose you've already done your homework and that you have selected the perfect puppy for your family. Let's imagine the pup is nine weeks old. This doesn't take much imagination on my part, as that's where I am now as I await the arrival of Piper, the golden retriever assistance-dog-in-training who is coming to begin her first formal training experience after leaving her mother and siblings. She is flying with Patty Dobbs Gross, executive director of North Star Foundation, in the bulkhead of an airplane. She has already had weeks of handling, stimulation, exposure, affection, and nurturing; Devin and his brother David have known Piper since she opened her eyes. The boys will be seeing Piper's brother Buddy on a regular basis while Piper is with us. They are very much on my mind as I drive to the airport to pick up Piper.

What do I have besides an overwhelming sense of excitement that a bundle of naive fur is heading west to find adventure? Healthy food and water bowls, new toys, a crate, a leash, several kinds of collars, a vet relationship, and lots of plans to prepare her for her future career.

It is now the morning of the first full day of Piper's presence in my home. She has successfully met and charmed all she has come across, something I anticipate she'll be doing almost daily for the rest of her life. Two other dogs in the household have already sized her up, the six cats that drape themselves over countertops have lifted their heads in greeting; a young kitten with a heart murmur daintily steps up to touch Piper's nose with hers. My husband and three daughters—ages three, six, and nine—have already fallen in love. Piper will be here through all three kids' birthdays, the rest of this fall, a full winter, and possibly into the beginning of spring. It was significant that on her first night here tornadoes and unprecedented thunderstorms ripped through the area: bright bolts of lightening, claps of thunder, drenching rain, and high winds. Through it all, Piper remained unflappable. A definite good sign.

Piper has now been here a full week. She has shown behaviors indicative of a great early upbringing, both through proper genetics and a variety of gentle interactions with many people in her short life. She's soft and fluffy; all light golden fur and dark expressive eyes. Her body is dense and weighs more than it looks like it should, 14 pounds on my bathroom scale. She's already showing great confidence in her ability to go both up and down the stairs throughout the house and leading downstairs to the backyard. The substrates (surface) of the floors include carpet, wood, and rubber-covered curved steps leading to the outside. She has played in wet leaves, learned to pay my two dogs their proper respect, and eliminated without fault when taken outside. She has bounded and shown increased curiosity with her environment. She has been up since 5 A.M., been taken out three times, gnawed on a bone, and is now resting comfortably at my feet, along with the other two dogs. Cats and husband and kids are still sleeping as dawn slowly lightens the sky. It is a peaceful, calm time that I use to reflect on the importance of the job I have undertaken.

In less than two weeks Piper has already learned a multitude of behaviors, both default and on cue. ("Default" means she's trained to assume a position based on where she is and what's going on; for example, sitting every time we approach a curb and waiting for permission to cross. "Cued" is something she's asked to do—for example, doing a "down/stay" at a movie theater.) Housetraining is going well. She is sleeping through the night without an issue and now when my husband or I put her in the bedroom with our already sleeping daughter, she will curl up to sleep without jumping on and waking up my fortunately tolerant child, as she did the first few days!

During the day she is given plenty of opportunity to eliminate outside on a variety of substrates and by day ten there were two consecutive days with no accidents (most accidents, by the way, were due to human error!) She learned almost immediately, without instruction, how to access the dog door that is at the bottom of a slightly winding stairway at the back door. She simply saw the opening of the dog door, passed through it, and trotted right up to me to receive a biscuit and complimentary mini-massage. Within a few days after that, after being shown just once, she learned how to navigate the second dog door, which is accessed by going down four brick steps, into the vastly cluttered and unfinished basement and up a flight of "scary" stairs into the kitchen.

It is my intent that during the initial period I want the puppy to eliminate in a variety of places and on a variety of substrates at all hours of the day and night and in all sorts of weather. This is to socialize her to all the possible future places she might be with Devin when she has public access. When she is a little older I will start to ask her to consistently eliminate on cue on a variety of substrates (as opposed to her choice). This is in case there will be a need to have her empty her bladder or bowels before a trip in a car or the need to be indoors for a fixed period of time.

Piper, as most golden retrievers, loves to eat. She has eaten everything offered to her. In addition to her meals, she gets treats, including carrots, broccoli (steamed or raw), peanut butter, and chemical/preservative-free dog treats. (She also seems to greatly enjoy gnawing on the toes and hands of Barbie dolls, but my daughters have been trained not to make them accessible to her! If they forget, it's their fault; Piper is still too young and unsophisticated to avoid craving such a delicacy!)

Piper has met a variety of other dogs, both in Puppy Class and out and about our town. She defers to all her elders by crouching low or lying on her side exposing her belly. Upon meeting a new dog she is not assertive or demanding. Once she understands another dog might play with her, she relaxes and engages happily in play. Finding a language to communicate with your dog is a critical aspect of the dog-training process. As Devin currently communicates using hand signs, it is our goal to have Piper respond to both verbal and signed commands. I am beginning to pair hand signs with my spoken commands and she is absorbing this new component of her training like a sponge.

I pull the pup onto my lap and touch her all over. Her ears, her nose, in her mouth, her soft body, her legs, joints, toe. I gently pinch into her toes and her paw pads. Throughout this inspection she remains calm and settled. I pull out a pair of nail clippers and let her sniff them, and as I manipulate her toes I clip the tip off one nail and give her a crunchy liver treat. If introduced patiently, kindly, slowly, a puppy can learn to enjoy one of the more commonly unpleasant grooming chores for dogs.

Piper gets a variety of chew toys and stuffed toys. She enjoys many of them, some with greater relish than others, but in no way does she show any reaction when I poke around her mouth and nose and eyes as she is chewing. She allows me to take away the toy and wait for another sit before I give it back. Throughout she shows great aplomb.

Next, I have my kids do the same thing. With each of them she shows calm deference and allows them to do anything. In fact, when the toys are taken away, she again cocks her little head and waits until she's given the toy back or the kids decide to put it a few inches away from her face. If they take it away, she lies quietly. If they place it back on the floor, she hoists her body up and goes for the toy, collapses again on the floor and gnaws the toy. I instruct my kids, under my supervision, to pet her head, stroke her body, tug gently at her tail, "coochy coo" under her furry chin. All the while she remains, as always, unflappable. It is interesting to me that of my three girls, the youngest is the most natural with dogs and really enjoys helping train. While the older two are comfortable and enjoy dogs too, it is the youngest who is most outgoing with animals. I am struck by what an important role she is playing in shaping Piper to accept children as leaders. Devin will be primed to step up to this role in just a few short months.

Now 12 weeks old, Piper weighs in at 20 pounds. She has one month left of puppyhood. We continue finding balance between activity and rest. While I want Piper to have great experiences and exposure, I also want to make sure, as she's in the heavy growing phase, that she's not overly exerting herself. For the medium- to larger-sized dog, it's always a wise idea to follow a trusted vet's advice about rate of growth. While genetics is a big part of the skeletal growth, early puppy development and exercise is also a factor, and so I make an effort to balance out her play and exercise with calm resting activities like bully stick chewing, sleeping beside the fire, and cuddling.

Despite the fact that Piper is being heavily socialized to children, dogs, cats, birds, and grand adventures, I also felt it would be a good idea to enroll her in a Puppy Kindergarten class with myself as the student instead of the instructor. And so Piper began her Puppy Kindergarten class at the age of 14 weeks in a large training center with lots of space and rubberized matting. In the first session there were ten other puppies and about fifteen people; included as the students were shy pups, confident pups, overly exuberant bouncy pups, all varieties of breeds, and all less than four months of age.

In our initial class Piper was overwhelmed with the social element and deferred to me whenever she felt stressed or confused, which I liked. As her ultimate goal is to become an assistance dog she needs to learn to defer to her handler and display a calm, stable demeanor in all social situations, even and especially when being overwhelmed. (Patty reported that when faced with the jostling and noise of her first plane ride, Piper either sat attentively at her feet or curled up to sleep through the unpleasantness. These reactions Patty naturally reinforced.)

Two weeks later in the second class Piper showed a much improved attitude socially and engaged one or two of the other pups in the class. She excelled at recall and came flying over towards me to lie down expectantly at my feet. (She was heavily rewarded for that choice!)

Her loose leash walking is excellent and she continues to excel in that area, looking to me as her handler with confidence. I'm going to allow my children to work with her as well, so when she is with a less confident, smaller person, she can walk politely without pulling. She defaults to a sit at every curb. In class the puppies are passed from handler to handler to accustom them to various people. She was hugged and cuddled and petted and treated by everyone and seemed to greatly enjoy the experience.

Thus far in her first month in our home Piper has met nearly three hundred people of all ages and both genders. She has met over fifty dogs of various ages, sizes, and temperaments. She has gone for both long and short car rides. She has walked on a leash to my daughters' school at least twice each week, happily greeting children as she went. She has hiked in the woods off leash and has learned "go home" from several houses away. She has learned to come when called indoors and out, from increasing distances with layered-in distractions. She has gotten exponentially better about eliminating in appropriate places, although she still has the occasional accident. (Puppies are not reliably housebroken until approximately four to six months, and must be taken out regularly to reinforce the housebreaking process.) She has been to the vet several times, sometimes just for a visit, twice for a checkup, and once for a booster shot and weigh-in. She has been to two puppy classes, with three more to go. She visited my daughters' dentist and endeared herself to everyone there.

Piper has enjoyed playing in snow and relished warming before a crackling fire. She has accommodated kittens and cats that snuggle up to her for warmth. In all her time here she has not shown one iota of aggression towards a human. I have never heard her growl or snarl or seen her snap at anyone. When overwhelmed by anything in her midst, which is rare, she will lie down or turn away. When in a situation that can be stressful she defers to her person and reacts calmly. I took her through a drive-through car wash and as the vehicle was encased in water sprayers and large equipment she worried a bit, but a little reassurance allowed her to eye the situation calmly and by the time it was done, she was no longer exhibiting stress.

She has also learned not to bark for food and will go quickly into her crate to assume a sitting position before being fed. In short, Piper shows all the hallmarks of excellent breeding and socialization. Her adaptability to different environments indicates a successful future as a service dog.

Shortly after her sixteenth week, which I consider officially the end of puppyhood and the beginning of early adolescence, Piper accompanied my two older children, three other adults, and myself to a local diner. Piper was all dressed up and ready to work (wearing her North Star Assistance Puppy in Training saddle). I brought along a fleece pad and bully stick, and she lay down on the pad beneath our booth and chewed the stick. She remained calm and well-behaved during the entire meal. Other diners periodically asked to pet her, and after being given permission, Piper calmly lay and allowed herself to be petted. This all bodes very well for her future role as assistance dog for a child with a developmental disability.

Piper will remain with us for the next several months, returning to North Star for her finishing touches before her placement with Devin and his family. She has far exceeded even my high expectations for what is involved in puppy raising. The next developmental phase, early adolescence, will continue in the same direction of varied experience, training, reinforcing, and raising the level of expectation for performance. We will be working on retrieval, increasing distances and duration for the basic behaviors, including sit, down, stay, and recall (coming when called) with both verbal and signed commands. We will layer in the distractions as she can accommodate them. We will continue to offer her a balance of structure and free time, with lots of toys, games, and adventures sprinkled into her days to make her training fun. We will take her sledding and to movies, stores, and friends' homes.

By now, at four months of age, she is fully housetrained. She has a regular elimination cycle and is in fact eliminating more or less on cue. She may vocalize in frustration but easily redirects herself if needed. This vocalization can in fact be turned to alerting if needed for her future family. She waits for permission to eat and adores car rides. She is a truly lovely and loving dog who shows great promise in being a valuable assistance dog for her future family.

I am of the opinion that rescue, shelter, or haphazardly bred pups can sometimes make fine service dogs with the right training. Due to experience, I also feel strongly that dogs intended for assistance work with children with special needs should be bred and selected for temperament, raised in a nurturing environment, trained throughout adolescence, and specifically socialized to work with children.

Housebreaking Tips

Tactile sensation received through the footpad is part of a pup's learning where to eliminate. A substrate is defined as the surface upon which the pup is standing. Is it grass? Cement? Sand? Carpet? Linoleum? Tile? Pebbles? Mud? Snow? Is it hot? Cold? Wet? Dry? When establishing a pattern of behavior to put on cue, designing a treatment plan with concrete training goals can be very helpful to maintain consistency as well as measure progress.

Here's an example of a treatment plan for housetraining:

Training Goal: Get all eliminations in desired area for five consecutive days to create establishment of appropriate elimination sites.

Management: Keep track of puppy's whereabouts around the clock until this training goal is achieved. This supervision is best accomplished by employing a tether to keep the puppy attached to you or a piece of furniture in the room you are in; crate your puppy if you are unable to provide this level of supervision. The duration of this level of management is not fixed, but depends upon the age, breed, level of intelligence, and temperament of the puppy in question. The general rule of thumb is to continue this management technique until your puppy is reliably indicating the need to go outside to relieve himself, along with his use of the designated elimination spot. It could be days, weeks, or even months before these goals can be successfully achieved.

Training: The puppy should be offered an opportunity to eliminate upon waking, within 20 minutes of eating, when he seems distracted and is sniffing the ground, or when the pup wanders to the door that leads to his elimination spot. Eventually the pup can be trained to bark or ring a bell when nature calls, but first you will need to learn to read the pup's signals that he needs to go out. It may be helpful to visually designate this spot, perhaps with survey flags you can purchase at a hardware store. When in the designated elimination spot, be patient to wait for your pup to eliminate (very young pups may need to urinate twice to completely empty their bladder due to distractibility), and when he is successful you can put this behavior on cue by saying, "go potty," or whatever you choose to serve as command for this action. (Having a dog trained to eliminate on cue can be very convenient, especially when traveling.) Gradually reduce the opportunities for your pup to relieve himself as time passes. No rough handling or anger is ever appropriate in this process, for the dog needs to learn how to internalize self-control along with how to communicate to you his need to go outside. Be lavish in your praise when your puppy achieves success in this rather complicated process, for this is truly an accomplishment!

Handling Tips

We need to make sure assistance dog that are slated to work with children know that people sometimes might do unusual things but that they aren't intended to be hurtful. This is especially true for children with developmental disabilities, for they are apt to behave in socially unusual ways, such as screeching with sudden joy or having a meltdown when angry; when these incidents occur your pup should be taught to melt into an extended down/stay to wait patiently for your next command. Having a dog that is genetically non-reactive is a plus here, but there are also things you can do when raising a dog for service work that can help to create a safe companion for a child with behavioral differences.

Here are a few exercises designed to prevent a dog from interpreting these activities in a hostile way. By pairing these annoying or uncomfortable (not painful!) stimuli with praise, reassurance, and rewards your pup will be more likely to demonstrate great patience with your child's efforts to interact with the pup.

Bonk the pup lightly on the head

Bump into the dog's side while he's eating

Tickle the hair between toe pads

Gentle ear tugging

Lip twisting

Nose "beeping"

Tail pulling (gentle!)

Finger into ear canal

Finger pressure on eyelid

Finger into nostril

Pull on tongue while dog's panting

Sudden touch to testicles/penis

Lean all over pup, put your head on them, etc.

Lie next to them on the floor while they chew their chewies

Slide them around while they're resting peacefully

Play with their toenails

Hug them clumsily, too tightly, and longer than they'd prefer

Yell, sing, howl, ululate (trill loudly)

Start to hand them food or a toy, then suddenly pull it away at the last moment

Jump up and down, wave arms, spin around, and fall down

There are sure to be other possible ways to bug innocent dogs that some unknowing child might try, this is by no means a complete list. Keep your particular child in mind when devising these activities, but keep safety in mind and be certain nothing you do is deliberately painful to your puppy. Teach your pup that the proper response to a face thrust close to theirs is to lick that face by rewarding this response.

Non-reactive dogs can be a reality, but they don't just happen; it takes the right genetic potential along with serious training to properly prepare dogs to work with a child with a developmental disability and "bombproof" them against the kinds of bite-provoking behavior many children and some adults unwittingly invite.

There is a certain amount of personal responsibility that an assistance dog user has to have or develop; the dog has to have impeccable manners and temperament and the level of control has to be so high that a simple whisper can turn a head. The dog has to be clean, in good condition and never have accidents in public places. Your goal is to shape your dog to work with your child unobtrusively anytime and anywhere you choose; it takes an enormous amount of time to do this, but as luck would have it, you can't teach a puppy anything outside the context of play, so at any given point the opportunity exists to enjoy yourself during this life-long process of shaping your child's canine companion.

Piper is now six months old and ready to return to Connecticut for advanced training. She has been a stellar, if temporary, addition to the family for these past few months. That's not to say that she hasn't tested my patience; she has been responsible for amputated Barbie appendages, shredded tissues strewn across the floor, occasional puddles on the carpet, and some broken sleep. But through it all Piper has displayed a consistently upbeat attitude, helping me to rise above the trivia of life to recognize its true purpose: to help those in need. I am happy our family found this way to help Devin to meet his social, emotional, and educational goals. I wish Piper all the best in the next leg of her amazing journey, even as she leaves some broken hearts in her wake.

Rachel Friedman combines her passion for and long experience in working with animals with her extensive social work training and work experience. She became a full-time dog trainer in 1999. Her background makes her uniquely qualified to help clients learn how best to teach their dogs, and thus how best to create a harmonious household. Rachel is a clinical member of the International Association of Animal Behavior Consultants (IAABC) and a professional member of the Association of Pet Dog Trainers (APDT); she also served as director of North Star during our formative years and helped to form our training philosophy.

18

Taming the Teenage Assistance Dog

Michelle Goldner

All teenagers have this desire to somehow run away.—Joan Chen

I would like to begin this chapter with a disclaimer. While I am a dog trainer with a number of years experience handling many different breeds and types of dogs, I still consider myself just barely scratching the surface of understanding—truly understanding, canine behavior. Additionally, training and working with assistance or service dogs is a new experience for me—one that I jumped into with both feet first taking on the training support role for North Star Foundation to train an adolescent female Lab named Lexi for a family with a six-year-old autistic child. For a number of years I have pursued a path to teach common, everyday pet owners that their dog can be so much more than just the family's pet. I feel very strongly that as a species, the dog is better suited than any other domestic animal to be worthy of a higher level of respect and understanding.

Dogs have long had a valuable role as allies to people, taking turns being our hunting partners, protectors, and faithful companions. In modern times, some dogs have gone even farther to help us, and there are currently many people with disabilities who owe a portion of their freedom to assistance dogs by their sides who have been carefully trained to meet their needs. But for as many successful partnerships, there are far more instances where a dog may be spun from a program and/or family due to inadequate temperament or training, or for the lack of resources needed to raise, train and support one of these special dogs.

The adolescent assistance dog is normally the picture of vitality and health. This is especially true when considering the special care that goes into breeding and selecting dogs that have the potential to become assistance dogs. Only the dogs of the soundest mind and body are given the training necessary to handle the tasks faced by a working dog. But what defines the "ideal" dog for an autistic individual will vary greatly from what defines an excellent canine partner for a physically challenged individual. Further, the path to a manageable adolescent dog must begin with the basics applied by the puppy raiser. From puppy to young adult, a dog is a sponge that, with the right plan, can develop into an animal with a lot of scope and adaptability.

The following is a suggested list of behaviors and the approximate time to teach them. By introducing a number of behaviors very early on, a puppy's ability to learn these and other future behaviors is greatly enhanced. Further, while puppy raisers are normally well-intentioned volunteers, often times their grasp of modern training methods can be greatly enhanced by support from a professional trainer. Dog training is both a physical and cognitive skill. A handler must develop timing and attention focus, while at the same time making quick evaluations as to why a dog is exhibiting behaviors (good and bad) and learning to anticipate behaviors before they happen.

One of the most important things you can do for the young assistance-dog-in-training is to socialize him to many different people, places, and things. A man with a beard or a lady with a funny hat can be very traumatic for a pup that has never seen this. There are many texts written about the stages of development for dogs. They go through an infant, toddler, pre-teen and teen stage just like humans, but they do it all in one year. Understanding the basics of canine stages of development will go a long way toward increasing your ability to guide your dog intelligently through adolescence.

For the novice dog handler, learning to use the clicker as a training tool can be cumbersome, but it is valuable to become skilled with this small but powerful device. The clicker allows you to shape behaviors at a very early stage in a positive manner. It is critical that puppy raisers "load the clicker" or teach the pup what to expect when the click is heard (a food reward) as soon as possible. When you acquire good timing to mark desired behaviors, the pup can quickly and easily be taught to respond to an unbelievable number of commands. It all starts by breaking every movement down into baby steps, then chaining these intermediate behaviors together to get a finished product.

8 Weeks to 12 Weeks

Supply list:

- A clicker
- A bowl of highly desirable treats
- A flat collar appropriately fitted to the pup's neck, with care taken that it is not tight
- A short lightweight leash for the pup to drag around
- A desirable toy with a squeaky (for breaks and play time)

Take advantage of the puppy's "window of opportunity." Until they are about 16 weeks of age, puppies are a very clean slate. They respond extremely well to lots of stimuli (when it is presented in a reasonable manner). In this time frame, the pup should be taught to sit, come in response to his name being called, lie down upon command, and begin to learn how to wait.

Sit

Show the pup you have a food reward, put the reward near the pup's nose and slowly bring the hand back over the pup's head forcing him to follow the movement back. No command is necessary at this stage, and gravity and physics will actually do the work of teaching the pup to sit. As he continues to follow the treat, his tail will go down and his shoulders will come back. Once he has achieved the sit position, click and deliver the treat. Repeat these steps a number of times until the pup will sit with just a small hand movement, or as soon as the food is presented. At this point you can begin to verbalize the sit command so that there is a spoken command, then a click for doing it right and finally the delivery of the food reward.

Down

Once the pup is sitting reliably on verbal command, begin to teach down. With the pup in a sitting position, draw a line with the bait hand from the pup's nose, down his chest (slowly) toward the floor. Once the bait hand reaches the top of the dog's paws, draw the line out over the floor away from the pup. If during this process the pup crouches to reach the food, or puts a paw forward, click and reward. Continue to click the crouch or the forward paw for several tries. Once the pup will consistently crouch or put a paw forward, move the bait hand out a bit further. If the pup gives up or stands, replace the sit and start over. If the pup crouches a bit lower, reward again, until that level of crouch is consistent. Finally, pull the bait further away until the pup fully lies down. Depending on the dog this may take several minutes, or even several training sessions. Once the dog understands this concept, the handler will find that the dog will quickly lie down as soon as the bait hand begins to draw the down and out pattern. When the pup is consistently offering the full down, begin to add the verbal command. At this point, you can have the pup go back and forth between the sit and down by luring with the food and clicking the proper position.

Recall

As far as I am concerned, the most important basic command is come. Ironically, recall is the easiest thing to teach a young pup and the most difficult to teach an adolescent or adult dog, so you are wise to master this skill early with your assistance-puppy-in-training. My favorite game is "Puppy in the Middle." Recruit friends and family, load them up with very high value treats and a clicker, and everyone takes turns calling the pup and clicking and treating when he shows up on cue to his name and the word come. Additional practice should take place inside the house, around the yard, and off your property (if there are no barriers to keep the puppy safe, a long lead should be attached to be certain this recall exercise remains safe). No matter how aggravating your puppy's resistance to coming when called might be, under no circumstances are you to call your dog to you and follow that compliance with anything other than food and praise. It only takes one or two negative reinforcements or punishments to ruin the recall forever.

Wait

There are so many uses for this command it staggers the mind! Wait to follow me through a door, wait to get your dinner, wait to get into a car, etc. The two methods I use with very young pups include waiting for dinner and waiting to go out a door. Armed with a meal and a clicker, ask the pup to sit. Lightly hold the pup's collar and tell the pup to wait while you place the bowl of food down on the floor, and then restrain the pup gently from moving forward. Give the command wait and pull gently back on the collar to position the pup back into a sit. At some point the pup will relax, take a deep breath and sigh, or just stop leaning on the collar. This is when you click and say OK to allow him to eat his meal.

12 Weeks to 6 Months

If a trainer has spent the time teaching a pup the nuances of the clicker, and has gained solid control of the aforementioned behaviors, the pup will be prepared to move on to more serious training. It is important to understand that the process of developing a well-trained dog takes a minimum of six months to a year; even more training past this point is required to produce a safe and reliable assistance partner. It is also important to remember that a young dog needs frequent breaks from regimented training to be able to relax and play in a safe area with abandon; at times this play should be alone with a fun toy and at other times with a friendly dog or variety of people. Play is a critical part of teaching a young dog that interaction with humans is fun, rewarding and worth his time!

Before introducing your puppy to a leash and collar, it should be understood that these are not meant to enable you to drag your pup around, but instead to serve as a tethering system to keep your pup safely by your side. To prepare for leash work, the trainer should have the following tools available:

A six-foot lead, preferably made of leather with a solid clip

A flat collar

A Gentle Leader or Halti head collar

A fanny pack or bait bag with a supply of high-value, small training treats

A clicker

Lessons first begin with introducing a new tool to the pup, the head collar. Head collars work because dogs hate the feeling of pulling with their heads (although they don't tend to mind pulling if it is felt in their necks). Because these collars fit over the dog's nose and around the ears like a horse's halter, some dogs find them very distracting. To get the pup accustomed to wearing (and ignoring) this type of collar, begin by placing the properly fitted device on the pup during meal times. Just before putting the bowl of food down, place the collar on, and as soon as the meal is finished, remove it. Spend about a week or more if necessary allowing the pup to associate the collar with the rewarding act of eating. Time spent here will keep the pup from constantly trying to remove the collar in the future.

Assuming the pup now accepts the head collar, begin by snapping the leash to the extended loop and letting the leash drag behind the dog. This feeling will be different from the earlier training period because now a slight weight will be felt from the pup's nose. Ignoring the leash and any fussing the pup may be doing, begin training sessions by running through behaviors already mastered. Once you have the pup's attention, pick up the end of the leash and place the loop over your wrist. Resist the temptation to steer the pup with the leash, and instead plan on using the lure of food and your voice to communicate.

Here are a few exercises that you can teach your adolescent dog to perform that will help him in his future role as assistance dog to a child with a developmental disability.

Exercise 1—Watch Me (eye contact)

This exercise should be very easy if the preliminary training has been consistent. The properly raised pup should look at you when his name is called. The "watch me" command puts this behavior on cue and asks the pup to hold eye contact with the handler for longer periods of time. While a simple behavior to train, "watch me" can be critical to keeping the dog's attention in highly distracting situations. This exercise is also valuable for the children with autism who are working on establishing and maintaining eye contact. By switching their role from student to teacher of this skill, many children with autism are able to improve their own eye contact with their dogs, which they can then transfer to people with appropriate guidance.

Begin by having the dog sit or stand in front of you. Show the pup the bait and bring the hand with the bait up to the front of the handler's face at the nose so that in following the bait the dog is also looking the handler directly in the eye. Once the handler gets the dog's eyes to hold that contact for even a brief moment, click and treat. This exercise is to be repeated a number of times and can, in subsequent training sessions, be made more challenging by asking the dog to hold the eye contact for longer periods of time.

Exercise 2—Loose Lead Walking

I am always amazed at how many dog owners never teach their dogs to walk on a leash correctly. One of my biggest personal pet peeves are dogs that pull their handlers around by the leash, straining for air because they have tightened their collars to the point of practically cutting off all air flow. This is where the Gentle Leader or Halti head collar can really prove itself a valuable training tool. The most difficult thing about the head collar is getting the dog to wear it without fussing. Make sure to do your preliminary work with the head collar before clipping on the leash.

Once your puppy accepts his head collar, begin to take walks around the neighborhood together; begin with your pup on the left, with the leash and clicker in your left hand and high-value treats in your right hand. Begin walking by stepping forward and giving a "let's go" command. The dog should readily follow, and more often than not, will try to surge ahead. If this happens, stop, call the dog to you and walk backwards a few steps while at the same time bringing the dog back into the heel position in the same manner described above. Once the dog is back in place, begin again, only this time, put a treat right at the dog's nose (near the seam of your jeans) and keep your hand there, allowing the dog to lick at, but not acquire the treat. As you walk, continue letting the dog have a bit of reward from time to time—don't withhold the treat too long, or the pup will lose interest and surge ahead again. At regular intervals, plan to stop your movement, give a slight backward tug on the leash (only enough to warn the dog you are about to stop) then stop your forward motion. At the same time, move the treat (still right at the dog's nose) up and back to encourage the sit. Give the verbal command for sit. Repeat this exercise daily, in many situations and incorporate many stops and sits. Eventually the dog will sit without the verbal command. Also practice this exercise on the right as well as the left.

Exercise 3—Teaching Stay

Begin teaching stay by placing the dog in either the heel or side position. Give the dog the stay command and either point to his nose, or push your flat hand up to, but not touching his nose. Take one step out, turn and face the dog so that you are standing toe-to-toe. Several things can happen in the moments between beginning this exercise and your arrival at your position in front of the dog:

The dog stays put—excellent. Reach down, click and treat and tell the dog "good stay." Count to three or four, then return to your position next to the dog, so that you are both facing the same direction; give the release command and reward the dog.

The dog moves to follow you—this is an understandable mistake. Up to this point you have encouraged the dog to move off with you, so asking him to remain in place is new. If this happens, stop your movement, tell the dog "oops" or "wrong," repeat the stay command and hand signal and try again. Don't punish, but don't reward the dog until he will stay in position while you change yours.

The dog stays while you position yourself toe-to-toe, but moves once you are facing him—again, not a big deal at this point. However, if you don't correct this reaction now, you will forever be battling the movement.

If the dog moves while you are toe-to-toe, quickly say "oops" or "wrong," and use your hand to lure the dog back into the sit, without repeating the sit command. It is important to have the stay command be that last thing you say to the dog. Once the dog is sitting, repeat stay, count to 4, click and treat if the dogs stays put, say "good stay" then move back into position. Chances are this dog will move again when you try to reposition yourself. Stop what you are doing, lure the dog into the sit, repeat stay and keep trying to move back to position. If the dog continues to move each time you do, a stern "eh, eh" can help remind him to stay put. It is critical to react to the dog moving immediately. If you are slow and the dog has time to wander about, you lose the effectiveness of the exercise.

Once the "sit/stay" has been mastered, begin making the exercise difficult by increasing the time the dog needs to stay still, and by increasing the distance between you and the dog. Your goal is to produce a dog that will stay up to 30 minutes with you sitting across the room. Note that this is a far longer period than would ever be expected from a pet or show dog, but this is a necessary skill to teach any assistance-dog-in-training.

Also of note, each time you practice this exercise, you must end the exercise by giving a release, or free dog command. Remember, when you allow the dog to get up, he should not jump and scurry about. His release should be low-key and organized.

The same exercise pattern should be achieved with the dog in a down position as well.

Moving On

The commands outlined above constitute the basics every young assistance dog should master before leaving the puppy-raiser's home. More important, however, is that the dog performs these exercises anywhere at anytime and for a variety of handlers. To really proof your dog, make sure you allow all different types of people to handle him. Look for men, women and children with various tones of voice, size and skin color to help with your dog's training. You have to teach the dog to be a generalist, a trait that does not come naturally. A young assistance dog must learn to trust humans, and must learn to learn. The successful assistance dog must also be non-reactive, and focused on his handler rather than the environment. Further proof of training needs to happen in malls, parks, other people's homes, on public transportation, in offices and at public gatherings such as fairs and festivals.

Spending the time and energy needed to intelligently guide a dog through his adolescence is a critical part of any assistance dog's training program. It is your important job to be sure that this dog will always be a help, and never a hindrance, to the child he will serve.

Michelle Goldner is a member of the Association of Pet Dog Trainers (APDT). In addition to running her dog-training business, "A Wag N' Time," Michelle also volunteers her time to the Humane Society of Indianapolis. She has also helped to trained a North Star dog named Lexi for a young boy named John, who is on the autism spectrum.

19

A Mother's Letter to Her Son

Kathleen Vranos

The mother's heart is the child's schoolroom.
—Henry Ward Beecher

April 18, 2004

Dear Jake,

Happy birthday to you and Nomar! It's been a whole year since the two of you partnered up to teach me a thing or two about life. How you've changed, Jake!

I remember the anxious, isolated seven-year-old boy who prompted my first call to Patty at the North Star Foundation. You were so devastated by the coming and going of our busy family that it seemed we were all just living from melt down to melt down. Your little brother, Mark, 5, whom you adored, was frightened by you, and Dad and I tried everything we could think of, but couldn't find a way to help. I could see all of the pain and confusion in your eyes, Jake, and could only imagine how hard it must have been for you to understand barely a portion of what we said and then be able to express even less. You had just begun to respond to our efforts with using pictures and symbols to communicate with you, but this was in the early stages and left so much unsaid between us.

Then one day when you were crying in our room after Marina, who was 9, had left for gymnastics, Dad and I finally had the divine inspiration! You needed a friend of your very own, Jake, a friend who would always be with you whenever you needed him, a friend you could count on every minute of every day. Dad and I have had a friend like that. Our beautiful golden retriever, Duke, who is 13 now, was the first family member to join us after we were married. Duke came to us when he was just 18 months old, afraid of everything and the most submissive creature either of us had ever seen. We both just loved him to pieces, and he became our devoted, gentle, 100 percent reliable best friend. In fact, Duke has been so in tune with me over the years, Jake, that he actually sensed my premature labor with you before I did. He intuitively adapted to all of your births, herding me to "our" babies whenever any of you cried, and he wouldn't miss stories at bedtime for all the bones in the world! But by your seventh year, Jake, Duke was growing tired. There would be no replacing him for Dad and me, but could we find a friend like that for you?

Thank God for the web! I began searching for help and there they were: "The North Star Foundation . . . We Help Children Find Their Way." I wrote a note explaining you and our hopes to someone out there in cyberspace, and lo and behold, I got a fast response back that was warm and friendly. "Yes, we place dogs with children with autism. Yes, your dog can be a friend to the rest of the family and your child's friends, too—friendship is the best medicine for autism! Yes, you can come meet our dogs and us soon. Yes, we've been through what you're going through as a family. Yes, we understand."

We were on our way, Jake! Nearly a year later, after many visits and e-mails with Patty Dobbs Gross and her family, we met the litter on your eighth birthday! Do you remember how (uncharacteristically) quiet you were, Jake? The puppies were just a week old, so fragile and small. You sat on the bench in Patty's kitchen with Marina and Mark so perfectly still and quiet, clearly appreciating how special the golden puppies were.

I had created a picture book for you explaining how tiny and fragile the pups would be, but I wasn't sure you had understood until I watched you with them. Despite your overwhelming motor impulses, your touch was so soft and gentle.

We couldn't stay away while the puppies grew, even with the 90 minute drive to Patty's. Although we immediately fell in love with all the puppies, as the weeks passed it became increasingly clear which pup was meant for us. Nomar, you would say, clear as a whistle, despite garbling every other suggestion we'd make. And a mighty puppy he was, even at eight weeks of age! Nomar was nearly twice the size of his littermates and clearly the leader of the pack. But what really made him stand out was his fascination with people, especially Patty's son, Chris, who had completely bonded with Nomar. Even as a little pup, Nomar showed great intelligence, courage and curiosity. Surely he was the one who could befriend a growing, physically active and emotionally intense boy like you, Jake.

"Now, he's the alpha," Patty said. "He might be harder to train at first, but his potential is enormous."

"No problem," we said. In our minds, Dad and I were so confident because of how things had worked out with Duke. And you loved Nomar, Jake. You were broken-hearted every time we had to leave him at Patty's, and the rest of us were just as crazy about him. Patty recommended she raise and train Nomar with her son Chris's assistance for at least the first six months, so we were sure things would proceed smoothly. And isn't an alpha just a highly intelligent dog with strong leadership instincts? Who wouldn't want that?

Now, Jake, this is the part of the story where I tell you how our family earned the dubious distinction of being one of the placements from which North Star learned the most!

Nomar came for his first sleep-over "visit" when he was just ten weeks old. You were so excited, Jake, an emotion you rarely showed at that time! I could see from your smiles and giggles that you loved having Nomar curl up in your bed for stories. But best of all, you thought Nomar's messing up your lines and lines of toys was just hilarious! For years, those lines drove Dad and me crazy, but particularly during the anxious year you were having, this ritual had become really important to you at certain times. How could we have guessed that only an extremely cute puppy could get away with turning your perseveration into the funniest game ever? Within a few days, you just gave up on lining up toys! You had a new toy who was far more interesting, didn't you?

The e-mails flew between Patty and me during these first days and we both questioned whether Nomar should just stay since you were benefiting so much from him already. Our goals for your assistance dog were ambitious. We wanted search and rescue training because of your tendency to "explore," and we wanted excellent obedience because this was required for public access. But above all, we wanted you to have a best friend who could comfort you, help you stay connected and play with you interactively. It was a tall order.

"What kind of guidance and support would we have if Nomar stays?" Dad and I asked Patty. "I'll be your trainer," she said. "We'll visit back and forth when we can and stay in touch by e-mail as much as you'd like." She gave us a long to-do list and guidelines.

And so we took the plunge.

To this day, no matter where we go with you and Nomar, people stop to ask, "What does he do?" There is an expectation among the general public, which we even shared at first, that an assistance dog comes with amazing bells and whistles, which enable him to perform stunning tasks for the disabled individual in his care. Now at a year of age, Nomar has some pretty amazing bells and whistles, Jake. But within your first few days together, the two of you taught me how the simple moments would be the most important.

"We walk together now," I like to answer.

You and I know what a miracle that is, don't we, Jake? It's so simple, and something most families can just take for granted. But before Nomar's arrival, it was so hard for us to simply walk together. You were fed up with people holding your hand, and I couldn't blame you. But the fact was that you usually lagged behind our busy family by ten feet or more, slipping into your own little world if left to walk on your own, and often even silently slipping away in a store or a park.

But with the help of a leash with two handles (something we rigged up by attaching two collars as handles to one short leash), you and Nomar could walk together with any member of our family. This was so remarkable to me, Jake, because you did it voluntarily and you did it during the most important times.

Throughout the year before Nomar's arrival, dropping your brother and sister off at school just broke your heart every day, didn't it, Jake? You would cry for an hour and have such a rough start to your own school day. We tried routines around saying "goodbye" and social stories, but it just seemed that the world was too hard and confusing, and the love you have always had for your family was one of your few comforts. Eventually, Dad had to rearrange his office schedule to drive Marina and Mark to school (something I missed terribly), so that you and I could focus on arriving at your school with a smile.

Then along came Nomar . . . I'll never forget how his North Star vest swam on his miniature body the first time he wore it. But he filled it out in other ways! Nomar took walking with you seriously, Jake, and with the help of a gentle leader, Nomar has always walked like a perfect gentleman between us. Walking with Nomar helps you to be more in tune with your surroundings; you seem happy to be responsible for holding Nomar's leash and for this time we share together.

You and Nomar and I are back to driving Mark and Marina to school, and we haven't had a tear all year, have we, Buddy? After we say a confident "goodbye" to your brother and sister, you and Nomar and I take a long walk, practicing traffic safety, and arrive on your playground all smiles, ready to greet the classmates who never tire of greeting you and your dog.

The beauty of the simple things, Jake . . .

But we also had our trials the first four months we spent with Nomar, didn't we Jake? We learned that goldens are not all the same, despite outward appearance, and that Nomar and Duke had some important differences in their temperaments that we needed to recognize in order to train Nomar correctly. Some have called Duke "just a pretty face" over the years, but Dad and I know that he's actually all heart. All it ever took for us to elicit Duke's unfailing devotion was lots of TLC. For a pat or a hug or few minutes of attention, he would follow us to the ends of the earth, perfectly mannered and always gentle, if not exactly energetic.

So if our whole family lavished loads of TLC on Nomar in between training sessions, he was sure to do our bidding, too, right? Wrong!

We thought we were following all of Patty's advice with training Nomar for basic obedience, and we were encouraging him to play hide and seek with you, Jake, all around the house and out in the yard, as instructed. He amazed us when we'd say, "Find Jake!" and he'd go tearing after you in the woods near our house at just four months of age! It seemed like a lot for such a little pup, and we sure didn't want him to be stressed, so we all coddled him in our laps and cuddled him in our beds, and on and on, whenever we got the chance.

But dogs are pack animals, Jake, and they pay attention to our signals to figure out their perceived status. Our coddling Nomar had convinced him that he was the boss, and this is a perception you don't want a dog to have in a household with three young children, especially when one of them is you!

After two stays at Patty's house (which we dubbed "Camp Rascal"), Nomar returned to us with model behavior, but these improvements would slowly fall apart as the weeks passed, and by the time Nomar was in the throes of adolescence we knew we were in trouble. With the distance between us, Patty couldn't see us often enough to put her finger on the problem, and we didn't have the perspective to see it ourselves. Although he was always reliable on leash with his vest on, Nomar was becoming a bit of a bully with you and Mark and Marina, with increasing mouthiness, and a generally imperial attitude. He had many great skills, which he picked up effortlessly due to his extraordinary intelligence, but his obedience was selective, even with rewards. Worst of all, in the absence of training on what to do when he "found" you, Jake, Nomar took it upon himself to "retrieve" you whenever he saw you begin to run, indoors or out. This meant that Nomar was trying to pull you by your clothing, and no matter what we did, we couldn't find a way to make him stop.

That's when you taught us our next lesson about life, Jake. You quit on Nomar. And rightfully so! We promised you a friend and instead you were getting pushed around by yet another entity in your life. Your giggles and smiles were replaced by screams of frustration. You wouldn't touch Nomar. Except for walking, you just didn't want him around. You couldn't have made your thoughts any clearer, even with words.

It was supposed to be about the relationship between you and your special dog and we lost the very heart of it. We all felt horrible, and we wondered if Nomar should stay.

Patty's a bit mystical, Jake, and so am I. As Irish women, we've felt special touches of guidance along the way as we've raised all of our exceptional children. There are reasons for things, Jake. There's a reason that you are mine and I am yours. There's a reason for our meeting Patty and choosing Nomar.

And there's a reason that Pam Murphy walked through our door last December . . . it was an incredible privilege to have this top-notch trainer here in our home that day, and it all came about because Patty heeded our call for "help!" and never gave up on us. At their request, I had kept you, Mark and Marina home from school so that Pam could get the "full effect" of the challenge before us. After watching what it took to simply get all of you, including Nomar, dressed for the deep snow, out-the-door, and pointed in generally the same direction for a walk through our woods, they sized things up in a hurry, while showing us nothing but support and encouragement.

"Nomar is a one-in-a-million dog and he's capable of anything," Pam said. "He clearly understands his responsibility for keeping track of Jake, and he'll certainly find a way to alert you should Jake wander. The challenge is to reshape his response to Jake in motion so that Jake can feel more secure with Nomar. Rather than thinking about this as 'search and rescue,' let's think about this as Nomar's staying with Jake in general, and 'blocking' Jake only on your command, or only when Jake passes certain designated, off-limits markers."

Right there on the spot, she began to break the blocking behavior down into chewable pieces, teaching Nomar specific name recognition and "targeting" games which were marked and rewarded with "clicks and treats." Before we concluded, Pam agreed to add her expertise in obedience training to our case and signed on as our local trainer with a promise to work with Nomar and I at the house and all around our community on a weekly basis. All the while, Patty and her trusty video camera captured what could be a turning point in the development of assistance dogs for kids like you, Jake.

Things were beginning to look up!

"There's only one way to deal with bullies," said Pam on our first day alone. "Nomar, you're about to learn that nothing in life is free."

I always have to smile watching such a gentle, funny person "teaching Nomar a lesson," Jake. Pam couldn't make the lessons more fun for Nomar and I if she tried. Nomar waits at the door for her as soon as he smells the coffee brewing. He loves the challenge and praise, and I love the changes in him from week to week!

"It's not just about teaching specific behaviors," Pam said. "This is about knowing when to use the behaviors to shape attitude. Nomar needs to know that he's low-man on the totem pole in this house, and that he's dependent on Jake and even six-year old, timid Mark for absolutely everything he wants. So nothing will be free! Not hugs, not play, not toys, not food, not time on the bed! Nomar will have to earn everything while we're turning things around!"

Whew! She's a toughie, Jake, but it worked!

For a meal, Nomar had to sit and stay at Mark's command or yours while you boys prepared his food and water and set it on the floor. Only after your, "O.K., Nomar," could he begin to eat.

To get into the car or go through a doorway with you, Nomar had to sit and wait until everyone else had passed. Then he could go only if called.

For a game of tug or fetch, Nomar had to sit or lie down while we got the toy. He had to "drop it" at our feet or "give" into our hands periodically throughout the game to keep it going. The game had to end with a child always winning and putting the toy away. Failure to follow the rules ended the beloved game.

For a hug, Nomar had to lie down in our laps on the command, "hug." He no longer had the option of choosing.

For pets and praise, Nomar had to be performing any of his basic foundational behaviors.

For food rewards (which account for half of his diet), Nomar had to gently eat out of our hands following good behaviors. While we had a lot of "training sessions," we put the emphasis on using and rewarding Nomar's skills in practical situations.

Above all, Mr. Alpha was banished from sleeping on the beds (you should've seen the look I got when I introduced him to the pillow on the floor, Jake!). After a couple of weeks on the new regime, he was allowed to sit next to the bed and make eye contact with a child by way of asking for permission to come up. If you kids said, "Up!" he could lie quietly at the foot of the bed for stories. Any shenanigans, and he was ordered, "Off!" Sleep throughout the night remains on the floor.

Finally, Pam taught me how to harness good ol' Duke to put Nomar in his place. Since he was always at my side anyway during training sessions, Pam suggested that I just reward Duke with food treats and praise every time Nomar chose to disregard my commands. This caught Nomar's attention in a hurry!

Obviously, a critical piece of this whole program was making sure that Nomar would be gentle with his mouth while playing games or eating out of your hands, Jake, or any else's. I was a little worried about this and told Pam.

Naturally, she had a plan.

"It's good that he's mouthy at this age," she said.

"Huh?"

"It's good," she repeated. "You can't teach bite inhibition unless you have some mouthy behaviors to work with. The most dangerous dogs are the ones who never use their mouths as puppies."

To teach Nomar bite inhibition she initiated a game of tug-of-war with Nomar, and sure enough within a few minutes he grabbed the rope too close to her hand and his teeth grazed her fingers. "OW!!!" she squealed in a high pitched tone, just two inches from Nomar's nose. He immediately jumped back, head down and tail tucked between his legs, and he has never used his teeth roughly with any of us again.

The power of appropriate communication, Jake! This was how his mother and siblings would scold Nomar for not being careful with his teeth, and so he was able to understand our message using this technique.

The last thing Pam wanted to shape up in terms of basic obedience was Nomar's recall. Like you, Jake, Nomar was selectively obedient to my calls outdoors, coming consistently during training sessions, but ignoring me during less structured times . . . easy to understand when I consider how much you two love our beautiful, wide-open landscape. But this was not a safe situation, to say the least!

"We're starting all over with a new command," said Pam.

Starting over?!

"You're going to use an Emergency Recall approach and he's going to be 100 percent consistent with it. Here's how it works. . . .

"Starting in the house from short range, you're going to call Nomar when he's distracted with something else, saying, 'Nomar, here!' You are then going to hold up a delicious treat for him.

"When he comes to you, you're going to feed him the treat over a 30 second period! This is long! All the while, you're going to tell him how wonderful he is. You might finish it off by giving him his favorite toy or playing his favorite game. You're going to do this indoors a lot, gradually increasing the distance, and going on different floors, and when he's out of your sight and during times of big distractions. But you're always going to do it when you're absolutely sure he's going to respond and you're going to be successful. You're always going to give him the 30-second reward! Always! Over time, 'Nomar, here!' will come to mean more satisfaction for Nomar than anything else he does. This will ensure that when you really need him to obey in an emergency, he'll do it . . . every time."

Of course, Pam was right, Jake. We built this up over the course of several months, very gradually. Just last week, when Nomar was tearing after you at full speed across the fields outside (with a vision of a torn jacket forming in my mind), I yelled, "Nomar, here!" He turned instantly from 50 yards away and came to me . . . as he does every time. After the reward, I allowed him to return to you, which he did eagerly, but submissively.

With Pam and Patty's guidance and upbeat, supportive natures, Jake, things really began to come together! We were figuring out our amazing dog and Nomar was stepping up to the plate, becoming all that we knew he could be . . . reliable and obedient, but also fun, adventurous, playful and affectionate with every member of our family. He learned many new commands during this time, but one of the most valuable was simply, "Go to (any member of the family)," which meant that Nomar should go and lie down at the individual's feet. Do you remember all the fun you, Marina and Mark had sending Nomar all over the house as we practiced "go to," Jake? You really ran poor Nomar around . . . this is my favorite command because it turned around Nomar's tendency to pull on your clothing when you moved. At last, I could see both of you beginning to relax together.

Now, with this solid foundation, Pam and Dad and I felt we were ready to tackle "blocking." The concept was to train Nomar to block your forward motion by having him run in front of you and hold a firm "stand/stay" on our command or by using visual markers to cue the behavior. Blocking could be used around our yard, at the park, or in any location where we felt your bolting was a risk. Pam added a nice touch to it by helping us teach Nomar to block in any direction you were running (frontward, backwards, sideways), since we thought you might respond to the block by bolting in a new direction. As always, Nomar picked up on the steps of this training quickly.

Next, Pam and Dad and I practiced giving Nomar the command to "block" someone else in motion. Once again, it was easier to practice this indoors, before we rolled our work outdoors. Nomar picked it right up, Jake, and we were ready to block you kids!

It's a fun game that we practice outdoors. We learned from our early work with hide-n-seek that we shouldn't ask Nomar to "block" within the limits of the yard, where we want him to feel relaxed and to play with all of you at ease. So we practice blocking at the edges of the yard, to reinforce the boundaries with everyone, especially you and Nomar. He is so aware of your every move, Jake, that you can't get near those boundaries now without Nomar alerting us with a bark or by running to you. And you've shown much greater awareness of those boundaries because of all of this, and now look to us for permission before you cross. Hooray!

But Dad and I know that boundaries in new places are not so obvious, so we're still working with Pam on using "Stop and Go" signs as the signals for blocking away from home as another layer in our safety net, and we'll see how that goes. Now that it's springtime, we'll go over boundaries with both of you in new places by walking the edges and practicing blocking when we first arrive. It's a valuable exercise for both of you.

A year ago today, we brought you to see what we hoped would be your new friend for the first time. How you've both grown! I've told you about Nomar's growth, Jake. Now let's talk about yours.

As I've said, you were so anxious. The two to five words you could get out at a time didn't come close to expressing all that was in your eyes. It was clear that there was so much you wanted to ask and say. It must have been so frustrating for you, Jake.

But thankfully, as the year went on, the Mayer-Johnson picture symbols began to help . . . more, and more, and more. We used them the way Dr. Greenspan and Dr. Wieder counseled—in many varied experiences, which were highly meaningful to you. We used them to challenge your reasoning, to help you ask and answer the "Who, what, when, where and why" questions related to your life. You were using them to make choices on places to go, foods to eat, games to play, and more. You used them to express your emotions in very simple ways. We used them to check in and out with you as each of us came and went around the house—bringing you to the "Bye, Bye Board" to show you where we were going and when we'd come back. We built a PECS book for you with 250 icons—including sentence starters, nouns, verbs, adjectives, adverbs and prepositions, all color-coded to make sentence-building easier. We included a schedule section in it to help you keep track and negotiate about what was happening. We carried the book with us wherever we went, loading it with new vocabulary as needed.

And you loved this, Jake! Pretty soon, you began showing a lot more initiative in getting your point across. You began dragging us around by the hand to point to things, gesturing and using the words you had to let us know what you meant. Finally, it seemed like trying to communicate was worth the effort for you!

The symbols were helping, thank God, but they were also limiting in so many ways. If only you could read and write, Dad and I thought. You'd known your letters and their phonetic sounds for quite some time, so we thought surely you were almost there! But your teachers felt that you couldn't seem to grasp the concept of reading "a word," and you were only tracing letters in handwriting practice. Reading and writing still seemed like a long way off.

That's when another divine inspiration came to us, Jake. Dad and I realized that we needed to harness your strength as a visual learner to help you make the leap to reading . . . What about learning to read while sounding out and typing the words that give you the symbols you understand?

There is a wonderful word-processing program developed by Mayer-Johnson called "Writing with Symbols 2000 (WWS)." Basically, it puts a symbol above the word and says the word as you complete typing the word. Visual . . . Auditory . . . Motor, all in one package. Hey, it was worth a try! We kept the Greenspan mantra in mind, "high-affect, meaningful situations related to Jake's life," and we began with baby steps. Several times a day, Jake, Dad and I asked you to come to the computer and type about your own experiences. At first, you couldn't even find the keys on the keyboard, much less the words to tell us what you did that day. So we gave you the words, and held your hands as you hunted for the keys while we sounded out:

"Today I went to the park with Mommy."

"I am going skating with Marina."

"I went to the store with Mommy."

It was a start. You were able to "read" back what you'd typed each time, and you clearly understood whether we were typing about the future or the past, but you still weren't spelling or composing on your own.

Then one day, you answered my question, "What did you do today, Jake?"

"Swim," you said.

"What??" (We did go swimming that day!)

"Swim."

"O.K., let's type about it."

You laid your hands into my trembling palms, Jake, and I felt you type on your own: "Today, I went swimming in the pool."

Alleluia!

It's a very original way to learn to read, Jake, but it's working! We all get it now, the folks at school, all of us at home. Sure, we work on the more traditional exercises, too, to polish up the edges of your curriculum. But we all know that the real action lies in helping you type about your life and yourself.

Around December, Drs. Greenspan and Wieder suggested that we stretch these Language Experience Stories you were typing into meatier dialogues which would challenge your reasoning and your ability to hang in there for longer interactions. You were still just typing one or two fairly concrete sentences at a time (occasionally on your own, but often with just a light, fingertip touch from us beneath your forearms for focus and connection), so it seemed like a tall order.

And then, another beautiful, small moment came our way.

You were in the bathtub on a dreary evening in March, Jake, laughing wildly for no apparent reason. Nomar was peeking at you over the edge of the tub, ever vigilant. I have to admit, I was really tired with Dad away on a business trip, and I wasn't exactly up for any shenanigans. Your laughing continued as you got dressed, and you weren't responding to any of my questions or interactions about the source. Mark came in to see what all the commotion was about, and as usual, was a little intimidated by your wildness. Fortunately, the computer was nearby . . ."Hi Jake," I typed.

"Hi Mommy," you typed.

"Why are you laughing a lot?"

"I am laughing at Nomar."

"Why are you laughing at Nomar?"

"I am laughing at Nomar because Nomar was playing with me my dog."

"Yes, Nomar is your special dog, Jake. I'm glad you were having fun with Nomar. Do you like Nomar?"

"Yes, I like Nomar."

"Why do you like Nomar?"

"I like Nomar because Nomar is my dog."

"Yes, Nomar is your friend, Jake. He will always play with you and love you very much."

(At this point, before I could type another question, Jake, you jumped in and typed again.)

"I am happy because Nomar and Mommy love me and play with me."

"Nomar and Mommy will always play with you and love you, Jake. What would you like to do now?" (The wild laughing had stopped.)

"I want to sleep now."

"O.K., can Nomar lie down in your bed, too?"

"Yes, Nomar can lie down too."

"Good night, Jake."

"Good night, Mommy."

(While this dialogue was occurring, Mark had been lying on the floor next to us, cuddled up with Nomar, listening to everything. For the first time, he asked to join you and Nomar in your bed for stories, Jake.) I typed . . .

"Hey, Jake, Mark wants to come in your bed, too. Is that O.K.?"

"Yes, Mark can come too."

Upon hearing the sweet giggles from your bedroom, Marina soon joined us, and the three of you, along with Nomar, snuggled up in your bed for stories. It was one of the nicest moments I've ever experienced as a mother. Jake, this was the first time you ever typed about a relationship, and it was the first time Mark ever asked for special time with you. This scenario has repeated itself many times since then in many different ways. And always, in the middle of it all, is our golden bridge, Nomar, just as we'd hoped.

At age nine, you're not an anxious little boy anymore, Jake. You're a tall, handsome guy with a beautiful smile and a calm, knowing look. You carry yourself with confidence and you're happy to express your thoughts and feelings if given a little time to type and read. You're eager to play and grateful for friendship. And you can't get enough of the beautiful friend you call "Nomar."

The future has never been so bright, Jake. May God bless both of you on your birthdays, and may He give you and Nomar all of the love and joy that you have given to us.

With all of my love,
Mommy

How to Train the Blocking Technique
Pamela Murphy and Kathleen Vranos

- Start by teaching a firm "stand/stay" against a wall indoors. Use a hand signal to reinforce the "stay" command. Tug on your dog's collar, trying to entice him forward to make sure he will hold the "stand/stay."

- Next, tackle the "stand/stay" away from the wall, walking into your dog a little and making him hold his stance, even against the pressure of your legs.

- Now use clicker training to teach targeting. Hanging an open hand down near a leg, click and treat when your dog touches his nose to your hand, moving him all around your body.

- Next, tuck hands in closer to your legs, and attach the command "block." Click and treat when he makes contact with your leg, and quickly use hand "stand/stay" signal to make him hold the stance, even as you lean into his body.

- Next, practice this in motion, walking or jogging forward slowly. Holding a hand close to your legs as the target, give the "block" command and click and treat when he makes contact with the front of your legs, nudging in and encouraging him to hold his stand/stay.

- Now try changing direction (backwards or sideways), using the hand as the target again, and giving the "block" command.

- Click and treat when he makes contact with legs in the right direction.

Kathleen Vranos is a mother of three who has been very successful in finding ways to communicate with her son, Jake, despite the challenge his autism presents. This letter is submitted to *The Golden Bridge* with special thanks to Patty Dobbs Gross of the North Star Foundation for her vision, and to Pam Murphy of NB Productions for helping to make it a reality.

20

Training an Assistance Dog for Public Access

Shari Dehouwer

It takes a whole village to raise a child.
—African proverb

Tommy and his family decided to take his assistance dog, Rex, out on a family outing to the mall. Though Rex had never been to the mall before, his family felt confident he would be the same well-behaved dog he was at home and in the neighborhood.

The family piled in the car with Rex. Remembering all the previous trips to play at the park, Rex paced and whined during the drive. Upon arrival, Tommy put the leash on Rex and walked toward the mall. Tommy tried to keep Rex walking quietly at his side, but Rex was just too excited.

When they entered the mall, Rex pulled Tommy over to an indoor garden and immediately lifted his leg to relieve himself. Tommy tried to tell Rex "no!" but it was too late. Embarrassed, Tommy's parents realized they had forgotten to let Rex relieve himself before entering the mall.

They went to the food court for lunch. Tommy struggled to handle Rex, so Mom took the leash while Tommy walked beside them. Rex settled down a little but continued to pull. As they got closer to the mall he began to lower his head to the ground and sniff the floor. Mom didn't think that was an appropriate behavior, but she wasn't sure what to do.

When they turned the corner near the food court, the family's neighbor appeared and waved excitedly at the family. Rex barked, ran to the neighbor and jumped up to greet her. The neighbor greeted Rex enthusiastically, while she rubbed and patted him. Mom struggled to regain control of Rex and finally got him calmed down.

The family decided to find a table to sit down and have lunch. Rex walked calmly to the table, but near the table he lunged toward the floor to grab two French Fries that had fallen on the floor. The family purchased their lunch and ate while Rex sat near the table begging and looking for more tidbits on the floor.

A security guard came to the table and questioned the family about having a dog in the mall. Tommy proudly announced that Rex was his assistance dog. The security guard had seen other assistance dogs in the mall but the behaviors Rex displayed just didn't seem appropriate. By this time Mom was exhausted from trying to walk with Rex anyway, so the family left the mall for home.

This situation occurred because the proper public access training did not take place. Assistance dogs that have been properly taught to perform trained tasks to mitigate their partners' disabilities should do so comfortably and reliably, regardless of what unexpected distractions they may encounter. Attentive to their handlers, assistance dogs are relaxed in situations they would never encounter as pets or working in a home environment.

Selecting an Appropriate Dog for Public Access

Assistance dogs working in public places must learn to disregard food on the floor in restaurants, navigate crowded shopping malls, ignore attention from the admiring public, be relaxed with new and possibly frightening situations and be on duty and focused on their handlers when asked to perform tasks. A properly trained assistance dog team can relax and enjoy public outings. The dog will have had many hours of experience learning to work amidst heavy distractions, and the handler will have been trained to give direction to and rely upon the dog's skills. A great handler/dog team works in partnership in public situations and the handler is knowledgeable of his access rights under the law. The handler should be able to comfortably deal with the access challenges, even if this involves calmly educating the people involved.

Not all dogs can work comfortably in public, though they may well be excellent pets and do helpful tasks around the home. An assistance dog can perform beautifully at home, but be stressed, distracted and reactive in public. The proper dog to work in public access situations is chosen for its stability and then given many, many hours of additional training with increasing levels of distraction.

A suitable candidate for working as an assistance dog in public access situations must be of sound temperament, with a quiet and mellow disposition. A dog showing reactivity and aggression would be a liability to the assistance dog partner and could possibly put the public at risk. Some reactivity can be managed, but ideally the handler would not have to manage the dog's problems and the dog would be comfortable and non-reactive to strange sights and sounds.

Debi Davis, assistance dog trainer and handler of Peek, recipient of the 1999 Delta Society National Service Dog of the Year award, feels that public access training is more challenging than training the specialized tasks assistance dogs perform. "Public access training is by far the most intensive and time-consuming part of service dog training, because the dog must be so rock-solid amidst tremendous distractions," she cautions.

"What makes public access work so challenging? It's asking a lot of any dog to work in an ever-changing human environment. At home, if you drop a toothbrush, your dog fetches it without a problem. However, asking the same dog to perform a simple retrieval on a busy city sidewalk, with buses backfiring three feet away, is another ball game. Add a dollop of screaming toddler trying to pull the dog's tail, a skateboard careening by, and the dog's stress can escalate astronomically.

"It takes a dog with a very mellow, stable personality to handle the stress of performing normal assistance tasks in public. While walking through a park with his owner, the assistance dog cannot lunge at or chase a squirrel, chipmunk, cat, loose dog or running child, even when full of energy and excitement. Inability to ignore these types of distractions may put the handler in jeopardy or cause an injury.

"For instance, if the handler is using a dog for balance, a quick movement or step away by the dog could cause the person to fall. An assistance dog with public access will be exposed to shopping carts with squeaky wheels, loudspeakers that blare, backfiring cars, inconsiderate joggers, and huge trailer trucks that will rumble past them. In a restaurant, no matter how hungry that dog may be, he cannot sniff the floor nor eat bits of steak, hot dog or french fries."

Public Access Training for the Dog

Before public access training, dogs are taught basic foundation skills. The dog is then taught to perform these basic skills with increasing levels of distraction. The dog learns to perform behaviors such as sit, down, stay, leave it and heel in the park, around other dogs, around other people, near traffic, around other animals, at ball games, in front of the grocery store, etc. There are a myriad of places available to train before taking the dog into restaurants or other public places.

As new skills are taught, they are "proofed" in new situations with increasing distractions. The trainer teaches the dog to maintain focus and ignore the surrounding sights and sounds. As Debi says, "In order to be comfortable working in public, there are certain basic skills that all assistance dogs must master, regardless of their partner's disability. While it is tempting to focus training on the amazingly complex tasks that assistance dogs are often taught, a primary focus of training should be on the more mundane foundation skills. Is the dog really comfortable doing a one-hour down/stay? Is walking quietly by his partner's side a well-entrenched habit for the dog? Does he have any fear of screeching children running towards him? Has 'leave it' been so thoroughly trained that he doesn't give a second thought to that french fry on the ground? Can the dog pass by another dog or a cat without becoming aroused?

"Fluency in these skills enables a dog to relax in public. Lack of attention to these skills will produce a dog who may be able to do impressive things, but who may always be somewhat on edge and tense in public. Assistance dogs must also be taught to accept a wide variety of situations and circumstances. Dogs do not generalize quickly, and often perceive situations quite differently than humans.

"Imagine being at a bus stop with your dog when the bus pulls up and people begin getting on board. From a block away, you see a large man in an overcoat waving a closed umbrella over his head while running toward the bus hollering, 'Hold the bus! Hold the bus!' The human knows this is no threat; it's just a man trying not to miss the bus. But what might the dog be thinking when he sees an unknown human running towards him, hollering and waving a threatening stick?

"Just because a dog seems unflappable in the mall does not mean that he will be comfortable at the airport or in a city park, where the distractions are quite different. And although a dog may enjoy riding in a car or bus, this doesn't guarantee his comfort on a plane when the landing gear comes up, or when a pocket of turbulence causes the floor to shake.

"The dog should be slowly and systematically acclimated to many different settings, including malls, grocery stores, medical facilities, airports, stadiums, restaurants, and any other place that their future partner might decide to go. Initial exposure should be to relatively calm, quiet places. As the dog gains confidence he can be taken to noisier, more crowded locations. It is important to recognize and prepare for new situations that might be stressful to the dog. Have treats readily available to reward the dog for calmness and acceptance of new situations while maintaining focus on the handler. As the dog gains experience in a variety of settings, his confidence and comfort level with new situations will increase."

Dogs that are performing reliably with many different distractions are then taught the special skills they will need to assist their partners. When a dog can perform specialized assistance tasks and focus on his handler no matter what the distraction, an assessment is made of the dog while he is working in public. Assistance dogs that can work reliably in all settings are then considered to be fluent in public access.

Public Access Training and Education for the Handler

The human partner in an assistance dog team must know how to work with the dog in public access situations, understand the laws that apply to access with a dog, manage the dog's toileting schedule, and keep the dog safe while navigating through crowds, on public transportation, during travel and in everyday situations that may be unusual and novel for a dog. The human partner must learn to recognize stress in the dog and manage errands, work, school and task time in way that keeps the dog comfortable and relaxed.

Access challenges do arise and the handler must know how to advocate for the team and, at times, diffuse concerned comments from the uneducated public.

Etiquette for the Assistance Dog Team in Public

An assistance dog should not interfere or inconvenience the public in any way. There are people who don't like dogs, are afraid of dogs or allergic to dogs. Many people have never seen a dog working in public and are quite startled when they sit down in a restaurant and see a dog lying under the table, or standing next to them in a small elevator. It's very important to leave a good impression with the public. We want to insure the rights of all people with disabilities to continue to work with assistance dogs in public access situations.

An assistance dog should:

- Lie quietly while the handler is dining without grooming itself or scratching.
- Be allowed to toilet only in areas where people do not sit or walk, and the handler should have a method for cleaning up and disposing of droppings immediately.

- Move purposefully next to its handler while working, staying between 12–18 inches from the handler's side unless it has been cued to perform another task.
- Work comfortable and reliably, giving its handler focus when necessary.

An assistance dog should not:

- Be allowed to wander in public.
- Initiate social contact without its handler's permission.
- Sniff, beg, or eat from the floor in a restaurant or public setting.
- Bite, snap, bark, whine, or growl, causing a disruption or danger to the public.
- Block the areas where the public will be walking.
- Press against, jump on, or sniff people.

Working in public access situations with a specially trained assistance dog is a privilege and a joy. A combination of the right dog with proper training of both dog and human partners will create a successful working team.

Shari Dehouwer founded Discovery Dogs in San Rafael, California in 1995; the program offers fully trained assistance dogs and dog training support and advocacy to individuals with mobility limiting disabilities interested in participating in the assistance skills training of their own dogs. Shari has also partnered up with North Star to help train a golden named Max for a young boy named Steven, who is on the autism spectrum.

The Evolution of a Professional Therapy Dog Handler

Roles and Goals for Success

Kris Butler

> *Children and dogs are as necessary to*
> *the welfare of the country as Wall Street*
> *and the railroads.—Harry S Truman*

Something important is happening in hospitals, treatment centers, and schools all across the United States. Creative educators, health care professionals, and savvy dog handlers are successfully connecting children with visiting dogs in ways that enhance healing, learning, and self-awareness.

"Visiting dogs" refers to those dogs that are brought into facilities by handlers who either work or volunteer there. Visiting dogs are neither resident dogs that live at facilities, nor assistance or service dogs that are partnered with people who are patients, students or clients at facilities. Professionally speaking, visiting dogs are considered modalities.

Several popular terms refer to the concept of dogs working in human service venues, including pet therapy, pet-facilitated therapy, animal-assisted therapy, animal-assisted activities, and pet visitations. The dogs themselves are usually referred to as "therapy dogs," but it is inappropriate to refer to everything that visiting dogs do as "therapy." This author believes that appropriate dogs not only assist, they enhance, opportunities for people to heal, learn, and improve the quality of their lives. For those reasons, I refer to educational and therapeutic programs that include visiting dogs as "animal-enhanced programs."

In 1976, Elaine Smith founded the first volunteer visiting dog and handler registry, Therapy Dogs International, Inc. The popularity of "therapy dogs" has grown among volunteers since then, and now there are at least two additional registries, Therapy Dogs, Inc. and Delta Society's Pet Partners. Thousands of volunteer dog and handler teams have registered through these organizations and visit with adults and children in local communities.

Volunteer animal-enhanced programs have introduced educators and health care providers to the benefits dogs can bring into professional environments. Now, growing numbers of visiting dogs are actually professional partners with the teachers, school counselors, mental health professionals, and therapists with whom they live. At the end of the workday, these dogs go back home with their handlers and become normal family pet dogs.

The popularity of these professional partnerships is most likely due to the growth of goal-directed animal-enhanced interventions, which are facilitated by human service professionals. Many human service professionals have determined that the best way to access a consistent canine modality is to have it available continuously. Sometimes, issues that surround confidentiality, scheduling, and the availability of teams that are appropriate to the task preclude participation of volunteer teams.

Educators and health care providers who work with their own dogs within their professional environments are referred to by this author as dual-role handlers. Dual-role handlers are the newest breed of handler—they handle their dogs and facilitate interventions.

Just as visiting animal programs have evolved from volunteer visitations into goal-directed and professional programs, I, too, started out with a volunteer's focus and later began working professionally with my dogs. My first steady visiting program was a volunteer "gig" with Partner, my son's golden retriever, at a residential long term care center for veterans, located in our city. During that same time frame when Partner and I were developing a relationship with our veteran friends, I began taking him to a church youth program. I can see now that I learned a lot about developing experiential education and therapeutic exercises at that church with Partner. Back then I was just trying to keep a small group of young children and a couple of teenage assistants actively engaged. My son and daughter were enrolled in Youth Club at our church on Wednesday evenings. To do my part, I helped with activities, about 45 minutes devoted to fun and fellowship. My group included six first- and second-grade children. I took Partner about once a month. Partner worked with me at church, off and on, for about three years.

Sometimes our small group sat on the floor, petting or brushing Partner, discussing our similarities as well as our differences. Partner's big golden head would fill up an entire six-year-old lap as, one by one, they took turns at "holding" the dog while they spoke. I learned that some children like to pet and nurture while they talk, and others prefer to brush and perform functional tasks. I learned that the best thing Partner did was the way he made the children feel simply by getting down on their level and gazing into their eyes while they spoke. He "received" them.

The children also loved that Partner would "do things" for them. We developed the "Tennis Ball Game," which included tiny pictures of crosses, arks, mangers, and stars taped individually to tennis balls. Each child identified one of the pictures, and gave the group an explanation or story about the picture. Then the child removed the picture, threw the ball and gave Partner the cue to retrieve. That game taught me that deep discussions can center on anything you want to stick on a tennis ball.

During Youth Club, high school-aged members of our church served as teachers' helpers. From the teens assigned to our group, I learned that what works well for young children and visiting dogs also works well for teens. I intended for the teens to be involved in a more adult-like role, but they enjoyed the games so much that they usually did not differentiate themselves from the younger children during these activities. The teenagers taught me that interactions with an appropriate visiting dog can bring out the inner child in almost everyone.

Back then, I learned how Partner's behavior effectively drew the children in and helped them feel safe about expressing their ideas. These early experiences were validated by experts years later as I explored ropes and adventure courses as models for new experiential programs to wrap my dogs around. Partner and Youth Club taught me ways to develop and deliver similar exercises and games for teachers and counselors in special education programs. I presented Partner in a manner consistent with meeting the goals of the church program and Partner received the children in a manner that encouraged participation.

I believe the fundamental canine behaviors that enhanced a church-based program back then are the same behaviors that are needed today to enhance the many settings that include visiting dogs.

In 1995, Partner and I got our first professional contract, offering weekly services with therapists at the largest rehabilitation hospital in Oklahoma City. Our pediatric patients worked hard to overcome the effects of disease, accidents, and developmental disabilities.

In this setting, when Partner's young patients brushed and petted him, they were practicing balance and motor skills. When they put a harness on him and took him for a walk, they practiced problem solving skills, motor integration, balance, trunk control and endurance. When his patients threw a tennis ball for Partner and gave him the cue to retrieve, they worked on speech, memory, and cognitive skills in addition to using their arms, hands and upper bodies. Beyond his skill, Partner made the children feel safe and accepted, simply by getting down on their level while they worked with him. He received them and encouraged them to participate, just as he'd received the children in the church program. I continued working at that hospital with Partner and the dogs that followed him for nine years.

While I was working with a soon to be retired Partner, Cookie came into my life. Cookie was a confident, friendly young adult standard poodle in need of a home, and so we became family and soon after that, we became professional partners.

She soared through training and socialization exercises, participating eagerly; her first months of work with me in the hospital were stellar. With exemplary walking, retrieving, and positioning skills and her solicitous behavior, Cookie was a huge hit. But after a relatively short time, I saw her behavior changing, first as she slowed down or hesitated when greeting some of our adult patients, and shortly after that, when I read "Do I have to?" in her body language. I reluctantly removed Cookie from the hospital program and replaced her with a less dynamic Labrador retriever named Scout, who excelled in that environment until his retirement several years ago.

At first, I was disappointed that Cookie hadn't shared my enthusiasm for the structured, goal-directed exercises we'd developed for therapists and patients at the hospital. What was wrong with her? Hindsight—and Cookie—showed me what a fine thing it was that Cookie wasn't the dog I originally wanted her to be.

I had begun exploring avenues for dogs to help special education students develop communication and social skills. I'd researched ropes courses, adventure courses, farm animal and equine programs and it seemed to me that hands-on exercises with dogs could prove equally successful at creating therapeutic and educational metaphor. Careful preparation, persistence, and Cookie being simply herself resulted in experiences beyond my imagination. Cookie and I worked together for the next three years with special education teachers and counselors in three different facilities. Our programs included an alternative high school program for adjudicated teens, elementary school children identified as having learning disabilities, elementary school children identified as having emotional difficulties, and a group of elementary school children identified as being at-risk.

We developed programs that taught individual students to work Cookie through modified obedience exercises while the group observed, identified, and discussed Cookie's behavior. When the children communicated their needs appropriately, Cookie responded. When the children communicated in ways that Cookie did not understand, or in ways that confused her, Cookie was free to respond naturally, which helped the children learn to manage their situations. Cookie did not shut down or become anxious as a more sensitive or less secure dog might have. When students stopped to breathe and reorganize, Cookie stopped too, made eye contact, and leaned in or nudged a hand in support. Through her connection with them, Cookie enthusiastically received each student with whom she worked. By completing tasks with them, Cookie contributed to feelings of success among groups of children for whom success was often elusive.

The exercises helped the children meet goals such as effectively communicating, following instructions, sequencing, offering and receiving compliments, and exercising self-control within a group. Important preparation and processing led to staff facilitated discussions that focused on a wide variety of topics that related to working with Cookie: overcoming obstacles, causes of stress in dogs, causes of stress in people, signs of stress, calming techniques, body language, personal territory and intimidation, boundaries, how dogs learn, how people learn, how behaviors change, and assertiveness without anger.

Cookie hadn't "fit" into a hospital environment, but she thrived in highly active experiential school programs. One job wasn't right for her, but a changed environment changed the dog's behavior. Interestingly, Cookie's national "therapy dog" registration was based on an evaluation given in a mirrored room used to teach dance at a community recreation center. The evaluation site resembled neither a hospital nor a public school.

Today, one of the most important challenges facing visiting dogs is human non-awareness of the complex, stressful environments in which the dogs are being required to participate for long periods of time. Creative professional people have developed high expectations of their dogs, yet most people still rely on assessment tools that were developed years ago to evaluate volunteer handlers and dogs for brief meet-and-greet visits that might occur once a week, at most. Additionally, no one gives as much attention to whether the dogs are actually enhancing therapeutic and educational processes, as much as they consider whether dogs have passed an often unrelated test or evaluation at some point in their lives.

The goals of visiting programs might be therapeutic in nature or they might be educational in nature, or both. Some standard concepts can be applied to every visiting process. Effective visiting processes consist of handlers who appropriately present their dogs and dogs that appropriately receive the people being visited.

Partner and Cookie taught me that dogs facilitate healing and learning when they contribute to feelings of safety, comfort, and connection. The behaviors that are required to make people feel safe, comfortable, and connected to visiting dogs remain consistent. However, dogs' and handlers' abilities to demonstrate specific behaviors depend on environmental factors, as well as team skills and talents. The best way to determine whether dogs are appropriate for specific environments is by assessing their behaviors moment-to-moment within those environments.

Every visiting dog's role is to receive the person or people with whom the dog is interacting. The process of being received is what gives people the perception that there is a connection or bond between themselves and the dog. Children safely assume that no dog is concerned with the young person's physical appearance, nor do dogs make judgments based on any human's social status. Dogs don't care about clothes or correct grammar. Dogs live in the moment. Past achievements, mistakes, and physical changes that have occurred in the lives of people they are visiting seem irrelevant to dogs. Children being received by visiting dogs do not have to earn approval; approval and acceptance are freely given. Appropriate visiting dogs communicate, "You are just right. We are just right. This is enough." It is primarily that perception which motivates children to participate in therapy, learning, discussion, or other targeted activities.

There are specific identifiable canine behaviors that tend to enhance the perception of a bond between the dog and the people being visited. Initiating physical contact, staying engaged, making eye contact, respecting personal boundaries, and allowing his behaviors to be redirected all suggest connection. It should be apparent that the dog wants to be there!

Canine behaviors that reduce the perception of a bond and hinder the visiting process include disinterest, reluctance to engage, disregard for personal boundaries, and any conduct that might be interpreted as aggressive or stress-related.

The first question handlers should address is whether their dogs want to visit. When invited (but not being ordered by their handlers), dogs that enjoy visiting with unfamiliar people will initiate contact. Dogs that are comfortable and enjoy unfamiliar people will remain engaged and will offer at least some eye contact. Conversely, dogs who are not willing to initiate contact or remain engaged probably do not want to be touched and petted by unfamiliar people.

Nothing else dogs do compares to the kinds of intrinsically stressful social interaction that takes place when they visit clinical, educational, or post-trauma situations. No other canine-related event, no sport nor competition requires a dog to enter the intimate zones of unfamiliar humans and remain there for several minutes of petting and hugging. Touching is the most intimate act of communication. Touching is an integral part of almost every animal-enhanced intervention and no one would suggest that people stop petting visiting dogs. However, it is crucial that handlers determine whether the dogs being petted are seeking out this intimate contact, or just obediently tolerating an invasion of their personal space.

Behaviors that can be redirected or interrupted give people a greater sense of connection and control. Simply being able to cause a dog to make eye contact by saying the dog's name is enough to create the sense that a connection has been made.

While friendliness and confidence are necessary qualities, visiting dogs must also respect personal boundaries. Dogs must wait for permission before initiating contact. Jumping, pawing, and licking (beyond the few quick and respectful face-to-face calming licks) can seem intrusive, even abusive, to the children we work with.

Dogs who demonstrate behaviors that can be interpreted as aggressive should not visit. Sometimes rumbles and moans are misinterpreted as growls; and sometimes handlers identify growls as rumbles and moans. Some dogs bark when they are excited. Barking dogs may be friendly to a fault, but children being visited will not feel safe if they interpret barking as a threatening behavior. The reasons behind a visiting dog's behavior are never as important as the effects of that behavior on the people being visited.

Most symptoms of stress are universal. People know stress when they see it, even in other species. Not only is it risky and abusive to visit with a dog that is stressing, but people being visited will ascertain that the dog does not wish to visit with them.

Unfortunately, the effects of real human emotion, the stress of having unfamiliar humans grabbing and hugging them, and overcoming sensory stimuli are too overwhelming for some dogs. These are not simple training issues—these are humane issues. Just because some dogs are willing to tolerate environments or populations that are overwhelming to them does not mean people have license to exploit their visiting partners.

Past experience tells individuals what to expect next. Experience is the teacher that causes dogs and handlers to anticipate visiting with either positive or negative expectations. It is important to note that a dog's perception can differ greatly from a human's perception of the very same event. There is a strong social connection between handlers and their visiting dogs. The dogs, after all, hold the admission tickets to activities handlers enjoy very much. It's understandable that some handlers—volunteers and professionals alike—measure a degree of their worth based on the recognition they receive from their dog-related services. Sometimes handlers want to keep the team intact, even when the dog is ready to break up the act. Effective, mature handlers are able to deal with the reality of their current situation and act as their dogs' advocates.

My craft combines the magic of dogs with the science of health care and education. We've begun an amazing journey with our dogs, and now it's time to discover whether what we ask of them measures up to what each dog is designed to give. Any of us who are handlers must examine the examples of unconditional acceptance our dogs offer to us daily, and return to them the courtesy of receiving them just as they are. That requires that we learn to see them as a species closely connected to us, but intrinsically different from us. It's important for handlers to examine our own feelings, and that we not project our ambitions onto our dogs. Ethical handlers will always defer to the dogs. The message from handlers to their dogs must be clear: You are just right. We are just right. This is enough.

Kris Butler is the author of *Therapy Dogs Today* and *Therapy Dogs: Compassionate Modalities* book and DVD. She owns American Dog Obedience Center, LLC in Norman, Oklahoma. In 1995, Kris and her dog, Partner, received Delta Society's Therapy Dog of the Year award. Parts of this chapter are reprinted from *Therapy Dogs Today: Their Gifts, Our Obligation,* with permission of Kris Butler.

22

Dustin's Paw

Including an Assistance Dog in the Classroom

Diane Rampelberg

Nothing happens unless first a dream.—Carl Sandburg

To soar through the air like a bird, with currents of wind lifting your wings ever higher, to be able to bank and turn and see the entire world below—to *fly*—this has been the oldest of dreams. I, too, am a dreamer with a desire not only to fly, but to also inspire and watch others take their own graceful flight.

The Dream

As a teacher, I am fully aware of the fact that one can create innovative programs and wonderful goals and objectives, but if the student is not motivated, those plans are nothing more than a good idea. Motivation is difficult for special children for whom simple movements require a major effort. The act of communication becomes a grueling task when muscles won't move at will and language processing is difficult. Sometimes a child's "will" to make the next step towards independence gets lost in the myo-

This chapter was adapted from *Dustin's Paw, 2003 Interactive Learning and Therapy Techniques*, copyright © 2003 by Diane Rampelberg. All rights reserved.

213

pic focus of therapeutic protocol. But what if there was a wind that could generate a lift beneath our special children's wings?

In 1997 my son who had wanted a dog for years—specifically a golden retriever—finally convinced my husband to let him have one. But, as is usually the case in life, there was a catch: he would eventually have to give the dog up. My husband was very concerned that when Thomas left for college we would be "stuck" with the dog. So, he consented to bringing a dog into our lives only if Thomas would give the dog up and the raising of the dog would in some way benefit others. On December 23, 1997 we brought home a very special Christmas present, an eight-week old Canine Companion for Independence golden Lab puppy named Dustin to raise.

Over the course of our adventure raising this puppy, I was amazed at what was occurring. Not only did I see what the puppy was doing in my son's life and my husband's life—not to mention my own, but I was seeing amazing things happen in others lives as well. As we worked through the various puppy-training exercises, particularly the socialization experiences with children, I was awed at how the puppy's gentle urging and unconditional love seemed to bring such joy into their lives.

Fourteen months later we turned Dustin in for more advanced training at CCI, and Thomas made the decision to raise one more puppy for CCI before he began college. We all missed the first puppy but busied ourselves raising the second. I don't think a day went by that didn't hear us pray for Dustin to do well in his advanced training and develop to serve the person for whom he'd been created. Each month we eagerly awaited his progress reports from CCI (Canine Companions for Independence) and were particularly pleased to find that he had been selected to participate in the new operant program under the direction of Bob and Marian Bailey.

In the meantime, the dream began forming in my heart and mind. It had now become abundantly clear to me that the bond between dogs and humans, particularly children, could not be overstated. I had heard of the tremendous effect that a therapy dog's presence can have but I wanted more. Would it be possible to train a dog in such a way that the handler/teacher could consciously direct the dog's behavior and positioning to motivate a child to accomplish IEP (Individualized Educational Program) goals? Armed with the dream, I applied for a CCI Facility Dog to work with disabled children.

In October of 1999 CCI called to let me know that I had been accepted into the November team training. When I arrived, I was overjoyed to see the bright-eyed puppy we had turned in several months before. He had made it though advanced training and was ready to begin working. Through what I believe was providential intervention, Dustin and I were partnered together, and on November 13, 1999, we graduated from CCI as a certified facility dog team.

Harnessing the Wind

The truth is that when Dustin and I began working as a facility team in January of the year 2000 at two schools for children with disabilities, we weren't quite sure how to work together to get our dream off the ground. Not only was I struggling with how to incorporate him into the children's structured learning activities, I was also fine-tuning my own handling skills with Dustin within the context of the classroom.

I needed to figure out how to harness the wind so he could generate the inspiration. Although Dustin was operant-trained, I was not. At home he'd do the weirdest things, and I couldn't imagine what was wrong with him. In passing I mentioned his unusual behavior to Mandy Book, a friend and dog trainer. She laughed and said, "He's offering behaviors." From this day forward my adventures with a "clicker" began. I will always be eternally grateful to Mandy, Bob and Marian Bailey, Cheryl Trotter, Dick Evans, Amy Speckard, and Helix Fairweather, who patiently shared their knowledge and experience at various times throughout my education, which still continues today.

There is no doubt in my mind that operant training is the secret to training a dog to accomplish the dream. First and foremost, Dustin needs to be responsive to the children—a responsiveness that is not contrived but genuine. He is naturally a very people-oriented, social dog. Dustin's spirit has remained intact and yet allowed me to direct his behavior for the children's benefit in a very gentle and subtle manner via operant training. He is eager to learn new behaviors on the spot, and as competent on a leash as he is off; training him in a reward-based manner has not held him back from developing his full potential as an assistance dog working with children in the classroom.

In fact, there is a great deal of similarity between the structure and methodology of Dustin's training program and that of the children's educational plans. We use a series of "successive approximations" to teach skills to many of the children with whom we work. Timing, criteria, and rate of reinforcement are valuable principles to understand, whether the student has two legs or four.

Utilizing the Wind to Fly

An aircraft is heavier than air and depends on the wind to overcome gravity to fly. So it is with our students. They range in age from infants to 22-year-olds. Some are visually impaired, hearing impaired, and autistic. Others are orthopedically impaired, developmentally delayed, and mentally challenged. There are children who are emotionally disturbed, socially inept, or who have multiple overlapping disabilities; with Dustin by their side these children have been able to overcome challenges that even adults would find daunting.

I soon discovered that if you understand the secret of reaching children through assistance dogs, taking flight is a rather simple matter; the number one secret I can share with you is to focus on developing interactive activities that are not only intelligently designed to meet the children's IEP goals, but that are also great fun for the children to participate in, regardless of the educational value of the exercise. Today, on any given day in the classroom you might find a small group of children pretending they are doctors, taking care of "sick" Dustin, who wears a hospital gown and a happy expression (for his participation earns him praise and food from his handler, along with the intrinsic reward of the kind attention of the children). Or perhaps they are showing their best manners at a tea party, all of them—including Dustin—decked out in fancy tea party clothes. These interactive activities and many others are so much more than just play.

While I direct Dustin in his role, the staff and I encourage communication. We focus on receptive (ability to understand speech) and expressive language (ability to use language). Many times I act as Dustin's voice or interpreter. At other times we introduce new vocabulary words by just talking about what we are doing at the moment with Dustin. We take the time to describe what he is doing or ask him questions—for example, "Dustin, would you like a drink of water?" Both he and the children are allowed to make choices. Those children working on articulation and voice disorder problems regularly give Dustin commands to encourage clear speech. Children using augmentative-speaking devices also give Dustin commands and chose the activities they'd like to do with him. For those children who focus and attend best when holding Dustin's leash, we take advantage of this window in time to present communication icons or practice social skills. We teach sign language as Dustin responds to commands in sign and as we "play" using his Baby Kit or Beauty Parlor, Barbershop and Spa.

Other children are challenged to become better motor planners as

Dustin leads the way through specially designed obstacle courses. We have a selection of leashes especially adapted to meet our children's specific needs, so that children sensitive to tactile input or those who are orthopedically challenged can take Dustin for a comfortable and safe walk. Gross motor skills are practiced when children take Dustin for a walk or play on our special playground equipment with him. Experiences in orientation and mobility are provided as Dustin retrieves child-thrown toys that sing catchy tunes or make animal sounds. Occasions are provided to work on sensory integration problems, functional academics, and self-help skills. We have found the possibilities to be endless!

At school we travel from room to room with our little red Radio Flyer wagon loaded with Dustin's theme kits for the month and other equipment. We have a selection of leashes especially adapted so the tactilely sensitive or orthopedically impaired children can take Dustin for a walk. Other equipment includes a basketball hoop, retrievable toys of various sizes and textures, incentive stickers used for potty training, a light-extender to turn lights on and off, a rope used to open doors, and several dog storybooks.

In fact, we have created Dustin storybooks for our hearing-impaired children. These books, complete with sign language, are designed to be acted out with Dustin at school, read in the classroom without Dustin, and read again at home with parents. Titles include "Dustin Gets a Bath," "Dustin Sits On," and "Dustin Goes In and Out." We've also made videos with Dustin and the children as the actors to teach numbers and colors. Selections include "Dog's Colorful Day" and "One-Dog Canoe." Each child actor then received a video to take home. The children tend to watch these videos over and over again, easily providing the repetition that is required by some children to "get" a concept.

The Magic of the Wind

There can be an unpredictable magic in the movement of wind, and Dustin often stirs up the children's will to take their next step, whether this is a figurative or literal movement forward: he has been a vital force in helping the lame to walk, the mute to speak, and the tentative to soar high above their fear. He delivers a warm breeze to young hearts frozen with fear of the classroom and breathes a soul into the children's educational life. He swirls in and out of the classroom with the children, accompanying them onto the playground as well as the community which surrounds us on field trips; he creates a bond between us all that is as invisible as air, but no less real as a strong and steady breeze.

Working with an assistance dog in a classroom to help children socially, emotionally, and educationally requires these key components:

1. A heart for bringing independence, joy and healing.
2. A desire and commitment to train yourself and your dog to bring that independence, joy and healing.
3. Acquisition of Therapy/Assistance Dog certification.
4. Continual commitment to training your dog and educating yourself.

What Are Interactive Dog Therapy Activities?

They are practical, creative, and effective synergistic activities designed to capitalize on a dog's special magic to bring independence, joy, and healing through the use of commands, positions, and any therapy/rehabilitation equipment involved.

A spoonful of sugar (interactive activity with a dog) helps the medicine (therapy/rehabilitation process) go down in the most delightful way!

Who Sets Up and Facilitates These Activities?

Whenever the dog is working with an individual, the handler is responsible for handling the dog. This means that the handler has trained the dog in the behavior(s) necessary to do the activity and then directs and supports the dog through the activity.

If the handler is a volunteer, it is very important that he or she work closely with the professional staff caring for the client in both selection and implementation of the activities. If the professional staff is not directly involved, it is the volunteer's responsibility to discuss beforehand what she plans to do with a client. In some cases, the professional staff will play a more active role by helping to design the activities and make the decision as to which activity is appropriate. Some will even work with the volunteer and dog by supporting and guiding the client during the activity. In most cases, this is optimal and by far most effective, especially when the focus is on a specific therapeutic/rehabilitation goal.

If the dog handler is also someone who is working with the child in a professional capacity (i.e. as teacher, speech therapist, occupational therapist, physical therapist, psychologist, social worker, etc.), then he or she will be responsible for handling the dog as well as designing and implementing the interactive activity.

Facilitating Interactions

Facilitating is both the *art* and *science* of deepening the interactions between the assistance dog and the child with the goal of bringing independence, insight, joy and/or healing.

The best facilitators/handlers are those who are not noticed. They plan and train, set up the activity, get the dog in position, and then quietly support and guide the interaction to meet the desired therapeutic goal.

Facilitators/handlers are quad-dexterous people. They are aware of where their dog is, what the dog is doing, and what the dog needs at all times. They are constantly monitoring the client's mood, reactions and general state. They are in communication with the professional staff, making sure the interactions with the client are appropriate and beneficial. And they are aware of and honest about their own personal skills, what they can and cannot handle, and personal preferences.

Interactive Commands

The basic interactive commands are the foundation from which all interaction is built.

Commands need to be trained to fluency. This means the commands are "bomb proof."

1. The dog performs them regardless of what the distraction(s) is.
2. The dog does them for minimum reward.
3. The dog performs them in any environment.

A good handler understands that in order for a dog to bring independence, joy, and healing a good relationship is essential. Good relationships are built on trust. This means you need to figure out how to get the interaction needed and keep the needs of all concerned in mind. First and foremost, you need to properly train your dog. Do not ask your dog to do something he is not prepared or trained to do. Set everyone up for success. This can be done through proper positioning of the dog and client as well as safe and wise management of the activity.

The focus of this chapter is on providing an overview of the concept of using assistance dogs within an educational setting, and therefore not all aspects of properly training assistance dogs for necessary skills to work with children within the classroom are covered. It is essential that you and your dog obtain the necessary positive training and become properly certified before you attempt to work as a team with children in a classroom.

Basic Interactive Commands

Command	Definition	Use
Dog's Name	Dog looks at person issuing command.	Used to get the dog's attention.
Sit	Dog places rear end on the ground. This command comes with an implied stay.	An all purpose command used to get a dog in position for interacting with client (i.e. petting/greeting position.) and foundational behavior for other commands and activities.
Down	Dog lies body flat on the ground. Can lie either on one hip or centered between hips. This command comes with an implied stay.	Used as a petting/greeting position, to keep the dog out of harm's way or to get the dog in position for other activities. This command is, also, a foundational behavior for other commands and activities.
Here	Dog comes.	Used to bring dog to the individual who gave the command. It is effective in bringing the dog back under control as well as being used to get the dog in position to interact.
Let's Go	Dog is on two or more leashes – one for handler and one for each client. Handler guides dog by walking beside, in the rear or in front of the dog and client. Dog moves forward keeping pace with the client.	Used as the primary command to get client and dog moving together whether the client is walking or using a wheelchair, walker or other assistance device.
Stay	Dog remains in position until released.	Used as the primary command for keeping the dog in position to interact with clients as well as being foundational in other commands.
Leave It	Dog will come and work regardless of food or other distractions in the environment.	Essential safety and good manners command.
Ok	Dog takes treat gently from open hand, off spoon, plate or dish and drinks from bottle, cup or dish in appropriate manner.	Essential good manners command when food and drink are presented.
Release	Dog no longer has to do the command.	Used to let the dog know that command given is no longer in effect, to release to play and to release dog to another handler.

Commands are necessary for communication. Therefore, when thinking of commands, think *communication*. How can you use them to encourage more effective communication between dog and client, client and other individuals, and/or client and a group? The communication between dog and client can provide speech therapy as well as provide the foundation necessary for a client to enjoy "working" with the dog.

Diane Rampelberg and her dog, Dustin II, now form the cornerstone of the nonprofit organization Dustin's Paw which is as dedicated as North Star Foundation to helping children to meet their social, emotional, and educational goals through the use of well-bred and well-trained assistance dogs. They are beginning their fifth year together helping to serve children with disabilities in San Jose, California. In addition to their work in schools they also do presentations to help educate members of their community, believing there is no better way to teach compassion than through the eyes of a dog trained to help a child with a challenge. To order a complete copy of *Dustin's Paw 2003 Interactive Learning and Therapy Techniques* go to www.DustinsPaw.org or contact Diane directly at diane@dustinspaw.org. This article also appeared in the November/December 2003 issue of *The Clicker Journal.*

Part 4

Home before Dark

23

The Path Less Traveled

Patty Dobbs Gross

*The day came when the risk to remain
tight in a bud was more painful than
the risk it took to blossom.—Anais Nin*

If a seed is planted in a place shadowed from the sun, the healthy seedling will twist its way into the sunlight, even if this causes it to stray from its intended growth. Should the seedling be successful in its journey toward light it would reach maturity with a unique shape. This plant would still be healthy and viable, even though it may require extra support if its path toward light has placed unusual stress on a stem designed for typical growth. The value of this vulnerable plant would be up to us, and its assigned value will determine the amount of time and energy we will choose to expend to provide the necessary assistance in order for it to thrive. We can support a hospitable environment, create a harsh one, or ignore the seedling altogether and allow it to fold up into the ground. This decision is up to us.

It has been our own misconceptions that held kids with developmental disabilities back in the past, our own false beliefs that kept them from reaching their sun. We now struggle as a society to absorb the rapid changes in both our knowledge and our attitudes toward autism and related challenges. We are playing catch up, and we need to do this before we can even begin to hope to educate young children with autism and mental retardation appropriately.

I believe as time passes most people are choosing to become more tolerant; we are learning how to see past the boundaries of our egos, to look beyond our own personal concerns and focus on those around us. Nature's most fragile and unique flowers reward us when they bloom instead of wither, and within our collective soul, as well as our society, something beautiful also unfolds. A tolerant and educated society is good for children who face all kinds of special challenges, but it is also good for all children in general, as well as for us. We all need tolerance, understanding and support, eventually; no one gets to slide through his or her entire life independently. And as this new millennium dawns, so does our understanding that we are both capable of, and frighteningly close to, destroying ourselves through our lack of knowledge and empathy for the people who share our planet. Intolerance ends up being the most limiting, and therefore the most dangerous, disability of them all.

Danny was launched into the roiling social waters of a large high school nearly four years ago. I have dropped him off every school day, and I don't leave until he has walked through the double doors, past my ability to follow him with my eyes. I am still a beached lifeguard, openly terrified that my love is his only life jacket. When I pick him up at the end of each day, I walk down corridors neither as myself nor as the popular ghost of my distant past. I walk these locker-lined hallways like a woman with autism, scanning for danger as though the building was a cave capable of swallowing us both up. Danny used to keep a finger along the mortared grooves of the white cinder blocks in his elementary school; he would literally bump into the walls if he did not regulate his feedback in this way.

Today Dan navigates high school hallways in a smooth but studied manner, his face a picture of concentration as he reaches his locker and carefully selects his books, perhaps dodging the occasional sling and/or arrow of a less enlightened peer. I have been wounded by those slings, too, and have had my psychic flesh pierced by these cruel arrows, though it was technically not my flesh that was targeted.

And what do I do with this pain? Like toxic waste, it collects and putrefies. There is a myth that pain purifies us, and sometimes this is true, but just as often the opposite comes to bear. I have been acquainted with bitterness, shaken hands with anger, climbed into bed with vengeance. The backwash of prejudice and injustice is corrosive; it can destroy you from the inside out. It is also unfair, and perhaps even unnecessary, for the most painful part of Danny's difference became society's reaction to it.

Discrimination grows in subtle patterns as it is woven into the fabric of our adult society. It becomes more painful to endure and harder to ignore. Anger can seduce you into thinking you can wipe out the world's prejudice, with your own personal blood and guts conviction serving as your only battle plan. Dan doesn't tell me many stories from the front lines anymore; I stay hunkered down in the bunkers and ask careful questions upon his homecoming. He edits incidents that might upset me, realizing the phone calls I am prone to make with clenched jaw could worsen the situation. He has quietly made this burden his own, and I have great respect for his decision. I have diverted my blocked energy into creating and presenting programs at schools to heighten disability awareness and discuss the importance of valuing any differences that children may find in their peers. This is my way of fighting the formidable enemy of intolerance.

I know that trying to change the entire world's opinion of kids who face special challenges one classroom at a time is idealistic. On my bad days I mix my overwhelming sense of futility with as much grace as I can beg, borrow or steal. But on my good days I know this is the only path I would ever want to take. After all, this is the path that led me here, to this very page at this precise moment in time, to write these words for you.

Danny wrote these words for an assignment in his English class during his first year of high school:

> There are times in life when I get a hint of the things about my personality nobody wants, but I do not immediately know how to fix. I mean, this is me! This has always been me! I've certainly never had a problem with it! Then, I realized how important it is to forsake old ways to be a better person.
>
> In third grade, a year after I moved to Mansfield, I instantly knew I had to be friends with a boy named Ryan. (He) was one of the cool kids that truly stood out from the crowd. Perhaps this was why I liked him so much. I made cardboard basketball cards for him. I always begged him to sit next to me during lunch. I always tried to dress like him. I even tried to be cool like him, and I never hesitated to help him, although sometimes he would not need it.
>
> I didn't notice I was being annoying as I continued to be his loyal friend through seventh grade, but I finally started to get the picture when I noticed the next year

that Ryan seemed less than thrilled I had almost every class with him. About two weeks later, Ryan announced that he was moving to Enfield and I was in denial. I thought it was a joke, and said, "I'll believe it when I see it." He replied: "You'll believe it when I'm gone."

After four years I finally realized I wasn't a good friend of Ryan's at all, I was that typical annoying, obnoxious guy you really hate but play along with for all the things he does for you. I thought I was being Ryan's best friend, and I wasn't. When Ryan left, I was having trouble accepting it. I was at first sad because I had really liked him although he never liked me. Then I was mad that he never had the guts to say to me I was annoying. He just milked me for all I was worth, as I kept blindly tripping over myself to do things for him. Then I accepted the fact that it was not his fault, it was mine, to be so ignorant to the fact that maybe I was just being too good a friend. I am now devoted to moderating my friendships and making sure I do not get carried away.

In some ways this essay could be read as a success story about a child developing social skills well enough to cringe with embarrassment at his past mistakes. Others might see it as an indictment of Dan's insensitive peers, or as a failure on the part of their parents or their schools to instill character. I view it as a story of a boy reaching adulthood with great insight about who he is and where he fits into society. He knows who loves him, who might use him, and who might cause him harm.

And so it goes . . . one step back, two steps forward, as I walk my son to adulthood.

We tried to get comfortable resting on the cutting edge of technology to help Dan spend his time creatively when growing up. As this is an expensive place to be, we searched for, and found, ways to utilize technology for free. Dan worked as an intern at the Benton Museum at the University of Connecticut and this position allowed him to receive in depth knowledge of a field at no cost. Dan also took a free internship at our local public access channel where he learned to be comfortable in the editing room as well as behind a camera. Volunteering has proved a valuable activity for Dan, as well as for my other children, to spend their time outside of school. Encouraging them to contribute to the wider circle of our community rather than concentrating on forming same-age-and-similar-social-standing cliques has paid off by setting us up for success. Dan is now talking about attending film schools in California, of buying cars and setting up apartments and I have come to understand that the most difficult part of my job of raising Danny will be to allow my role to fade to insignificance.

I think the most important thing my husband Ron and I did while raising Danny was to keep his happiness our prime focus, and his education the cornerstone of our lives. This concept sounds deceptively simple when boiled down to a sentence, but at times it was as hard as sculpting rock with fingernails. Patience was as necessary a resource as both money and time in meeting challenges; Ron and I routinely ran out of all three in various ugly combinations. Doubt often camped out in our living room, and she still returns from time to time to make a mess of our psychic house.

But there is freedom granted people on the outskirts of society; if you're not accepted then you have to invent your own universe where you can fit right in. For us it ended up a relief to loosen ties to conventional society, and to quit trying to uphold beliefs that were inherited rather than invented. To create our own reality out of the whole cloth of our experiences and hard-won beliefs is both exhilarating and exhausting.

I am not autistic, and neither is Danny according to the accepted definition of the word. They took the unusual step of taking away his label last week at his PPT, or at least they downgraded it to reflect a learning disability (this is like downgrading a hurricane to a mere tropical storm). It seemed too obvious to all concerned that a young man on the high honor roll, with a small but close knit group of friends, no behavior problems and a sophistication beyond his years did not warrant an industrial strength label weighed down by past misperceptions. It is simple wordplay, I know, and I think it's as misleading to say Danny is "recovered" as it was to say he was "autistic." After so many years of testing him for labels and then fighting them, I have decided I don't ever again want my son to be vulnerable to anyone who would seek to define him, to those who think they can try to contain him within the space of a few words, or to those who want to play pin-the-tail-on-the-autistic-trait game.

I have been advised by well meaning friends to move, to pick up the pieces of our present lives and leave Dan's past in the dust. This advice is well meaning, as the prejudice against anyone who has been branded with the label of autism is tremendous and obvious. But to separate him at this point from his brothers and sisters with autism feels false and cruel. It is perhaps the best thing about human nature to want to turn around and offer the people coming up behind you a hand when you finally reach a safe ledge. Denying Danny ever had a label would be abandoning people who I know already feel quite alone. It's the label that has withered and yellowed with age, like something stuck inside a locked trunk in a distant attic; Danny himself has opened like a flower facing the sun.

I would be lying if I said the symbolic removal of Danny's label didn't make me happy, however. There are no traditional markers on the autism trail, so few ways to measure success or places you can stop to rest for a moment. As I sat at that table at the only PPT I've ever actually enjoyed, I felt triumphant, even as I knew the triumph was cut from the same false cloth that had been used to fashion his label.

We went out to eat to celebrate that night, although we did not tell Danny what we were celebrating. We never actually got around to telling him that he supposedly had autism, and now it all seems a moot point to underscore the fact that he supposedly doesn't. And what does a normal 18 year-old care about spectrum disorders, anyway? It seems to me that we all possess a mixture of unusual qualities and traits that are eminently human and uniquely individual. Being blessed with a child who faces a special challenge can end up a valuable gift of knowledge if you know how to receive it. When I understood that my husband, my children and I were perfect creatures forced to struggle too hard and too long to fit into an imperfect society, I was finally able to slip out of the tight grasp of society's expectations. Making this escape reminds me of the colorful Chinese finger traps I played with as a child; the more you struggle, the tighter the grip that holds you. Relaxing is the only way you can truly set yourself free.

We could afford to relax. The changes that Danny brought to our lives didn't require hard work to incorporate, only a willingness to change our thoughts. This paradigm shift in our thinking was like opening a window when a door had been slammed shut, leaving us in a dark and airless room.

But before we create and believe the mythology of acceptance in our society for children with autism, even for children who do well enough to shed their labels due to ill fit, consider this: just last week Danny came home from school quiet and confused. I pressed him a bit, and then waited for him to tell me his story. It took awhile to learn that a classmate had hit him when he refused to leave a group of kids, and had called him some very painful names, which everyone knows hurts more than sticks, stones or a sucker punch. . . .

I was overcome once again with my familiar beached lifeguard feeling, on guard but seemingly powerless to even try to save my son. I did not want to go to the administration as Danny is now 18 years old and over six feet tall, with the boy in question shorter and more physically frail. Dan could clearly defend himself, yet he was speaking to me of strategies whereby he could avoid this boy.

I stressed about this all afternoon: do I advise him to stand his ground, or is it best for him to slink away and hide from potential danger? Should I advise him to slice his enemy to ribbons with his tongue, or merely to wound him with the razor sharp edge of his wit? Do I talk to a friendly guidance counselor, a trusted teacher, or my own mother, who still dispenses the wisest council of anyone I know?

Or do I choose to listen to my gut and part the generational curtain that separated this bully from myself, to call this boy directly, thereby eradicating danger and correcting misinformation at the source? I felt like the antiquated giant tin-can robot on *Lost in Space* that does awkward half spins, waving its useless accordion arms so pathetically in the air . . . (Danger, danger, Will Robinson!). I knew I would be seen as a clueless intruder, a middle-aged Connecticut housewife, the mother of all mothers (and not in a good way).

But I still watched myself as I flipped through the phone book and dialed this boy's number with shaking fingers, a bit horrified that I couldn't even begin to stop myself. He answered on the second ring, not even allowing me any time to form a plan (have I mentioned I tend to be impulsive when emotional?). I will end this story here for privacy reasons, but will let you know that neither one of us was unkind in our conversation. I told him only that I wanted him to know I loved my son and needed him to treat him kindly. He told me he was angry and tired of Danny "making fun of him" and it was then I then came closer to true understanding. Danny does have a dry and biting sense of humor, and he sometimes misjudges the thickness and capability of someone's skin to deflect the sharp arrows of his insights. Just as it was not up to Danny to change completely to fit into society, so it wasn't up to this boy to have to deal with honest, perhaps true but certainly uninvited and mistimed sarcasm. A punch is not an accepted method of communicating this thought, perhaps, but I have become quite good at not throwing out the baby with the bath water; I accepted and explored this boy's feelings and found myself in the position of having to suggest to him that his behavior was socially unacceptable. This ironic thread is still being woven in the tapestry of our present day life.

To me what remains when all else about this embarrassing incident falls away is that Danny and I are no longer isolated, either from each other or the larger world. Moving closer to his way of thinking, while subtly shifting him toward mine, ends up being more an art than a science, and our lives together reflects this creativity. Frequently our worlds blend, transpose; I am free at last from the pressure to "intervene." I have decided to be judicious when censoring Danny, even if it makes those around him uncomfortable, for I have noticed it is his tendency to observe carefully and speak truthfully that is winning him friends and influencing people.

Here is an essay Danny wrote in his last year of high school:

> The question "Who am I?" is a very complicated question for anyone, but it is an especially complicated one for me, since at this point in my life I don't entirely know who I really am, or who I want to be or don't want to be, or who I'm inevitably going to end up becoming in the distant future. But what I can tell you are the bits and pieces, the little things I think I know about myself; about who I think I am with no outside influence whatsoever. I may not be able to put this mental jigsaw puzzle together myself at the moment (and even if I did, there's no guarantee I would know what to do with it), but hopefully this essay will allow you to give it a try.
>
> When I think about my entire life story to date, it gets me thinking about my personal characteristics, little things about myself that contribute to who I am. There are things about myself that I like, that I don't think I want to change in the future. For instance, I like the fact that I have a very good sense of humor. Whenever something is said that strikes me a certain way, I can often come up with a short, sweet joke or wisecrack that generates laughs almost instantly. I often possess a very potent, incisive, tongue-in-cheek wit that shines through when I say something like a bit of social or political commentary, a brief anecdote, a personal passionate opinion of mine, or a joke at my own expense. I'm glad I have this sense of humor because I feel happy when I make someone else happy, and I feel smart whenever I make an insightful observation or offer an opinion that surprises the person I'm talking to. I also like the fact that I can be very artistic. I have accomplished making a few good short movies so far, and I have gotten very good reactions from my peers, and I am proud of this because

I feel happy and talented whenever someone says they like my video.

When it comes to values, I've lived by them for so long that they're ingrained into my daily life. For instance, always doing as good a job as I can on something is very important to me, and very often it shows in my grades. I would never, ever want to be someone who consciously does a lousy job on something important and doesn't care. Being a good friend is important to me, too, and I would never want to consciously do anything disrespectful to one of my best friends. It is also important to me to be as honest as I can, and never lie to, or withhold, important information from someone invaluable in my life.

When I think of my hopes and dreams, I think right now I have a very good idea about what I want to do with my life, and I have a very clear goal. My goal is simply to get into the filmmaking business because I have dream of having a job I love that I can be happy and fulfilled with as I live and die. I dream of having people in my life that I love who love me back. And, above all, I dream of affecting the world with my work and, if just for a brief moment, of being remembered after I die.

As for my beliefs, this is simple: I believe in God, I believe in a peaceful democratic future, and I believe in love. . . .

24

Harmony Revisited

We don't see things as they are,
we see them as we are.—Anais Nin

It has been over a decade since I created North Star Foundation, and nearly two full decades since I delivered Danny. I have discovered that whether people appreciate the concept of my nonprofit or the value of my son depends more on who the person in question is rather than the intrinsic value of either Danny or North Star. We see things and people in our lives through a filter distorted by our preconceived notions and blind spots. The concept of "mindblindness" should be expanded to include not just those on the autism spectrum, but also those who would presume to judge them as inferior.

A butterfly emerges from a cocoon with infinite grace, the transformation as delicate as the wings that, when dry, will lift her away. My own transformation came in painful spurts that were not as beautiful as nature would have designed. Gradually, if not gracefully, I have begun to twist my way out of my own psychic cocoon. April is no longer my cruelest month; spring breezes now mean hiking with my children, taking them on vacations, and accepting the invitations that have begun to trickle in. And if it occurs to me that some people now offer me invitations because I am more socially acceptable, I try to put this thought aside as carefully as something hot from the oven. Feeling superior is dangerous, for it would soon be discovered that I aid and abet the crime of intolerance on a daily basis by my own acceptance of society's questionable values. I know that we all are prejudiced in our own way, against various populations of people that are equally innocent. My house is glass, and really messy to boot. I have no desire to pretend to be above, or below, anybody in my life.

I have discovered how connected we all are, and how, like family, our fortunes rise and fall in harmony. We influence each other and take turns playing teacher and student, usually not realizing just when it is our turn to teach or to learn; I am nearly a half a century old, and only just now beginning to understand how much I still don't know. But I think I understand what is important in this life, and for this I am very grateful.

One of my fondest memories is from the summer when Danny finally learned to skip, something he had tried to learn for years, but didn't fully master until he was a teenager well over six feet tall. Even though it was developmentally late to acquire this skill, he appreciated the fun of finally being able to skip with abandon, and he didn't want to miss out on this experience just because he was tardy. One afternoon while running errands with all four of my children, I found myself following them to the car, with Danny taking the lead and skipping all the way. People were turning their heads at the sight of a boy as tall as a man skipping past them on the sidewalk, but before I was enveloped by that familiar feeling of being judged, my son Chris, also over six feet tall, turned and caught my eye with a bright smile. He then turned and joined his brother and they both skipped side by side toward the car: one with a smooth and studied motion and the other a lanky, fluid grace. My girls, Jennie and Kelsey, only watched their brothers for a moment before they followed suit, and I was then treated to the sight of all four of my children skipping to the car that would take them home with me. Bystanders were now smiling or frowning, depending on how they chose to interpret this sight. It was hard for me to tell, because I was moved to tears.

There's an essay that parents of children newly diagnosed with any disability will eventually run across; it compares having a child with a difference to flying to the Netherlands when you thought you were on your way to Italy. I remember hearing this story from a well-meaning friend, but not quite believing it rang true to my experience.

Only recently have I discovered a better analogy. It came to me one night after driving home from Cape Cod. Our entire family had driven up just that afternoon, arriving frazzled after four hours jammed into the car following a frenzy of making arrangements and packing suitcases.

When I finally got to the hotel's counter and saw the puzzled look on the clerk's face I realized with horror I had gotten it wrong; we were there exactly a week early for our reservations. I then had to walk back to the van, where Ron and all four kids sat waiting to unpack for our long-awaited vacation, and tell them I had messed up, big time. Our complicated schedules would now need revision, co-workers would have to be convinced to cover for us, appointments would be missed and sleep unnecessarily lost. We would be lucky if we still got to come back the following week with all the smoothing out of details to be done. And we would first have to drive the four long hours home, unpack all our stuff, and struggle to return even to square one. I told them all this with an unfamiliar and very sharp lump in my throat, for in my family it is usually up to me to play spin-doctor to fate's whims.

About halfway home Chris mentioned that a comet was scheduled to pass by us that very night, supposedly a once-in-a-lifetime opportunity to watch thousands of meteors as they streaked across the night's sky. Could we stay up way past any thought of bedtime, until dawn perhaps? Could we bake cookies at midnight and eat them under that crazy night sky?

Was it possible to find joy here, even if we had to invent it ourselves?

As we drove, our spirits rose like a phoenix from the ashes of my mistake, and by the end of our trip we had all agreed we would watch the stars until they finally blended into daylight. We arrived home happy that night, despite the multitude of superficial reasons not to be. Danny volunteered to drag chairs onto the front lawn, Jennie pointed out constellations she knew and told us the stories behind them, and Kelsey fell asleep on my lap under the layer of covers Ron brought out for us. Madison lay in front of Danny, his grey muzzle resting lightly on his feet. Madison is twelve now, and it suddenly occurred to me that accepting his death would be the last lesson he would end up teaching our family. I tried not to let this unwelcome thought sink my mood, nor the weighty chores of the coming week. I consciously struggled to let go of my ever-present fear of the future, and to escape for just a moment from the past, which still haunts me with its long, cold shadow of painful confusion.

I concentrated instead on the moment I was in and the family that surrounded me: we were bound together by love, stitched to each other by our shared challenges, and fully aware of how greatly we needed each other.

The last time this comet passed by our planet the sky's crazy behavior was cause for concern; a sign to some that the world as they knew it was about to end. Two passes ago someone might have been blamed for the alarming celestial activity and been burnt at the stake, a cruel stab at protection from a twisted fear of fate. But thanks to the astronomers who enlightened us, we now know that this light show is a rare but natural event. They have even named this comet and can tell us with reasonable certainty that it will return again to pass us by one hundred years from now for a new generation to view.

And so we sat like this until morning, our lawn chairs lined up in a row and our heads tilted back at the same angle, watching the sky while our neighbors slept.

This is when it hit me: this is what having a child with a challenge is like. It's true that you think you are going one place when you are actually going to another, but the place you are going is actually home, and the sky you are under is, for a moment, unusually alive with movement and possibility.

And if, like us, you and your family ever find yourself in a place like this, may I suggest you stay up together until morning, appreciating each other along with nature's wild beauty. And if you begin to long for your old familiar sky you can always search for the North Star, that bright and constant point of light in a galaxy of endless change.

Or you could find us, who wait for you as patiently as the real North Star, ready to guide you on your journey home . . .

25

Parting Thoughts

We shall not cease from our exploration
And at the end of all our exploring
Will be to arrive where we started
And know the place for the first time.
—T. S. Eliot

Fifteen years have passed since I started to write the book you are about to finish. It began as an article tapped out on a typewriter at my kitchen table with four small children, countless jars of white out and a golden retriever named Madison to keep me company.

Today I write these words on a brand new computer with a high-speed cable modem. I have a proper desk now (which is still messy, for some things never change), but most mornings now find me alone with my four teenagers at various schools and activities. Through the years my fingers have moved over my various keyboards like dancers' legs, occasionally resting lightly on my lap while I stared out windows, conjuring up words (which, when forced into existence, tend to lie woodenly on the page and not like I had envisioned them at all). My eyes have traced the line of bittersweet that forms around the edge of the forest that surrounds my home while I yearned for these words to come . . . but now I wait for them to stop, for today is the day I have chosen to end this book.

Dan was accepted to the University of Connecticut at Storrs last week, on his own merit but with an interesting twist: my power and skill at being his advocate had to be tamed as surely as the beast that I'd become; I had to promise to the powers that be to let Dan advocate for himself on campus, just like any freshman is expected to do. . . .

So now I am a beached lifeguard with a restraining order in my dry pocket. And, of course, this is just the way it should be, for Dan is infinitely capable of navigating his own world, of sailing into the unknown on smooth water or frothy swells.

But he leaves me on the shore of my own life, fearing the tsunamis of fate and Poseidon's careless vendettas. I am growing both sentimental and superstitious as I get older; I avoid stepping on sidewalk cracks and my eyes fill up at the tiniest of things. Last weekend I took pictures of Danny trying on his graduation robe with far too much import, and when he graduates next month I will search for him in a sea of caps and tassels with a heart that beats much too fast, as if my immediate attention alone could keep him safe. I catch myself glancing over my shoulder lately, waiting for disaster to pounce like some calculating lion, but after all these years on such an inward journey do I really expect to find my peace or my peril in the tangled jungle of outward circumstance? It ends up me that needs taming, not some crouching creature in the brush.

Madison died yesterday and I, who tend to search for signs, now choose to take this as one. It is time to move on. After a lifetime of service, the last thing Madison ends up teaching Danny is how to move forward without him.

I am struggling to learn this, too.

They say that starlight can reach us long after a star has imploded, its light born of energy untouched by the illusion of loss . . . and so I trust that Madison's love, like light, can find us.

Appendix

Choosing an Assistance Dog Organization or Trainer

As the demand for assistance dogs for children with challenges increases, so does the need for knowledgeable and competent trainers. It is becoming evident that some individuals entering the assistance dog industry have little experience in the field, even though their websites may claim otherwise. Obtaining an assistance dog is a major commitment, and one that requires thorough research and investigation to make it effective for the child and safe for all concerned.

The vast majority of assistance dog organizations and trainers are reputable and experienced professionals, working exceedingly hard to fill the tremendous need for well trained dogs. It is only a very few that have ventured into the assistance dog industry for all the wrong reasons. In an effort to increase consumer awareness related to this emerging field, my colleague Bev Swartz of All Purpose Canines and I suggest the following guidelines when seeking an assistance dog to work with a child with a social, emotional, or educational challenge.

1. Visit the organization's website and carefully read all the information provided. Remember, if something sounds too good to be true, it probably is.

2. Does the website contain pertinent information and specifics regarding their philosophy of placement and experience in training or working with children, or does it have poorly written stories that play toward your personal desire to help your child?

3. Ask for all the trainers' credentials (how long have they been in the industry, what is their background, etc).

4. Ask about the organization's specific experience working with children with developmental disabilities; remember, the task at hand is not just to train your dog, but to teach your child how to communicate and care for his canine companion.

5. Check with the secretary of state inthe organization's home state for information regarding the date the organization was incorporated and any other relevant information. Remember, it takes time to properly train any assistance dog. Be very wary of any organization that has been in existence for a short period of time yet claims to have trained numerous dogs.

6. Is the assistance dog provider/trainer a member of any professional organization, such as Assistance Dog International (ADI), International Association of Assistance Dog Partners (IAADP), or International Association of Animal Behavior Consultants, Inc. (IAABC)?

7. Will the organization provide references from families who have been pleased with their experience working with it? If so, check these references out.

8. Are the dogs they use screened for genetic diseases such as hip, heart, and eye problems? Are they vaccinated? Are copies of veterinarian records given to you at time of placement? Is the organization willing to give you the name of the veterinarian who conducted the testing?

9. Are you able to trace the background of the dog they offer to train for your child? If so, has the dog received optimal care, nurturing and socialization to children in its crucial formative months?

10. Contact a number of assistance dog providers asking the same questions of every one. Compare your answers and choose the one that best fits your needs. If you have any doubts or concerns, please feel free to contact me at northstarfoundation@charter.net, as education is an important part of our mission.

North Star Foundation

*Never doubt that a small group of committed
people can change the world. Indeed, it is the
only thing that ever has.—Margaret Mead*

Please consider supporting our work at North Star Foundation.

We are a nonprofit organization and your donation is tax-deductible along with being greatly needed to fund our work helping children who face challenges to reach their social, emotional, and educational goals through the use of an assistance dog. Together, we can help these children find their way with the help of a canine companion.

Checks should be made out to North Star Foundation and sent to my attention at the following address:

Patty Dobbs Gross
Executive Director
North Star Foundation
20 Deerfield Lane
Storrs, CT 06268
www.NorthStarDogs.com
northstarfoundation@charter.net

Thank you in advance for your kind donation!

References

Atwood, Tony. "The Profile of Friendship Skills in Asperger's Syndrome." *Jenison Autism Journal* 14, no. 3 (2002).

Battaglia, Carmen. "Developing High Achievers" (originally published as "Early Neurological Stimulation"). B.E.I. Publications, 2001. Available online at http://www.breedingbetterdogs.com/achiever.html.

Clothier, Suzanne. *Bones Would Rain from the Sky: Deepening Our Relationships with Dogs.* New York: Warner Books, 2005.

Courchesne, E., R. Carper and N. Akshoomoff. 2003. "Evidence of Brain Overgrowth in the First Year of Life in Autism." *JAMA* 290 (2003): 337–344.

Davis, Kathy Diamond. *Therapy Dogs: Training Your Dogs to Reach Others.* Howell Book House, 1992.

Feddersen-Petersen, D. U. "Communication in Wolves and Dogs." *Encyclopedia of Animal Behavior,* ed. M. Bekoff, vol. 1, pp. 385–394. Westport, Conn.: Greenwood, 2005.

Gernsbacher, M. A. "Is One Style of Autism Early Intervention 'Scientifically Proven'?" *Journal of Developmental and Learning Disorders* 7 (2003): 19–25.

Grandin, Temple, and Johnson, Catherine. *Animals in Translation: Using the Mysteries of Autism to Decode Animal Behavior.* New York: Scribner, 2005.

Grandin, Temple. *Thinking in Pictures and Other Reports from My Life with Autism.* New York: Vintage, 1996.

Gutstein, Steven E. *Autism Aspergers: Solving the Relationship Puzzle: A New Developmental Program That Opens the Door to Lifelong Social and Emotional Growth.* Arlington, Texas: Future Horizons, Inc., 2000.

Hacking, I. *The Social Construction of What?* Cambridge: Harvard University Press, 1999.

Hare, Brian; Brown, Michelle; Tomasello, Michael; Williamson, Christina.

"The Domestication of Social Cognition in Dogs." *Science* 298, no. 5598 (22 November 2002), 1634–1636.

Kane, Ed. "Animals Healing Children." *Interactions* 19, no. 3 (2001).

Kennedy, Jr., Robert F. "Deadly Immunity." *Rolling Stone,* June 20, 2005.

Kirton, A., Wirrell, E., Zhang, J., and Hamiwka, L. "Seizure-Alerting and -Response Behaviors in Dogs Living with Epileptic Children." *Neurology* 62 (2004), 2303–2305.

Lemer, Patricia S. "Diagnosis: Autism What Families Can Do." *Mothering Magazine,* May/June 2000.

Nagengast, S.L., Baun, M.M., Megel, M., and Leibowitz, J.M. "The Effects of the Presence of a Companion Animal on Physiological Arousal and Behavioral Distress in Children during a Physical Examination." *Journal of Pediatric Nursing* 12(6) (December 1997: 323–330.

Nash, J. Madeleine. "The Secrets of Autism." *Time Magazine,* July 15, 2002.

Neergaard, Lauran. "Advanced Scanning Being Used for Autism." *Newsday,* April 14, 2004.

Park, Clara Claiborne. *The Siege: A Family's Journey into the World of an Autistic Child.* Boston: Back Bay Books, 1982.

Park, Clara Claiborne. *Exiting Nirvana: A Daughter's Life with Autism.* Boston: Little Brown & Co., 2001.

Peyton, Jeffrey L. "Position Paper." Emotions, Learning & Education Symposium, Copenhagen, Denmark, November 2004. Available online at http://www.puppetools.com/.

Pryor, Karen. *Don't Shoot the Dog! The New Art of Teaching and Training.* Rev. ed. New York: Bantam, 1999.

Rice, John, and Clothier, Suzanne. *Following Ghosts: Developing the Tracking Relationship.* St. Johnsville, NY: Flying Dog Press, 1996.

Ridley, M. *Nature via Nurture: Genes, Experience, and What Makes Us Human.* New York: HarperCollins, 2003.

Ross, Emma. "Study Shows Dogs Able to Smell Cancer." Associated Press, 24 September, 2004.

Rugaas, Turid. *On Talking Terms with Dogs: Calming Signals.* 2nd ed. Wenatchee, Wash.: Dogwise Publishing, 2006.

Silberman, S. "The Geek Syndrome." *Wired,* December 2001.

Spector, Morgan. *Clicker Training for Obedience: Shaping Top Performance—Positively.* Waltham, Mass.: Sunshine Books, 1999.

Ontario Veterinary College, University of Guelph, "Evaluating the Benefits of Service Dogs for Children with Autism Spectrum Disorder," Sept. 2003–April 2005. Researchers Dr. Cindy L. Adams and Kristen E. Burrows. Available online at http://www.nsd.on.ca/research.htm.

Index